AIA Guide to the Archit

AIA Guide to the Architecture of Washington, D.C.

FOURTH EDITION

by G. Martin Moeller Jr., Assoc. AIA

for the Washington Chapter of the
American Institute of Architects

with an introduction by Francis D. Lethbridge, FAIA

William Gordon IV, AIA, LEED AP, Photo Editor

THE JOHNS HOPKINS UNIVERSITY PRESS   BALTIMORE

This book has been brought to publication with the generous assistance of Pepco, Grunley Construction, Jackson & Campbell, and National Reprographics, Inc.

The Johns Hopkins University Press
2715 North Charles Street
Baltimore, Maryland 21218-4363
www.press.jhu.edu

AIA Washington DC
1777 Church Street, NW
Washington, DC 20036

Library of Congress Cataloging-in-Publication Data
Moeller, Gerard Martin.
    AIA guide to the architecture of Washington, D.C. / G. Martin Moeller Jr.—
4th ed.
        p. cm.
    Rev. ed. of: AIA guide to the architecture of Washington, D.C. / Christopher
Weeks. 3rd ed. 1994.
    Includes bibliographical references and index.
    ISBN 0-8018-8467-5 (hardcover : alk. paper)—ISBN 0-8018-8468-3
(pbk. : alk. paper)
    1. Architecture—Washington (D.C.)—Guidebooks.   2. Washington (D.C.)—
Buildings, structures, etc.—Guidebooks.   3. Washington (D.C.)—Guidebooks.
I. Weeks, Christopher, 1950– AIA guide to the architecture of Washington,
D.C.   II. American Institute of Architects.   III. Title.
    NA735.W3M64 2006
    720.9753—dc22·   2006003575

A catalog record for this book is available from the British Library.

In memory of

Charles Atherton, FAIA

Long-time secretary of the

U.S. Commission of Fine Arts and

Great friend of the Chapter

Contents

Preface and Acknowledgments

In the early 1960s, a quartet of Washington architects—Warren J. Cox, Hugh Newell Jacobsen, Francis D. Lethbridge, and David R. Rosenthal—accepted the daunting challenge of producing a handy but thorough guide to the architecture of the nation's capital. Written and published for what was then called the Washington Metropolitan Chapter of the American Institute of Architects (AIA), the book, which contained brief descriptions of buildings in the District of Columbia, northern Virginia, and suburban Maryland, appeared in 1965 and quickly sold out. A second edition, incorporating modest revisions, was published in 1974.

During the 1980s, the Washington area grew rapidly, and dozens of major new buildings were added to the cityscape. By the end of the decade, many members of the chapter—then known simply as the Washington Chapter / AIA—were clamoring for an updated guidebook. The original four authors, who were young Turks when they prepared the first edition, had become well established in their careers (in fact, a couple of them had gone on to enjoy national reputations), and were in no position to take on the third edition, which would require substantial new research and writing. In 1989, the chapter, under the leadership of Arnold Prima, FAIA, and Bill Hooper, AIA, engaged Maryland-based writer Christopher Weeks to produce a substantially updated and expanded guide.

Given the tremendous increase in the number of potential entries between the second and third editions, the chapter's leadership quickly concluded that it was necessary to narrow the scope of the new book to the District of Columbia proper (an exception was made for Arlington National Cemetery, which was deemed a crucial component of the capital's monumental core even though it lies across the river in Virginia). The chapter assembled an advisory committee to decide on the list of buildings to be included in the book. The committee consisted of Charles Atherton, FAIA, secretary of the U.S. Commission of Fine Arts; Donald Canty, former editor of *Architecture* magazine; and Benjamin Forgey, architecture critic for the *Washington Post*. (The committee was

later joined by Deborah Dietsch, also a former editor of *Architecture*.)
The third edition hit the bookstores in 1994.

In the decade or so following the publication of the previous edition of the guide, Washington experienced yet another impressive construction boom, and also benefited from a nationwide resurgence of interest in urban living. By 2003, it was becoming clear that another rendition of the popular guidebook was needed. The chapter once again gathered a group of experts—this time comprising Charles Atherton, FAIA, Heather Cass, FAIA, Benjamin Forgey, Mary Oehrlein, FAIA, Marshall Purnell, FAIA, and Judith Robinson—to advise on which new buildings to include (and which of the old entries to delete). Research and writing began in earnest in 2004.

The text of this edition is almost entirely new. While occasional words, phrases, and even a few extended passages have been carried over from previous editions, every existing entry has been rewritten and all factual data have been reinvestigated. This is not to say that the current guide does not owe a great debt to Messrs. Cox, Jacobsen, Lethbridge, Rosenthal, and Weeks—indeed, much of the spirit and fundamental information in this book is built upon the important foundations they laid. Nonetheless, this edition is intended to provide a thoroughly fresh look at the built heritage of Washington, while also providing a snapshot of the city's architectural character at the beginning of the twenty-first century.

Writing guidebooks is a tricky business. Accuracy and currency can be elusive goals, as buildings are constantly being built, renovated, enlarged, demolished, or sold, and institutions change their names, their locations, and occasionally their basic missions. Even seemingly pedigreed landmarks can pose challenges, as historians sometimes disagree about "facts" such as dates of construction or the roles of specific people in their design and construction. In preparing this guide, the author sought credible sources for all data, relying heavily on the documents of the Historic American Buildings Survey, specific institutional archives, local governmental agencies, and authoritative articles and books. To the extent possible, all essential information presented in a given entry was verified with the building's owner, architect, or another person presumed to have relevant knowledge, such as a curator, archivist, or historian. If, despite this diligence, an error has slipped through, the author would welcome a correction, which may be submitted through the Washington Chapter / AIA.

This guide is not intended to serve as a purely factual historical record; much of the content, in fact, is utterly subjective and may take the form of positive or negative criticism. The reader should remember that the opinions expressed herein are just that—opinions—and are solely those of the author. Reasonable people may disagree as to whether a given work of architecture is good, bad, gorgeous, or hideous—a negative comment about a particular building is not intended to give offense to the architects or any others involved in its creation.

It is unfortunate, but perhaps inevitable, that architecture guidebooks tend to emphasize prominent public, institutional, and commercial buildings at the expense of smaller, privately owned structures, especially single-family residences. The reasons are simple: there are limits on the number of entries that may be included in such books without compromising readability and portability; the vast quantity of distinct houses makes selection of representative examples difficult; and privacy concerns can complicate research into the history of residential buildings. The author is acutely aware that row houses, in particular, are underrepresented in this book. Row houses—in all their variations—collectively constitute one of the most important building types in the nation's capital, and contribute a great deal to the architectural and urban character of the city. Washington also, of course, boasts many beautiful streets lined with detached houses of various scales and styles.

So, once you, the reader, have faithfully completed every tour in this guide (as the author is confident you will), take some time to stroll through some of the residential areas of Washington. Note the characteristic scale and texture of the houses, consider the varied relationships of the buildings to yards and sidewalks, and observe the vital role of trees and other plants in defining the streetscape. Enjoy the quotidian details that make these distinct and culturally rich neighborhoods the true heart of Washington, D.C., overlooked though they may be by the typical tourist. Then perhaps you can head back to the Lincoln Memorial, gaze down the Mall toward the Capitol, and contemplate the broader course of civilization.

G.M.M.

The Washington Chapter / AIA is indebted to the following groups and individuals, without whom this fourth edition of the guide would not be possible:
- Our patrons, whose financial support helped to underwrite a lot of new research: PEPCO, a PHI company; Grunley Construction Company, Inc., Jackson & Campbell, PC, and National Reprographics, Inc.
- The architects and contractors who designed and built all the beautiful new projects in this book and who were so generous with their time and images.
- G. Martin Moeller Jr., Assoc. AIA, who researched and wrote this guide. His attention to detail and interest in the story behind the

story make this volume both a great resource and a joy to use. Martin adds his own thanks to the many architectural historians, architects, and others who reviewed the draft text and provided comments, corrections, and insights, most notably Richard Longstreth, Cynthia Field, Judith Robinson, Heather Cass, FAIA, Lonnie Hovey, AIA, Linda Lyons, and especially Steven K. Dickens, AIA.

- Our advisory board, including the late Charles Atherton, FAIA, Heather Cass, FAIA, Benjamin Forgey, Mary Oehrlein, FAIA, Marshall Purnell, FAIA, and Judith Robinson.
- William Gordon, IV, AIA, LEED, our photo editor, who worked tirelessly over two years to make sure the images and maps were perfect.
- Our photographers, principally Alan Karchmer, Assoc. AIA, and Boris Feldblyum, with additional photography by Brian Becker, George Cott, Carol Highsmith, Dan Cunningham, Dan Redmond, David Patterson, Ezra Stoller, Gary Fleming, Hedrich Blessing, James Oesch, Fred Sons Photography, Julie Heine, Ken Wyner, Mary Randlett, Michael Dersin, Michael Moran, Michael Houlahan, Paul Warchol, Peter Aaron and Wolfgang Hoyt of Esto, Phil Portlack, Prakash Patel, Ron Soloman, Sunny Odom, Timothy Hursley, Walter Smalling Jr., Arthur Cotton Moore, Alex Jamison, Max MacKenzie, Anice Hoachlander, the late Andrew Lautman, Robert Lautman, Hon. AIA, and Ronald O'Rourke.
- KUBE Architecture for its design assistance with the tour maps.
- Robert J. Brugger and his team at the Johns Hopkins University Press for their interest in producing a fourth edition.
- And last but not least, the members of the Washington Chapter of the American Institute of Architects who not only underwrote a substantial part of the production of this publication but are also its real stars.

Mary Fitch, AICP
Executive Director
Washington Chapter / AIA

AIA Guide to the Architecture of Washington, D.C.

The Architecture of Washington, D.C.

FRANCIS D. LETHBRIDGE, FAIA

The selection of a site for the federal capital was finally settled in New York City one evening in the summer of 1790, when Thomas Jefferson and Alexander Hamilton dined together and concluded what might be described as a political deal. Bitter political enemies though they were, Jefferson and Hamilton that year each wanted something that only their combined influence in Congress could bring about. And so it came to pass that sufficient southern votes supported the Funding Bill; Pennsylvanians, wooed by the prospect of removal of the federal capital to Philadelphia for the next ten years, cast their votes for the Residence Bill; and, to the accompaniment of cries of rage from New York and New England, the federal government assumed the debts of the states and made plans to set up its home on the shores of the Potomac River.[1]

The planning of the city of Washington is a familiar tale, yet one that bears repeating, for the quality, durability, and persistent effect of that plan upon the city must always be a central theme in the story of its architecture. We must first, however, go somewhat farther back in time, for long before the construction of the federal city began, there was a flourishing colonial society on the shores of the Potomac near the place where the tidewater country ends. The fall line—that abrupt rise from the eastern coastal plain that marks the end of navigable water—may be traced as an uneven line from New England southward and westward. The cities of Trenton and Richmond, for example, lie at the falls of the Delaware and the James, and if the capital had never been established on the Potomac, the ports of Georgetown and Alexandria would doubtless have prospered and grown into thriving cities by virtue of their location at this crossroads of travel by land and river.

The Chesapeake Bay had been explored by the Spanish before the end of the sixteenth century, but not until 1608, when Captain John Smith sailed up the Potomac River, quite possibly as far as the Little Falls, north of the present site of Georgetown, was very much known of the area that became the capital of the New World. Smith's *General Historie of Virginia, New England and the Summer Isles*, published in England in 1627, was accompanied by a remarkable map that was the basis for all cartography of the Chesapeake region for nearly a hundred years. His description of the river is still a vivid one:

> The fourth river is called Patawomeke, 6 or 7 myles in breadth. It is navigable 140 myles, and fed as the rest with many sweet rivers and springs, which fall from the bordering hills. These hills many of them are planted, and yeeld no lesse plentie and varietie of fruit, then the river exceedeth with abundance of fish. It is inhabited on both sides. . . . The river above this place maketh his passage downe a low pleasant valley overshaddowed in many places with high rocky mountaines; from whence distill innumerable sweet and pleasant springs.

In the next twenty-five years the Potomac became a scene of increasing activity on the part of traders, who began to tap a rich supply of furs, not from the adjacent country alone, but from the lands beyond the Alleghenies, from which they were carried by the Indians to the headwaters of the river. These adventurers were necessarily a hardy and resourceful lot, who plied their trade, in small shallops, from the lower reaches of Chesapeake Bay; and some of them, such as Henry Spelman and Henry Fleete, knew the Algonquin language well from having lived with the Indians as hostages or captives.

In March 1634 Leonard Calvert arrived upon this Potomac scene in two ships, the *Ark* and the *Dove*, with a cargo of Protestant and Roman Catholic settlers, the Catholics seeking their fortunes but also haven from English religious persecution. Near the mouth of the river they founded St. Mary's City, which served as the capital of Maryland until a Protestant revolt late in the century. The St. Mary's City Commission has been engaged in an ambitious reconstruction program on the site of the old capital, and a visit there repays the trip. But there are, in fact, very few remaining examples of seventeenth-century construction on either the Maryland or the Virginia shores of the river. You must travel farther south, to the banks of the James River, to the sites of the Thomas Rolfe house (1651), the Allen house, or "Bacon's Castle" (1655), and St. Luke's Church (c. 1650), to see the only recognizable survivals of Jacobean architecture in the tidewater country. It is ironic that the most famous example of the period, Governor Berkeley's mansion "Greenspring" (1642), which Thomas Tileston Waterman terms "probably the greatest Virginia house of the Century," was destroyed in 1806 to make way for Benjamin Henry Latrobe's house for William Ludwell Lee, which in its turn was demolished during the Civil War.[2]

Despite recurring troubles with the dwindling Indian tribes until the beginning of the eighteenth century, settlement along the Potomac continued steadily. Large land grants were taken up in both Virginia and Maryland, and estates of many thousands of acres were not unusual. Compared to the lands of Robert Carter of Nomini Hall, who owned 63,093 acres, and William Fitzhugh of Bedford, who had acquired over 45,000 acres, the 8,000-acre holdings of George Washington at Mount Vernon and George Mason's combined holdings of about 15,000 acres along the river seem modest in size. Cheap land, abundant labor, easy transportation from private landings to ships, and a ready market for tobacco in England made possible the development of the great plantations of the tidewater country.

At least for the planters who prospered, the country offered a gracious life, which flourished in the early and mid-eighteenth century and resulted in some handsome houses. Within a relatively few miles of Washington you can see many noble examples of these country mansions,[3] and a short trip to Williamsburg, Virginia, will help you to imagine what life was like in a provincial capital of that period.

The prosperity of the plantations and the settlements of tracts beyond the borders of the river and its navigable tributaries stimulated the founding of the ports of Alexandria (1748) and Georgetown (1751).

Another earlier port, Garrison's Landing, known later as Bladensburg (1742), on the Eastern Branch, or Anacostia River, sank into commercial obscurity at the end of the eighteenth century when the river silted up beyond that point. Two of these Potomac ports were the scene of an important event in colonial history not long after they had been established. In the year 1755 General Braddock embarked with his army from Alexandria, landed near the foot of Rock Creek, and marched up the path of what is now Wisconsin Avenue, on the ill-fated expedition against the French and Indians that ended in disaster near Fort Duquesne. One of the few provincial officers to return unscathed from the campaign was a young Virginian who had been spared to play a greater role in history.

Georgetown and Alexandria still retain some of the atmosphere and much of the scale and texture of colonial river port towns. From the accounts of travelers it would seem that by the latter part of the century they were thriving, pleasant places. Thomas Twining, after a rough all-day wagon journey from Baltimore in 1795, described Georgetown as "a small but neat town. . . . the road from Virginia and the Southern States, crossing the Potomac here, already gives an air of prosperity to this little town, and assures its future importance, whatever may be the fate of the projected metropolis."[4] The fate of the future "metropolis" was, in fact, frequently in doubt during the succeeding seventy-five years.

At George Washington's request, the act of 1790 specifying the location of a federal district of "ten miles square" to be located at any point *above* the Eastern Branch, was modified to include the town of Alexandria, several miles below that point. (Alexandria was ceded back to Virginia in 1846.) Congress enacted this change on March 3, 1791, and by the ninth of that month Major Pierre L'Enfant [who went by the name Peter] had arrived in Georgetown to commence the planning of the capital city. Andrew Ellicott and Benjamin Banneker had already been employed to survey and map the federal territory, and they proceeded without delay to carry out as much of this work as they could before Washington's arrival at the site.

On the evening of March 29 a crucial meeting took place after dinner at the home of General Uriah Forrest,[5] at which the president, the newly appointed commissioners, and the principal landowners of the federal district were present. The next day Washington recorded in his diary:

"Plan of the City of Washington, in the Territory of Columbia ceded by the States of Virginia and Maryland to the United States of America," by Andrew Ellicott, published in The Universal Asylum, *and* Columbian Magazine, *March 1792. This was the first published plan of the proposed city, and while at first glance it appears to be a replica of L'Enfant's original plan, in fact there are many subtle differences between the two.*

The parties to whom I addressed myself yesterday evening, having taken the matter into consideration, saw the propriety of my observations; and whilst they were contending for the shadow they might lose the substance; and therefore mutually agreed and entered into articles to surrender for public purposes, one half the land they severally possessed within the bounds which were designated as necessary for the city to stand.

This business being thus happily finished and some directions given to the Commissioners, the Surveyor and Engineer with respect to the mode of laying out the district—Surveying the grounds for the City and forming them into lots—I left Georgetown, dined in Alexandria and reached Mount Vernon in the evening.[6]

It was only fitting that the commissioners agreed in September that the federal district be called "The Territory of Columbia" and the federal city "The City of Washington"!

L'Enfant had less than a year to prepare the plan of the capital city before he was dismissed for his failure—or his temperamental inability—to acknowledge the authority of the commissioners over his work. To the end, he maintained that he was responsible to the president alone, and when Washington himself reluctantly denied that this was so, L'Enfant's dismissal was inevitable. He had sufficient time, nevertheless, to set the mold into which the city would be formed, and with the sole exception of Washington himself, no one's influence upon its conception and development was greater.

The architecture of the area since 1791 may be conveniently divided into four major phases. The first, which extended to the middle of the nineteenth century, is generally characterized by work in the Late Georgian and Classic Revival styles. Some designs in the Gothic Revival style also appeared in this period, but they were limited principally to small examples of ecclesiastical architecture. The second phase, in a variety of styles that might be grouped under the term *Romantic Revival*, dominated from about 1850 to the end of the century. The third period, Classic Eclecticism, was to a large degree an outgrowth of the Columbian Exposition of 1893 and the McMillan Plan for Washington of 1901–2. The fourth and last phase can be said to extend from about the beginning of World War II to the present day.

From the first, the federal capital attracted the talents of many of the most gifted designers of the period. They included architect-builders or "undertakers," such as William Lovering; self-taught gentleman-architects like Dr. William Thornton; and trained professional architect-engineers, of whom Benjamin Henry Latrobe was the most notable example. Some, like James Hoban, architect of the White House, and

Philip Hart proposed this design for the new Capitol, which would have had a rather collegiate character were it not for the cartoonish human finials.

Charles Bulfinch, who succeeded Latrobe as architect of the Capitol in 1818, do not fit neatly into any of these categories.

In an era that was not distinguished by temperance of speech and writing in the political arena, architects frequently indulged in bitter personal invective. Architects have been inclined to disagree with one another since the beginning of time and will probably continue to do so until the end, but they have seldom expressed themselves so forcefully in writing as in the case of:

(a) Thornton versus Latrobe:
   This Dutchman in taste, this monument builder,
   This planner of grand steps and walls,
   This falling-arch maker, this blunder-roof gilder,
   Himself still an architect calls.
(b) Latrobe versus Hoban:
   . . . the style he [Jefferson] proposes is exactly consistent with Hoban's pile—a litter of pigs worthy of the great sow it surrounds, and of the wild Irish boar, the father of her.
(c) Hadfield versus Thornton, et al.:
   This premium [for the best design of the Capitol] was offered at a period when scarcely a professional architect was to be found in any of the United States; which is plainly to be seen in the pile of trash presented as designs for [the Capitol] building.[7]

Paradoxically, the men who hurled such violent criticism at one another lived in an age of harmonious urban architecture, for, despite personal animosities and professional jealousies, they were all working within the limits of generally accepted standards of taste, and perhaps just as important, within fairly narrow limits of available construction materials and techniques.[8]

Although work on the first major public buildings, the White House and the Capitol, had begun in 1793—seven years before the government moved to Washington—they were virtually built anew after British troops sacked and burned Washington in 1814. The rout of the hastily assembled militia at the Battle of Bladensburg (known thereafter as "The Bladensburg Races") caused President Madison, Madame Madison, and the rest of official Washington to beat a hasty retreat to the suburbs. The president returned to take up temporary residence in Colonel John Tayloe's town house, the Octagon; the Treaty of Ghent, which ended the War of 1812, was signed in the round room on the second floor.

In the early 1830s the commercial leaders of Washington City thought its future lay in the success of the Chesapeake and Ohio Canal, which was supposed to connect the Potomac with the headwaters of the Ohio River. After 1850 the canal did tie Washington to Cumberland, Maryland, and it continued in operation until 1923. But it was never a

Published in London, this engraving marks the day the British took Washington in the War of 1812 and, according to the caption, the invading army "burnt and destroyed their Dock Yard, . . . Senate House, President's Palace, War Office, Treasury, and the Great Bridge."

The C&O Canal was popular with early twentieth-century schoolchildren, but not with merchants, who preferred the speed and reliability of the B&O Railroad out of Baltimore. The canal was closed to commercial traffic in 1923.

profitable investment, because the more successful Baltimore and Ohio Railroad, following much the same route and with its eastern terminus at Baltimore, had been begun at exactly the same time (a remarkable act of optimism, since steam locomotives had not yet been tried on such a scale). The canal today provides a valuable recreational area—an attractive stretch for hiking, cycling, and canoeing.

When Robert Mills served as architect of public buildings in 1841, he supplemented his modest income by producing the *Guide to the National Executive Offices and the Capitol of the United States*, a slim paperbound volume of only fifty pages that is of interest today chiefly because within those covers he was able to include plans of the Capitol and of all the executive buildings, to list the names and room numbers of all federal employees, and to have room left over to print the menu for the congressional dining room or "Refectory for Members of Congress."[9]

Mills (who had been a pupil of Latrobe), Ammi Young, and Thomas U. Walter were probably the last federal architects of the period to design work in the Classic Revival style. In 1849 Robert Dale Owen, son of Robert Owen, leader of the utopian colony of New Harmony, published *Hints on Public Architecture*. A former representative from Indiana, the younger Owen served as chairman of the building committee of the Smithsonian Institution, and his book supplied an elaborate presentation of, and argument for, the honest functional qualities of James Renwick's design, "exemplifying the style of the twelfth century," as contrasted with the false qualities of the Greek and Roman manners of other public buildings in Washington. The book and the design appear to have been strongly influenced by the writings of A. Welby Pugin and Andrew Jackson Downing. Some of the text gives one the impression that, though time may pass and styles may change, architectural jargon remains usable for any occasion: "to reach an Architecture suited to our own country and our own time. . . an actual example, at the Seat of Government, the architect of which seems to me to have struck into the right road, to have made a step in advance, and to have given us, in his design, not a little of what may be fitting and appropriate in any manner . . . that shall deserve to be named as a National Style of Architecture for America."[10]

Not many architects chose to follow Renwick's new "national style" (Renwick himself, when he designed the old Corcoran Gallery some years later, adopted the style of the French Renaissance), but most architects thereafter seemed determined to submit their own candidates for that honor.

Before his death in a Hudson riverboat explosion in 1852, Downing had laid out the grounds of the Smithsonian and the White House in the romantic, meandering style of the period. His popular books on landscape design and rural architecture publicized residential designs by A. J. Davis, Richard Upjohn, and Downing's own partner, Calvert Vaux, who planned houses for some of the fashionable and wealthy citizens of

This engraving, published c. 1854, exaggerates the scale of the almost completed Smithsonian "Castle" but vividly conveys the building's picturesque composition.

Georgetown. Vaux's houses show, in an interesting way, the transition of residential design from the late Classic Revival through the relatively chaste Italianate or Tuscan Villa style to the heavily ornamented, mansard-roofed houses of the latter part of the nineteenth century.

The Civil War turned the city of Washington into an armed camp. The location of the capital, selected so carefully to be near the line between the North and South, became a position at the edge of the battlefront. A ring of defensive forts appeared on the hills surrounding the city, and although in 1864 a Confederate army led by Jubal Early reached the outskirts of the federal district at Fort Stevens, the city's defenses were never penetrated.[11]

Apart from the completion of the new Capitol wings and dome, work on which continued despite the war, little construction of a permanent nature went on in the city until the end of hostilities. A significant aftermath, however, was the increased influence and activity of the U.S. Army Corps of Engineers—not restricted to works of engineering alone, but extending to the design or supervision of construction of major public buildings such as the Pension Building and the old State, War, and Navy Building. Most prominent in the corps at that time was General Montgomery Meigs, the talented officer who had earlier challenged Thomas U. Walter's authority as architect of the Capitol. Meigs designed

Georgetown merchant Francis Dodge built this "suburban villa," designed by A. J. Downing and Calvert Vaux, at 1517 30th Street, NW. From the glass-enclosed tower, Francis, whose brother Robert commissioned his own house nearby based on the same design, could watch over the family's warehouse near the C&O Canal.

The Franklin School, designed by Adolf Cluss and completed in 1869, as depicted in Joseph West Moore's Picturesque Washington, *of 1886. A model of the school building, which still stands at 13th and K streets, NW, was featured in the 1873 World Exposition in Vienna, Austria, and earned for the Washington public school system a Medal for Progress.*

the astonishing post–Civil War Pension Building but left what may be his most enduring monument in the Washington aqueduct system, extending to the city from above the Little Falls of the Potomac. Two of the bridges along its route are especially notable—the Cabin John Aqueduct Bridge, which for many years was the longest stone arch in the world (220 feet), and the Rock Creek Aqueduct Bridge, where the road was carried on the arched tubular metal pipes of the water supply system.

Construction of the old State, War, and Navy Building after the Civil War was considered by many to signify the permanence of Washington, D.C., as the site of the national capital. If cost of construction and permanence of materials were any measure of that intent, it must have served admirably to make the intention clear. Alfred B. Mullett was not an architect whose work rested lightly upon the earth (the Post Office Building in St. Louis is another good example of his work). Like MacArthur's Philadelphia City Hall, his buildings expressed as much civic confidence as architectural diligence.

The Smithsonian's Arts and Industries Building, designed by Cluss and Shulze, is an interesting survival from the exhibition architecture of the 1876 Philadelphia Centennial Exposition. The Oriental flavor of its form and polychrome decorations was echoed in some of the city's market buildings, schools, railroad stations, and residences of the 1880s, of which relatively few remain. The influence of H. H. Richardson and the Romanesque Revival made an impression on Washington architecture from about 1880 to 1900, and although Richardson's Hay and Adams houses were destroyed to build the hotel that bears their names, the Tuckerman House, built the year of his death, 1886, on an adjoining site, was carried out by Hornblower and Marshall in a direct continuity of style and exterior detailing. The Presbyterian Church of the Covenant, designed by J. C. Cady, architect of the Museum of Natural History in

New York, and the old Post Office on Pennsylvania Avenue, are other important examples of the period.[12]

The Washington firm of Smithmeyer and Pelz was prominent on the architectural scene toward the end of the nineteenth century, with buildings to its credit as widely different as Georgetown's Healy Hall, a Victorian neo-Gothic college building, and the Library of Congress, a competition-winning design in the Renaissance style. Some of the more startling designs of this versatile firm were never built; they included a Gothic multitowered bridge across the Potomac, a new White House spanning 16th Street at Meridian Hill, and Franklin Smith's proposal for the "Halls of the Ancients," a sort of permanent world's fair of architecture that would have extended from the west side of the Ellipse to the river.

The lack of any effective controls over its rapid and haphazard growth was gradually destroying any evidence of the capital as a uniquely planned city, but in the year 1901 the American Institute of Architects (AIA) played a central role in the initiation of the McMillan Plan, which modified, enlarged, and reestablished L'Enfant's plan of Washington. Glenn Brown, an architect whose deep interest in the history of the Capitol later produced a monumental two-volume account of its development, had been appointed secretary of the institute in 1899, and it was largely through his efforts that the program for the AIA convention of 1900 was prepared. The meeting convened in Washington on the centennial of the establishment of the federal city, and the papers delivered at that meeting inspired Senator James McMillan, chairman of the Senate District Committee, to appoint a commission to study the planning of the city. He asked the institute to suggest who would be most qualified to serve, and the names of Daniel H. Burnham and Frederick Law Olmsted Jr. emerged by common consent. The Chicago Columbian Exposition of 1893 was still fresh in the minds of all, and Burnham, having headed the group of architects and artists who planned the exhibition, was a logical choice, as was Olmsted, son and successor of the famous landscape architect who had designed the grounds and terraces of the Capitol. Burnham and Olmsted, in turn, asked for the appointment of architect Charles Follen McKim and sculptor Augustus Saint-Gaudens, both of whom had worked intimately with Burnham during the Columbian Exposition. The report of this group, the Park Commission, was published in 1902 and was a remarkable document. These talented men—bound together by friendship, respect, and common purpose—made the most of the opportunity to describe and delineate a vision of what the city might become.

Some of the Park Commission's recommendations were never carried out—among them ideas that could be profitably restudied today—but many of them were, and the effect upon Washington's architectural style was just as pronounced as the effects upon its plan. The formality of L'Enfant's plan was restored, and the argument that an architecture derived from classical antecedents was the only suitable style for such a plan was persuasively presented in visual terms. Whatever weight or merit this argument may have had, some of the finest buildings in Washington date from the early decades of [the twentieth] century quite simply because the best architects in the country designed them.

It was a time of great optimism, clients wanted and would pay for the best, and art was respectable enough to sit at the table when the money was being served. Not only were prominent architects of the period, such as Burnham, the firm of McKim, Mead and White, Henry Bacon, Paul Cret, and Cass Gilbert, given important commissions in the capital, but their buildings were embellished by the work of sculptors such as Saint-Gaudens, Daniel Chester French, and Lorado Taft.

The spirit pervading the best work of that period seems gradually to have been lost. Whether it was dried up by the Depression, squeezed out by the weight of bureaucracy, or simply enfeebled by lack of conviction and talent would be hard to say. Whatever the cause, work in the style of Academic Classicism, with few exceptions, seemed to become progressively larger, more sterile, and less graceful in conception and execution.

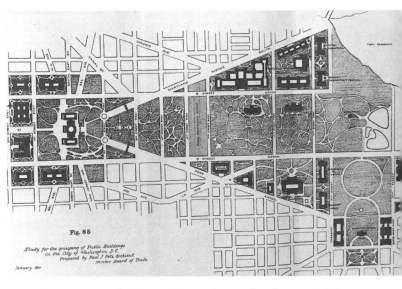

"Study for the grouping of Public Buildings in the City of Washington, D.C.," prepared by architect Paul Pelz in 1901. Pelz's efforts to tidy up the unkempt Mall did not go nearly as far as those of the Senate Park Commission, which released its ambitious plan the following year.

It is difficult to view architecture in Washington since 1940 in any clear historical perspective. Dating a new phase of architectural development from a period at the beginning of World War II is in itself a somewhat arbitrary decision, but the Saarinen competition-winning design for the Smithsonian Gallery of Art in 1939 (which was never constructed) and William Lescaze's Longfellow Building in 1940 [later modified beyond recognition] probably mark as distinct a point of change as any that might be named. Since that time, certain other isolated examples, such as the Dulles Airport Terminal building, loom up as important and serious works of architecture, but a leveling influence of sorts has been at work. The majority of contemporary commercial office buildings and governmental office buildings tended to become larger and more standardized to the point where they were virtually indistinguishable in form. This was perhaps inevitable, since the functions of these structures were very nearly the same. The great variety of industrially produced materials and building components that became available after World War II, along with the economies of modern curtain wall construction, created a new element in the cityscape that was both monotonous and distracting: monotonous because many of the newer buildings were wrapped, like packages, in an overall pattern of windows and spandrels; distracting because there seemed no limit to the number of unsuitable patterns that one could place in juxtaposition to one another.

Washington is a horizontal city. The maximum building heights Congress established in 1910 to prevent our principal federal monuments from being overshadowed by commercial construction are in general

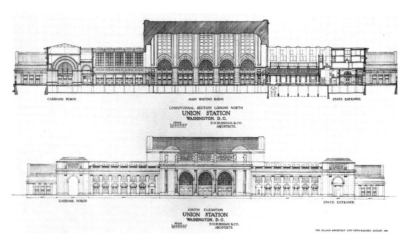

Cross-section and main elevation of the new Union Station, designed by D. H. Burnham & Co., the first building to be executed in the spirit of the Senate Park Commission's plan of 1901–2.

still considered to be a desirable limitation. But these height limits, coupled with building programs calling for hundreds of thousands of square feet of construction, have created architectural and planning problems within the city that remain unresolved.

Southwest Washington remains interesting to architects and planners, not only as one of the first large-scale applications of the powers of urban renewal, but also as an architectural sampler of the mid-twentieth century. Rarely may one view such a variety of architectural solutions to essentially the same problem, constructed in such a relatively concentrated area, over such a short period of time. Some examples of planned communities near Washington—ranging from Greenbelt, Maryland, the most famous of the government-sponsored resettlement housing projects of the 1930s, and Hollin Hills in Virginia, a pioneer example of post-war contemporary development planning, to Reston, conceived as a New Town, in nearby Fairfax County—also are of particular interest.

The 1960s and 1970s brought significant changes in the expectations, attitudes, and demands of the city's people, both black and white. The riots of 1968, Resurrection City, and the outpouring of young demonstrators against the Vietnam War offered dramatic evidence of change, but there were less dramatic shifts just as important to the architectural and topographical future of the city. Concern for the preservation of older buildings and places within the city grew, contributing to its cultural vitality and variety. Disenchantment with the wholesale demolition that accompanied (and the overbearing scale that characterized) so much of the federal city planning and reconstruction mounted in these years. Resistance to the construction of more freeways within the city, organized opposition by communities within the city to overly permissive zoning, and, on a smaller scale, the struggle to save the old Post Office on Pennsylvania Avenue all reflected changing beliefs of what constitutes progress. These movements questioned the sanity of any planning that fails to sustain and encourage the humane qualities of the city—those qualities making life within it bearable.

Reconstruction of Pennsylvania Avenue supplied a good case in point. Early plans, unveiled in 1964, swept away all existing buildings on the north side of the avenue from the Treasury Building to the Capitol and retained only the tower of the Post Office on the south side as a relic of the nineteenth century. Ultimately, however, those plans gave way, as had earlier proposals to "Federalize" Lafayette Square, to less drastic reconstruction. The Pennsylvania Avenue Plan, after being restudied and modified, saved some fine older buildings instead of demolishing them and brought more mixed commercial and residential uses into the area. It was well that planners reconsidered, for the FBI Building (as the first block to conform to the earlier plan, but without the arcaded street façade recommended by the commission) hardly warmed one's enthusiasm for an avenue filled with a succession of such structures. To the credit of Nathaniel Owings and others who were active in the planning process, they remained receptive to changing needs and conditions in their efforts to move this important project ahead.

From the Rayburn Building, to the Kennedy Center, to the FBI Building and Washington Convention Center, the planning and architectural problems of such immense, relatively low buildings within the city were nearly insurmountable. The area south of Independence Avenue, as it parallels the Mall, has been filled with federal office buildings just as monumental and just as lifeless as those spawned by the Federal Triangle project of the 1920s but lacking that undertaking's unity of concept and style. The Mall has become the site of a newer group of buildings for the Smithsonian Institution, which share only the general discipline of their location. Fortunately, the scale of the great central lawn, with its flanking panels of trees, is so vast that aberrations of form are visually submerged with scarcely a ripple.

If the work of any architect during the 1970s is to be singled out for its contribution to the city, one must note I. M. Pei's Christian Science Church at 16th and I streets and office buildings at L'Enfant Plaza. Both stand well above the level of quality of similar buildings of the period in their maturity of concept and execution. Pei's East Wing of the National Gallery [completed in 1978] stands as one of the capital's most original and exciting structures—complex but complete in its logic and form.

In 1967 President Johnson requested the development of a new "racially and economically balanced community" on one of the largest single undeveloped sites still remaining within the District of Columbia. Fort Lincoln New Town, to be built on the grounds of the former National Training School for Boys, was conceived as an urban community, a prototype for other federally sponsored new towns-within-towns, and a laboratory for innovative social, ecological, and educational planning. The project never received the support that had originally been envisioned; it remains, under the aegis of private developers, an architectural (as well as social) disappointment.

Mushrooming construction in Rosslyn, just across the river from the old port of Georgetown, and in Crystal City—an office and residential complex close to the National Airport—has transformed parts of the nearby Virginia skyline (someone called it Houston-on-the-Potomac) with a forest of high-rise office buildings unrestricted by the height limits of the city of Washington. The Georgetown waterfront, long depressed by anachronistic industrial zoning and by the blighting influence of an unattractive elevated freeway, now constantly stirs to the sound of new construction, and an effort is being made to reconcile opportunities for residential and commercial development on what is potentially one of the most advantageous sites in the city with the need to preserve the valuable historic buildings and enclaves that enrich the area.

And last, one must mention the Metro, the Washington Metropolitan Area Transit Authority. Washington's Metro was one of the most extensive, and expensive, public works projects in history, spending more than $3 billion on construction. The architectural design of the system was under the direction of Harry Weese and Associates, with DeLeuw Cather and Company acting as general engineering consultants. The subway, with rail extensions reaching far out into Maryland and Virginia, unquestionably has had a profound influence upon the present and future development of the city and its suburbs.

NOTES

This introduction is reprinted, with bracketed revisions, from the 1974 edition.

1. See Kenneth R. Bowling and Helen E. Veit, eds., *The Diary of William Maclay and Other Notes on the Senate Debates*, vol. 9 of the *Documentary History of the First Federal Congress of the United States of America, March 4, 1789–March 3, 1791* (Baltimore: Johns Hopkins University Press, 1988), 307–8. Maclay, a senator from Pennsylvania, had no illusions. His journal entry for June 30, 1790, reports: "I am fully convinced Pennsylvania could do no better. The Matter could not be longer delayed. It is in fact the Interest of the President of the United States, that pushes the Potowmack, he by means of Jefferson Madison Carroll & others Urges the Business, and if We had not closed with these Terms a bargain would have been made, for the Temporary Residence in New York."

2. Thomas Tileston Waterman, *The Mansions of Virginia, 1706–1776* (Chapel Hill: University of North Carolina Press, 1946).

3. Gunston Hall, Virginia (1753); Mount Vernon, Virginia (1757–87); Montpelier, Laurel, Maryland (1770). See also Mills Lane, *Architecture of the Old South: Virginia* (New York: Abbeville Press, 1987) and *Architecture of the Old South: Maryland* (New York: Abbeville Press, 1991) for other examples.

4. Thomas Twining, *Travels in America 100 Years Ago* (New York: Harper & Bros., 1893), 98–99.

5. The building that was Forrest's home, 2550 M Street, though mutilated by commercial alteration, remains standing.

6. Donald Jackson and Dorothy Toohig, eds., *The Diaries of George Washington* (Charlottesville: University Press of Virginia, 1979), vol. 6.

7. Talbot Hamlin, *Benjamin Henry Latrobe* (New York: Oxford University Press, 1955), 285, 294; George Hadfield, *The Washington Guide* (Washington, D.C.: S. A. Elliott, 1826), 22.

8. See, for example, Thornton's "Tudor Place," and the Octagon; Latrobe's Decatur House and St. John's Church, Lafayette Square; The White House—central façade by Hoban and Latrobe; and Hadfield's Arlington House and Old City Hall.

9. Some of the fixed prices were: venison steak, 37½ cents; beefsteak, 25 cents; pork steak, 25 cents; mutton chop, 25 cents; veal cutlet, 25 cents; one dozen raw oysters, 12½ cents; ham and eggs, 37½ cents; one plate of common

turtle soup, 25 cents; one plate of green turtle soup, 50 cents; wine and water, and malt liquor, per tumbler, 6¼ cents.

10. Robert Dale Owen, *Hints on Public Architecture* (New York: G. P. Putnam, 1849), 104, 109.

11. See Barnard, *Defenses of Washington* (Washington, D.C.: U.S. Government Printing Office, 1871). The remains of this chain of earthwork defenses are now under the jurisdiction of the Park Service. Fort Stevens, at the head of Georgia Avenue, NW, is probably the most interesting, historically if not topographically.

12. Of these three buildings, only the old Franklin Post Office still remains, the Tuckerman House and Church of the Covenant having been demolished in the late 1960s to make way for new speculative office buildings.

The Architecture of Washington, D.C., 1970s–2006

G. MARTIN MOELLER JR., ASSOC. AIA

There was a time around the 1960s when Washington was widely considered to be moving toward the vanguard of modern architecture. Internationally recognized architects, including Marcel Breuer, I. M. Pei, Philip Johnson, and Gordon Bunshaft, were designing prominent governmental and institutional buildings that celebrated pure, abstract geometry. Nathaniel Owings was leading a presidentially appointed advisory council that proposed an audacious and comprehensive plan for the redevelopment of Pennsylvania Avenue. Talented local firms, such as Chloethiel Woodard Smith & Associated Architects and Keyes Lethbridge & Condon, were producing in Southwest Washington some of the most convincingly livable "urban renewal" projects in the country. At the same time, years before the preservation movement took root, the nation's capital seemed ahead of the curve in this regard, too, as John Carl Warnecke was devising a scheme that saved Lafayette Square from demolition and Arthur Cotton Moore was finding a way to turn an old industrial facility in Georgetown into a model of adaptive reuse known as Canal Square.

While Washington was still a small city compared to New York, Chicago, and the great European capitals, and was not exactly a Mecca for newly minted architects, the city's architectural scene during this period certainly seemed to be emerging from its reactionary past. Particularly during the early 1960s, when the Kennedy administration infused the city with an air of youthful exuberance, the capital was viewed by many architects as an up-and-coming, modern metropolis.

Even so, the city's population at that point was already declining steadily as suburban development, here as elsewhere in the country, was exploding. When the last D.C. streetcar disappeared from the tracks on January 27, 1962, long-standing assumptions about civic scale, neighborhood viability, and urban density evaporated. The prevalence of the private automobile, which both government and industry went to great lengths to accommodate, dictated urban planning and development. Downtown retailers were already struggling to hold their own against new suburban shopping malls when riots in the wake of the 1968 assassination of Martin Luther King Jr. laid waste to once thriving commercial thoroughfares along 14th Street, NW, and H Street, NE. Urban emigration accelerated into the 1970s and even the 1980s amid a classic vicious cycle of crime, poverty, poor schools, and deteriorating infrastructure.

In this increasingly desperate urban context, the bold and sometimes heroic architectural gestures that had made Washington a poster city for high modernism began to look stale and barren to many designers and clients alike. Of course, a reaction to the purism of the modern movement was not unique to Washington and was not a new phenomenon—Robert Venturi had published his *Complexity and Contradiction in Architecture* in 1966, and the two most widely heralded (and derided) early works of postmodern architecture were not in Washington but in Portland, Oregon (Michael Graves's Public Services Building) and in New York (Philip Johnson's AT&T—now Sony—Building). By the mid-1980s, local architects were firmly on board with the counterrevolution, creating buildings such as 1300 New York Avenue (now the Inter-American Development Bank), which moved away from pure modern abstraction in favor of a more traditional hierarchy of forms, articulated windows, and allusions to historical architectural motifs.

The postmodern movement essentially developed as two different, if sometimes overlapping, strains—a playful, "mannerist," often jokey school, as exemplified by Charles Moore's Piazza d'Italia in New Orleans, and a quite serious, unabashedly historicist school that celebrated specific "styles," traditional materials, and contextualism. In Washington especially, the former strain never took hold, but the latter quickly became predominant. The ideals of the City Beautiful movement, of course, had never really fallen out of favor here. In retrospect, even during the heyday of high modernism, most of the capital's official and commercial architecture had always adhered to a monumental purity that never seriously challenged the fundamental precepts of Daniel Burnham and his cohort, even though the strictly classical vocabulary they favored had been abandoned. So a return to historicism—especially but not exclusively a kind of classicism—was an easy switch for many Washington architects. Soon, downtown was becoming filled with polite buildings, each with a clearly articulated base, middle, and top, typically with punched windows, and ever respectful of the street line. The better ones had well-controlled proportions and carefully conceived ornament, while the poorer ones were simplistic, formulaic, and ultimately quite dreary.

The ease with which the city climbed onto the historicist bandwagon prompted one Washington architect to quip that his local colleagues constituted "the avant-garde of the rear guard." Another, more cynically, dubbed Washington in the early 1990s "Stepford, D.C.," alluding to the fictional Connecticut town populated by what seem to be attractive, happy, but soulless housewives. His moniker reflected a profound ambivalence about the architecture of the day: on the one hand, he relished how buildings seemed to work together to form coherent and pleasant streetscapes, but on the other, he missed the excitement, the exuberant inventiveness, and even the occasional bold mistakes that made other large cities so interesting.

Washington may have avoided most of the postmodern excesses that now tend to engender embarrassed throat-clearing at cocktail parties, but it also turned into something of a caricature of itself. The majority of the large-scale buildings erected in Washington in the 1980s and 1990s seem to out-of-towners to be cast-stone-and-mortar versions of stereotypical Washingtonians—well-bred, tidy, and smart, to be sure, but also reserved and perhaps a little dull. Washingtonians, of course, know that the demographic stereotype is just that—it fails, for example, to recognize uniquely local aspects of African American culture, or the many creative young professionals who moved to town with the high-tech boom. Similarly, locals know and appreciate the unique character of Washington neighborhoods, and may favor certain cleverly designed restaurants, clubs, and shops that reveal a hipper side of the city's personality. Nonetheless, one must acknowledge that the core of late twentieth-century Washington was a place in which architectural invention—the spark of design genius—had generally been sacrificed in favor of urban unity and surpassing civic order.

Around the turn of the twenty-first century, however, several events suggested that this circumstance might be about to change . . . or not. In 1999 came the news that Frank Gehry had been selected to design the addition to the Corcoran Gallery of Art, and thus to bring his signature metallic squiggles to the city of marble and limestone. Washington skeptics cheered the prospect of a bona fide piece of trendy design to help put the city on some unspecified map presumably carried by members of the cultural elite. After half a decade of trying to raise the money for the addition, however, the Corcoran announced that it was abandoning the project. The skeptics threw their hands in the air and said that they had always known that staid old Washington could not pull it off. Largely missing from the public debate was the point that, even by the time the new wing was proposed, Gehry's basic architectural vocabulary had already become something of a cliché. Had the structure gone ahead, the same skeptics might well have scoffed "it's been done," and dismissed the city as a cultural backwater anyway.

More promising, but no less controversial, is the new undulating glass roof by Foster & Partners of London being built over the courtyard of the Old Patent Office Building (now the National Portrait Gallery

Computer rendering of the new roof, designed by Foster & Partners and scheduled for completion in 2007, that will enclose the courtyard at the Old Patent Office Building, which now houses the Smithsonian American Art Museum and the National Portrait Gallery.

and Smithsonian American Art Museum). Admittedly, this, too, seems a derivative work—in this case, of the firm's similar project at the British Museum—but the effect will be quite distinct because of key differences between the two projects (in the British Museum, for instance, there was a historic structure in the middle of the courtyard, whereas in the Washington building, there is not). The proposal angered many preservationists, who felt that it represented a desecration of one of Washington's oldest federal buildings, and at one point, the National Capital Planning Commission brought the project to a halt over unauthorized changes to the existing structure during early construction of the roof. The commission, the Smithsonian, and the design team eventually came to terms, and the project is back on. While the roof enclosure will inevitably change how the existing structure is experienced, it also represents an innovative and skillful marriage of old and new, bringing a fresh identity to an existing building without irrevocably altering the historic fabric. This is an approach that has been followed successfully on many occasions in Europe, from the new glass dome on Berlin's Reichstag, to unapologetically modern infill buildings inserted in the medieval core of Tallinn, Estonia, to stunningly sleek and sculptural storefronts bursting from the stoic old buildings of Vienna. Such projects can be done well or badly, of course, but numerous examples from the past two decades indicate that a combination of ardent preservation of existing structures and highly progressive new architecture can enhance the appeal of each component.

Washington, of course, does not have the exceedingly long history of Berlin, Tallinn, or Vienna. By global standards, even now that it has passed its bicentennial year, Washington is something of an upstart. L'Enfant, the Senate Park Commission, and many of the individual architects and firms that have practiced here over the last two centuries have actively tried to manufacture a coherent urbanism for Washington, and by doing so, to give it a sense of place. Their efforts speak for themselves. Compare Washington to most any other artificial city in relatively recent history, and the advantages of the U.S. capital's architectural development become evident. Canberra? Beyond a handful of monumental structures, one could search in vain for any landmark or memorable streetscape. Brasilia? Home to several absolutely brilliant buildings, the place is otherwise an unmitigated horror—a beautiful plan on paper rendered vacuous in three dimensions. In contrast, Washington works as a city in a meaningful sense. The famous building height limit has had the

A classic view of a row of attached houses in one of Washington's residential neighborhoods, exhibiting great variety in materials, colors, and details, but creating a consistent and unified streetscape.

(presumably) coincidental effect of keeping the urban core reasonably dense, as developers have sought to fill their maximum allowable building envelopes. Washington has thus avoided the hodge-podge patterns of many American cities, in which skyscrapers alternate with surface parking lots, creating haphazard and inhospitable streetscapes. Meanwhile, Washington's famous row house neighborhoods provide block after block of rich texture, intermingled with flourishing commercial nodes. And a variety and scale of parks that most cities can only envy yield a good balance between the natural and the human-made environments.

Charles Dickens snidely labeled nineteenth-century Washington a "city of magnificent intentions." A century-and-a-half after his comment, many of those intentions have been realized at last in stone, steel, and concrete. Wrought out of political compromise in the earliest days of the republic, Washington remains a city of compromise in terms of its architectural character. Perhaps, however, the numerous talented architects who now call Washington home—many of whom have never known the city as anything other than a vibrant and cosmopolitan place—will at last feel free to use the solid and stable built environment that has been bequeathed to them as a starting point for more inventive design explorations. Already, neighborhoods that had been the very symbols of urban decay for decades after the riots are sprouting funky, loft-style apartment buildings that are challenging preconceptions about how Washingtonians want to live. Hardly a month goes by without a trendy new restaurant opening its doors, and huge new cinema complexes have opened in Georgetown and the East End of downtown. A number of recent projects have been successful in simultaneously reinforcing the broader urban fabric and injecting elements of more forward-looking design.

Perhaps Washington's third century will be its golden age, in which rich layers of history, cutting-edge works of architecture, and thriving street life form a harmonious and sustainable city that will be the pride of the nation.

Governmental Capitol Hill

The Washington Monument may be taller, and the White House the more potent symbol of political power, but the primary architectural icon of Washington, D.C.—and, by extension, of American democracy—is undoubtedly the Capitol. Standing at the intersection of L'Enfant's cardinal axes, it is both the conceptual center of the city and the majestic terminus of the Mall. Refined and, in some places, lavish in its materials and details, and surrounded by expansive, well-landscaped grounds, the Capitol is simultaneously urbane and bucolic, making it the perfect emblem of a capital city forged out of a compromise between northern urban and southern agrarian interests.

Its architectural primacy notwithstanding, the Capitol today is just one element of a vast complex accommodating the U.S. Congress and its adjuncts. The jurisdiction of the Architect of the Capitol, in fact, extends to the House and Senate office buildings that bracket the Capitol grounds, the three major buildings of the Library of Congress, the Supreme Court, and the U.S. Botanic Garden, among other structures. Several prominent private institutions, such as the Folger Shakespeare Library, are interspersed among these landmarks.

An aerial view, c. 1920, of Capitol Hill, with Union Station in the left background and the Library of Congress in the right middle ground.

This chapter explores the public and private buildings at the core of the Capitol Hill neighborhood, the site of so many workings of the national government, from the petty and mundane to the noble and momentous.

A1   The Capitol

1793–1802 William Thornton, with Stephen Hallet, George Hadfield, and James Hoban
1803–17 Benjamin Henry Latrobe
1818–29 Charles Bulfinch
1836–51 Various modifications: Robert Mills et al.
1851–65 Extensions and new dome: Thomas U. Walter, with Montgomery C. Meigs
1951 Remodeling of House and Senate chambers: Associate architect: Francis P. Sullivan; Consulting architects: Harbeson, Hough, Livingston & Larson
1962 East Front extension: Advisory architects: Roscoe DeWitt & Fred L. Hardison; Associate architects: Alfred Poor & Albert Swanke
1976 Restoration of old Senate and Supreme Court chambers: DeWitt, Poor & Shelton
1987 West Front restoration: Ammann & Whitney; New structures in courtyard: Hugh Newell Jacobsen
1993 Addition below West Terrace: Hugh Newell Jacobsen

TEL: (202) 224-3121   www.aoc.gov

Now that it is surrounded by a twenty-first-century metropolis, Capitol "Hill" seems little more than a mound. But in 1791, the eighty-eight-foot rise then known as Jenkins Hill (or Jenkins Heights) impressed L'Enfant as "a pedestal waiting for a monument." For him, this was the most logical site for the principal building of the new capital city, and the rest of his plan was organized around the placement of the "Congress House" there.

The original design for the Capitol was the result of a competition, albeit only indirectly. None of the submissions received by the deadline in July 1792 fully pleased either President Washington or Secretary of State Jefferson. They therefore decided not to select a winner but instead to invite one entrant, a professional builder named Stephen Hallet, to redevelop his proposal for further consideration. After the deadline had passed, William Thornton, a physician from the West Indies, submitted another proposal, and the president and secretary of state invited him, too, to develop his scheme further. A revised design by Thornton was ultimately selected. Although architecture as a true profession was virtually unknown in eighteenth-century America, Thornton's blunt admission of his amateurism ("I got some books and worked a few days, then gave the plan in the ancient Ionic order which carried the day") worried Washington and Jefferson, so they hired Hallet to supervise the construction of Thornton's design.

On September 18, 1793, President Washington, following Masonic ritual, laid the cornerstone using a silver trowel and a marble-headed gavel. The spirit of optimism that prevailed on that auspicious day soon faded, however, as conflicts arose among the project's principal players. Hallet was fired and replaced by George Hadfield, who was replaced in turn by James Hoban, who already had won the design competition for the President's House. Construction of the Capitol proceeded very slowly due to fiscal limitations and political bickering. As Irish journalist Isaac Weld noted in 1799, "numbers of people . . . particularly in Philadelphia"

William R. Birch's 1800 drawing of the Capitol's north (Senate) wing shows an idealized Executive Mansion floating in the misty distance.

When Congress fired Latrobe in 1817, the House and Senate wings were con-
nected by only a wooden walkway, as shown in this c. 1819 watercolor.

tried to sabotage work on the Capitol by withholding funds. Given this
penny-pinching and intrigue-filled atmosphere, Jefferson and Washington
had laborers concentrate their efforts on the north wing alone, which was
finished in 1800. Congress met there for the first time that November.
Looking at the present building from the Library of Congress, one can
still see the small dome (to the right) that crowned that earliest structure.

The small dome to the left, atop the House of Representatives wing,
dates to a section completed in 1807 under architect Benjamin Henry
Latrobe, whom then-President Jefferson had appointed surveyor of
public buildings in 1803. Latrobe refined Thornton's design, introducing elements that brought a uniquely American flavor to a building
that, like most prominent buildings in the young nation, was obviously
based on European precedents. His signature "corncob" column capitals, for example, were conceived as a truly American successor to the
acanthus-leafed capitals of ancient Greece and Rome. Frances Trollope
wrote in 1832 that "the beautiful capitals . . . composed of the ears and
leaves of Indian corn" were "the only instance I saw in which America
has ventured to attempt national originality; the success is perfect. A
sense of fitness always enhances the effect of beauty." Latrobe later added
columns with capitals featuring tobacco leaves, continuing the decorative theme in the Capitol based on native American plants. Another of
Latrobe's contributions was the masonry vault structural system, a rare
American example of such a system at the time.

Detail of one of Latrobe's acclaimed corncob columns. He replaced the traditional acanthus leaves in the capital with indigenous maize, and made the shaft a bundle of cornstalks.

The War of 1812 brought the British to Washington, with devastating results for the Capitol. On August 24, 1814, British admiral Sir George Cockburn torched "this harbor of Yankee democracy," leaving what Latrobe called "a most magnificent ruin." After the war, Congress moved temporarily to the "Brick Capitol," on the site of the present Supreme Court, and Latrobe was brought back to reconstruct the earlier building. When he resigned in 1817 over a contract dispute, Latrobe left a curious structure on Jenkins Hill—the completed Senate and House wings and a walkway connecting them, creating a U shape in plan. President James Monroe then brought in Boston architect Charles Bulfinch to continue work on the building, and specifically to fill in the gaping U. Bulfinch's link was topped by a copper-clad dome of wood, stone, and brick, modeled on the one he had designed for the Massachusetts State House in the 1790s. Under his supervision, the Capitol finally reached what everyone hoped was completion in 1829.

As the government and the nation grew, however, the Capitol began to bulge, so in 1850 Congress authorized an expansion and launched another competition. Like the original competition for the building's design, this one produced no clear winner, but President Millard Fillmore selected entrant Thomas U. Walter, a Philadelphia architect, to undertake the work. Walter designed the huge extended wings—the outermost elements of the building as it exists today—to accommodate new chambers for the House and Senate, which were spanned with state-of-the-art iron trusses. Congress soon became concerned about Walter's management of the project, and brought in engineer Montgomery C. Meigs to oversee its completion. The House extension was finished in time for that body to convene there on December 16, 1857. The Senate moved into its completed quarters on January 4, 1859.

Walter's tour-de-force, however, was the enlargement of the Capitol's dome. The 1850s extensions had more than doubled the building's length (to about 750 feet), thus reducing Bulfinch's dome to visual insignifi-

Bulfinch added the center section and dome to Latrobe's wings, as depicted in this 1849 engraving of what most everyone assumed was the finished Capitol.

cance. So in 1855 Walter designed a soaring replacement consisting of two trussed cast iron shells, one inside the other, painted to resemble marble. The dome was still under construction as the Civil War began, and, according to an apocryphal story, President Lincoln directed that the work continue because he believed that "if people see the Capitol going on . . . it is a sign we intend the Union shall go on." The construction came to a climax on December 2, 1863, when Thomas Crawford's nineteen-foot statue, *Freedom,* was lifted into place at the peak of the cast iron dome.

Predictably, given the building's complex history, the Capitol's interiors are a hodgepodge, reflecting the tastes of the various eras during which major work was undertaken. The principal ceremonial space is the Rotunda, beneath the great dome, which is 180 feet high and profusely decorated. At its apex is Constantino Brumidi's fresco, *The Apotheosis of Washington,* in which the Father of Our Country hobnobs with various allegorical figures. Because the fresco is applied to the inside of the *outer dome,* it appears to float above a hole at the top of the *inner dome,* creating the illusion that the figures in the fresco are hovering in the sky. Closer to eye level, the Rotunda's walls are embellished with historical paintings by John Trumbull, known as the "Artist of the Revolution."

Beyond the Rotunda, the building contains a dizzying warren of rooms, punctuated by a few major spaces such as the original House and Senate chambers and the old Supreme Court chamber (the judicial

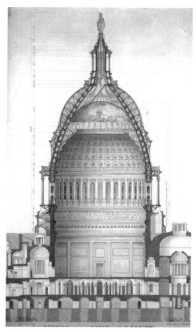

Sectional drawing, from 1859, of the new Capitol dome by Thomas U. Walter.

branch did not have its own separate quarters until 1935). The sprawling wings are full of delightfully excessive Victorian elements, from elaborate fireplaces to intricate cast iron grilles, but most of these are in suites that are not accessible to the general public. Unfortunately, the current House and Senate chambers were stripped of their gilded grandeur in 1949–51, and now look a bit like run-of-the-mill convention hotel ballrooms.

In 1958–62, the center of the East Front was extended outward thirty-two-and-a-half feet. This single stroke added 102 rooms and provided a deeper base for the dome. The stonework was changed from local Aquia Creek sandstone to Georgia marble in the process, but the old sandstone columns were preserved and now stand starkly and rather hauntingly on an open lawn at the National Arboretum [see S22]. Although wildly controversial at the time, such an extension had actually been proposed by Thomas U. Walter a century earlier. Another expansion scheme arose in the 1970s, but this time public outcry was so great that Congress scrapped the plans and voted to restore, rather than enlarge, the West Front. Accordingly, in 1988, the façade was reinforced with steel rods and roughly one-third of the crumbling sandstone was replaced.

Currently under way is a vast and complicated project to create a new visitor center, designed by RTKL Associates, under the Capitol's east lawn. Spurred by growing security concerns and a desire to handle huge numbers of visitors more efficiently, the project became all the more challenging in the wake of the terrorist attacks of September 11, 2001. However this new facility turns out, citizens making the pilgrimage to the seat of American democracy will surely be relieved to find any semblance of order following years of messy construction and ad hoc security procedures. Even so, it will be only a matter of time before some new project to extend or renovate the Capitol building arises to accommodate the needs of an ever-growing nation.

A1A Capitol Grounds

Primary grounds: 1st Street, NE, to
1st Street, NW, between Constitution
and Independence avenues

1874–92 Frederick Law Olmsted

It was perhaps inevitable that Frederick
Law Olmsted, whose name is virtually synonymous with the profession
of landscape architecture in America,
would be called on to redesign the Capitol grounds. Congress commissioned
him to do so in 1874, and the plan he devised was bold and comprehensive, addressing elements at all scales, from tree-lined walkways to cast
iron planters. A surprising amount of Olmsted's original street furniture,
such as the lampstands at the East Capitol Street entrance, endures *in
situ* on the leafy grounds.

A1B Waiting Stations

Near the East Front of the
Capitol

c. 1876 Frederick Law
Olmsted

These two stations testify to
the thoroughness and consis-
tency of Olmsted's design for
the grounds surrounding the Capitol. The stations were once known
as "Herdics," after the Herdic Phaeton Company, whose line of horse-
drawn, plushly upholstered trolleys they served.

A1C Summer House

Near the West Front of the
Capitol

1890 Frederick Law Olmsted

Olmsted envisioned this sheltered spring as a "cool retreat
during hot summer." The hex-

agonal grotto, with its brick and terra cotta walls and red tile roof, still serves its intended purpose, although it now flows with city water, since the original spring soured and had to be diverted. A nearby stone tower, also designed by Olmsted, served both aesthetic and functional purposes: its upward thrust balanced the declivity of the grotto, while a vent within carried fresh, cooled air into the Capitol through a series of underground tunnels.

A1D West Terrace

1884–92 Frederick Law Olmsted
1993 Hugh Newell Jacobsen

Olmsted questioned the emphasis that earlier plans had placed on the Capitol's East Front. He designed an elaborate system of terraces and walkways to provide a more substantial visual base for the west façade and, simultaneously, to ease the transition between the grand building and the then-informally landscaped Mall. The view from the west side had been commended by Ralph Waldo Emerson, who in 1843 wrote, "If Washington should ever grow into a great city, the outlook from the Capitol will be unsurpassed in the world. Now at sunset I seem to look westward far into the heart of the Continent from this commanding position."

A 1990s renovation of the terrace by Hugh Newell Jacobsen entailed filling in courtyards to create additional meeting space and offices. Glass panels at the base of the Capitol's west façade serve as skylights for the new spaces below.

A2 Grant Memorial

1st Street and East Mall

1922 Pedestal: Edward Pearce Casey;
Sculptor: Henry M. Schrady
1976 Reflecting pool: Skidmore,
Owings & Merrill

Over 250 feet long, this is the largest statuary grouping in the city and it includes the second largest equestrian monument in the world (after the bronze Victor Emmanuel in Rome). At the center sits General Grant astride his horse, Cincinnati. Peripheral figures represent the artillery and cavalry units Grant commanded during the Civil War.

The six-acre reflecting pool in front of the memorial sits atop a tunnel that carries Interstate 395 under the Mall. Because no substantial trees could be planted on the roof of the tunnel, the designers opted instead for this shallow water feature, the surface of which captures, in reflection, the entirety of the Capitol dome.

A3   U.S. Botanic Garden

1st Street, Maryland Avenue, and Independence Avenue

1933 Bennett, Parsons & Frost
2001 Restoration: DMJM Design

TEL: (202) 225-8333   www.usbg.gov

For much of its history, the Botanic Garden, established in 1820, occupied a site at the foot of Capitol Hill, not far off the centerline of the Mall. The McMillan Plan of 1901–2, however, demanded a clear vista along the Mall's central swath, and the garden's facilities were in the way. Though it took several decades, the government eventually demolished the fanciful Victorian conservatory that had housed the institution since 1850, and built this new Beaux-Arts building at the edge of the Mall.

The rusticated north façade, evocative of a seventeenth-century French *orangerie,* relates the Botanic Garden to its classical neighbors. Behind this formal front lurks an exuberant conservatory, recently restored and now incorporating sophisticated systems to maintain humidity and temperature levels. The structure's tall ribcage, manufactured by the venerable greenhouse firm of Lord & Burnham, is made of noncorroding aluminum, and when built was the largest such structure in the world.

A3A Bartholdi Fountain

1st Street and Independence
Avenue, SW

1876 Sculptor: Frédéric
Auguste Bartholdi
1877 Moved to Mall
1932 Moved to current site

As originally created for the
Philadelphia Centennial Exhibition in 1876, this fountain audaciously
juxtaposed fire and water in a single work, with gas flames flickering
amid spouting jets of water. When the exhibition closed, the federal
government bought the fountain and moved it to Washington, where it
originally stood on the Mall, almost on axis with the Capitol. Electric
lights long ago replaced the gas-fired flames, but the conceptual strength
of the work is still evident. Bartholdi is best known as the sculptor of the
Statue of Liberty.

A4 Cannon House Office Building

New Jersey and Independence
avenues, SE

1907 Carrère & Hastings
1913 Addition: Architect of
the Capitol, with Carrère &
Hastings
1932 Renovation: Architect of
the Capitol, with Allied Architects

The commission to erect freestanding office buildings for the Senate and
the House was divided between the two principals of one architectural
firm. Thomas Hastings was responsible for the House Office Building
(pictured here), later named for Speaker Joseph Cannon; John Carrère
took the lead on the design of its Senate counterpart, now named the
Russell Senate Office Building. The result was a set of fraternal Beaux-
Arts twins that, with their giant columns and gleaming Vermont marble,
visually merged to form a unified backdrop for the Capitol, at least until
the more sober Longworth Building and the irredeemably hideous Rayburn Building came along and spoiled the view.

A5 Library of Congress (Thomas Jefferson Building)

1st Street and Independence
Avenue, SE

1888–97 John L. Smithmeyer
& Paul J. Pelz; Interiors:
Edward Pearce Casey
1910–65 Renovations and
additions: Various architects
1986–97 Restoration: Arthur Cotton Moore/Associates

TEL: (202) 707-5458   www.loc.gov

As the government was preparing to move to the new federal city in
1800, Congress approved an expenditure of $5,000 to buy books and cre-
ate a library for its own use. Housed in the Capitol, these original tomes
were destroyed during the British invasion of 1814. To replace them, former President Thomas Jefferson, who declared that "there is . . . no subject to which a member of Congress may not have occasion to refer," sold
his remarkably broad-based private library of precisely 6,487 volumes to
the government. From this core, the Library of Congress has grown into
the largest and best-equipped library in the world, containing over 130
million items housed on some 530 miles of shelves.

The library did not have its own dedicated facility until this imposing
building (now named in Jefferson's honor) opened in 1897. While almost
certainly inspired by the principal façade of the elegant Paris Opera
House by Charles Garnier, the exterior of the library is somewhat overwrought, and the monumental structure was not universally admired
at first. The architect and critic Russell Sturgis, for instance, criticized
the entry façade and "that false idea of grandeur which consists mainly
in hoisting a building up from a reasonable level of the ground, mainly
in order to secure for it a monstrous flight of steps which must be sur-
mounted before the main door can be reached."

Once inside, however, even the most skeptical visitor is likely to be
dazzled. The principal interior spaces, which are credited to Edward
Pearce Casey, are among the most regal rooms in Washington. Casey
oversaw a team of more than fifty sculptors and painters, who brought
the architecture to life through an artistic program of appropriately en-
cyclopedic proportions. The heroic central stair hall is replete with statues set amid a sea of marble, stained glass, and bronze. The octagonal
main reading room, topped by a 160-foot-high dome, is the grand finale.
Here, the opening of a book becomes a noble rite.

A6   Folger Shakespeare Library

201 East Capitol Street, SE

1932 Paul Philippe Cret;
Consulting architect:
Alexander B. Trowbridge
1983–92 Additions and
renovations: Hartman-Cox
Architects

TEL: (202) 544-4600
www.folger.edu

The Folger Shakespeare Library, which was commissioned by Standard Oil Chairman Henry Clay Folger and now boasts the world's largest collection of Shakespeare's printed works, is one of the city's premier examples of the modernist-classical-hybrid style sometimes called "stripped classicism," "Greco-Deco," or, more wittily, "Stark Deco." This severe yet elegant style was popular in Depression-era Washington, as architects and clients tried to have things both ways—formal and hierarchical, in keeping with the city's conservative traditions, but also simple and spartan, perhaps in recognition of the economic crisis that had pervaded the country's psyche, but also to pay lip service to the burgeoning modern movement.

Cret's design, therefore, seems to be a perfectly exemplary building of the period, until one ventures inside. Within that fashionable 1930s envelope lurks an astounding neo-Elizabethan fantasy in dark, heavy wood. Cret explained the sharp difference thus: "The reason is quite simple. Mr. and Mrs. Folger desired surroundings . . . reminiscent of England. . . . On the other hand, the architect . . . could readily see that the site selected, facing a wide, straight avenue in one of the most classical of cities . . . would be inappropriate for an Elizabethan building." In short, the outside was a direct response to the architectural and cultural context of Washington, while the interior was designed to evoke the spirit of the era during which the Bard wrote his plays.

The new reading room, added by Hartman-Cox a half century after the building opened, suggests the inspiration of French visionary architect Etienne-Louis Boullée's hypothetical Bibliothèque nationale, with its semicircular-vaulted ceiling and skylights that bathe the interior with a soft glow. While examining original drawings by Cret's office for the building, the architects of the addition noticed that several of the documents bore the initials "LK." It is safe to assume that these drawings were produced by none other than Louis Kahn, the great modern architect who had worked for Cret during the period that this project was on the boards.

A7 Supreme Court Building

1st and East Capitol streets, NE

1935 Cass Gilbert with Cass Gilbert Jr. and John R. Rockart

TEL: (202) 479-3030
www.supremecourtus.gov

The Supreme Court Building was one of the last major works of academic classicism in Washington. Though well on the wane by then, the style continued to be favored for prominent public buildings in the 1930s since the nascent modern movement was still regarded with suspicion by many federal officials. The new edifice had its detractors: Dean Acheson complained, "the massive building . . . seems to shrink the members of the Court," and Justice Harlan Fiske Stone fussed that Gilbert's structure was "wholly inappropriate for a quiet group of old boys such as the Supreme Court."

Conceived as a temple of justice, the building draws heavily on Roman precedents. The wings are completely subordinate to the central spine and its end porticos, where ornament is concentrated. The panels on the great bronze entrance doors, which weigh thirteen tons, were sculpted by John Donnelly Jr. and depict the history of the legal system from ancient times into the twentieth century. The architect himself, Cass Gilbert, is depicted toward the left of the sculptures in the pediment (by Robert Aiken), next to chief justice and former president William Howard Taft.

Currently under way is a comprehensive modernization of the building, overseen by Hillier Architecture, including the construction of substantial new space beneath the existing structure.

A8 Sewall-Belmont House and Museum (National Woman's Party Headquarters)

144 Constitution Avenue, NE

1800 Robert Sewall, owner-builder
1820 Reconstruction: Robert Sewall
1879–81, 1922–29 Various modifications: Architects unknown

1941 Conversion of carriage house to library: Elise Dupont

TEL: (202) 546-1210   www.sewallbelmont.org

This restrained brick building, though heavily modified over the years, is notable as a rare Capitol Hill example of a freestanding, Federal-style house. The "Belmont" in the house's name was Alva Smith Vanderbilt Belmont, an Alabama-born socialite who married two of the world's richest men (William K. Vanderbilt and Oliver H. P. Belmont), then abandoned high society and threw herself into politics. She became a leader in the women's suffrage movement, organizing conventions, writing articles, and picketing the White House. After suffrage was achieved with the Nineteenth Amendment, Belmont went on to serve as president of the radical National Woman's Party (NWP). In 1921, she bought the Old Brick Capitol to serve as the NWP headquarters, and when the government took the building through eminent domain to build the Supreme Court, she allowed the NWP to use the compensation it received to purchase the Sewall House across the street.

The house itself is now a museum exploring the struggle for women's rights. Much of the museum's collection relates to the work of Alice Paul, a pioneering feminist who founded the NWP in 1916 and wrote the original text of the Equal Rights Amendment—in 1923!

**A9   Thurgood Marshall
Federal Judiciary Building**

Massachusetts Avenue at
Columbus Circle, NE

1992 Edward Larabee Barnes
Associates

Edward Larabee Barnes's attempt to reinterpret the Beaux-Arts splendor of Union Station in a modern governmental office building next door is half-hearted and unsatisfying. The arches on the judiciary building and the sculpturally impoverished pilasters that bracket them are anemic in contrast to their richly detailed and finely crafted antecedents. The new building's most successful element is its unapologetically modern atrium, which is quite inviting, particularly at night when brightly lit, although it does look more like the centerpiece of a shopping mall or entertainment center than the entry to a judicial office building. The flat, grassy lawn between the building and Massachusetts Avenue cries out for an inventive landscaping plan.

A10 Union Station and Plaza

Massachusetts and Louisiana
avenues, NE

1908 D. H. Burnham & Co.;
Sculptor: Louis Saint-Gaudens
1912 Columbus Fountain:
Daniel H. Burnham; Sculptor:
Lorado Taft; Landscape
architect: Frederick Law Olmsted Jr.

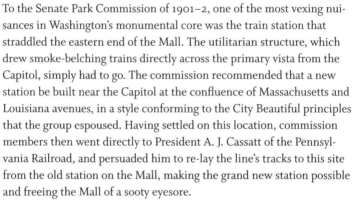

1988 Renovation and new retail facilities: Harry Weese & Associates;
Benjamin Thompson & Associates

To the Senate Park Commission of 1901–2, one of the most vexing nui-
sances in Washington's monumental core was the train station that
straddled the eastern end of the Mall. The utilitarian structure, which
drew smoke-belching trains directly across the primary vista from the
Capitol, simply had to go. The commission recommended that a new
station be built near the Capitol at the confluence of Massachusetts and
Louisiana avenues, in a style conforming to the City Beautiful principles
that the group espoused. Having settled on this location, commission
members then went directly to President A. J. Cassatt of the Pennsylvania Railroad, and persuaded him to re-lay the line's tracks to this site
from the old station on the Mall, making the grand new station possible
and freeing the Mall of a sooty eyesore.

The new Union Station thus became the first building erected in
conformance with the McMillan Plan's recommendations, and it was
designed by none other than Senate Park Commission member Daniel
Burnham. Sheathed in white Vermont granite (not marble), the station
bears a vigorous Beaux-Arts aesthetic that set the tone for much of the
city's early twentieth-century official architecture. The most prominent
feature of the main façade is the central pavilion, which directly recalls
the triumphal arches of ancient Rome. Running the entire length of this
façade is an open-air loggia, composed of a row of vaulted bays with suspended light fixtures. The view from one end of the loggia to the other is
among the most beautiful in Washington.

The station's primary interior spaces create just what the Senate Park
Commission had in mind—a triumphant gateway to the capital of an
increasingly powerful nation. The waiting room, inspired by the Roman
Baths of Diocletian, measures 219 feet by 120 feet, and lies beneath a
gilded, coffered, barrel-vaulted ceiling. Visitors to this space may notice
adolescents amusing themselves by attempting to determine whether
the scantily clad statues along the upper levels are anatomically correct
behind their shields (they were designed to be, but supposedly only one

of them ended up that way). Behind the waiting room is the 760-foot-long Grand Concourse, which, in its day, was among the most ambitious public spaces in the United States. It is still astonishing despite the enfilade of shops that now compromises the sense of expansiveness that so impressed early travelers.

After a period of neglect and an abortive, misguided scheme to turn the facility into a visitors' center for the city, the station underwent a $160 million restoration and was reopened in 1988. Today, the movie theaters, souvenir shops, and fast-food joints have turned Union Station into something of a mini-mall, yet these intrusions have not destroyed the grandeur of the building, which once again superbly fills the role of ceremonial gateway to the nation's capital.

In front of the station is a D-shaped plaza organized around a fountain honoring Christopher Columbus. As an urban space, the plaza is a bit nebulous, its curving side lacking architectural definition and its center crossed by a tangle of driveways. The fountain and the street furniture in the plaza are nonetheless engaging, with the Columbian theme carried through to such smaller elements as the light standards, which bear appendages designed to suggest the prows of Spanish galleons.

A11 Postal Square/National Postal Museum (City Post Office)

Massachusetts Avenue and North Capitol Street, NE

1914 Graham, Burnham & Company
1935 Addition: Graham, Anderson, Probst and White
1959 Interior alterations: Turpin, Wachter and Associates
1992 Renovation and addition: Shalom Baranes Associates; Preservation architects: Oehrlein & Associates Architects
1993 Postal Museum: Florance Eichbaum Esocoff King

TEL: (202) 633-5555   www.postalmuseum.si.edu

Cognizant of the 1901–2 McMillan Plan, the architects here took pains to make the City Post Office, with its central Ionic colonnade and slightly projecting entrance pavilions, harmonize with, but defer to, Union Station across the street. Graham and Burnham continued the Ionic order inside in the former main service room, marked by opulent decorative details that were hidden by a disastrous 1959 remodeling but have now been restored. The 1992 renovation entailed an almost invisible expansion of the building's floor space by 50 percent, which was achieved by filling in the courtyard, adding a mezzanine, and capturing unused space in the attic. The building now incorporates a mix of uses, including the Smithsonian's National Postal Museum, while still accommodating a working post office.

A12 U.S. Government Printing Office (GPO)

North Capitol Street between G and H streets, NW

1903 710 North Capitol Street: U.S. Army Corps of Engineers (under the Office of the Supervising Architect of the Treasury)
1930 45 G Street: J. J. McMahon
1940 732 North Capitol Street: Louis A. Simon

The world's largest information-processing and printing facility does not occupy an anonymous industrial structure, as one might expect, but rather this complex of robust brick buildings just blocks from the Capitol. A few architectural devices counter the bulkiness of the massive original structure—note the three-story arched "loggia" halfway up the façades, the two-story rusticated "basement," and the whimsical crest of terra cotta shells and cast iron. The head of this agency, by the way, enjoys the charmingly archaic title of public printer of the United States.

A13 800 North Capitol Street, NW

1991 Hartman-Cox Architects

Obviously inspired by the GPO across the street, this new office building evokes the spirit of postfire Chicago, when muscular neo-Romanesque commercial and institutional buildings sprang from the ashes. Although it looks expensive, given its apparent mass and careful detailing, the building was built on a relatively low budget using brick and cast stone.

A14 Georgetown University Law Library

Massachusetts and New Jersey avenues, NW

1989 Hartman-Cox Architects

For two decades, Georgetown University's Law School was relegated to a dreary, if monumental, box of a building designed by Edward Durrell Stone, located in what was then a rather dodgy part of town. This library was the first of several new structures that Hartman-Cox designed for the Law School, all of which now work together to create a compact but credible campus (meanwhile, fortunately, the neighborhood has also grown livelier and safer). The exterior of the library is polite, with precast concrete panels bearing subtle ornament that provides just enough visual texture to save the building from blandness. Inside, the wood-paneled main reading room captures the very essence of what the words *law library* bring to mind.

A15 National Association of Realtors Building

500 New Jersey Avenue, NW

2004 Design architects: GUND Partnership; Architects of record: SMB Architects

It's bluish green, but it's also just plain green—in the environmental sense, that is. This was the first newly constructed building in the District of Columbia to earn certification in the U.S. Green Building Council's LEED (Leadership in Energy and Environmental Design) Rating System. This was achieved through such measures as high-efficiency ventilation systems, a sophisticated curtain wall that minimizes thermal transfer, and the copious use of recycled materials in the construction of the building. The land was previously occupied by a service station, requiring substantial site cleanup before the National Association of Realtors could begin construction. The sliver of a building is particularly dramatic when viewed from the north—the tower at the apex reads rather like a ship's mast, with the sleek, sail-like curtain walls billowing behind it.

A16 Japanese-American Memorial

Louisiana and New Jersey avenues at D Street, NW

2001 Davis Buckley Architects and Planners; Sculptors: Nina A. Akamu, Paul Matisse

This monument, officially known as the Japanese American Memorial to Patriotism During World War II, recognizes both the service of Japanese American veterans and the American government's internment of more than a hundred thousand people of Japanese descent during the war. The most compelling feature of the memorial is a long tubular bell by sculptor Paul Matisse, grandson of Henri, which may be rung by pumping a lever to lift and release a clapper. The bell emits a profound and sustained tone—actually a pair of tones that gradually merge, symbolizing the healing of emotional wounds.

A17 101 Constitution Avenue, NW

2002 Shalom Baranes Associates

If real estate is all about location, then this property—so close to the U.S. Capitol—was destined for prestige. Fortunately, the

design of the structure befits its prominent site. The architects skillfully wove together several bold geometrical forms, including a cylinder at the apex of the roughly triangular block and a tall slab with a shallow curve facing the Capitol. The long Louisiana Avenue façade is enlivened by a continuous rectilinear bay that, though largely enclosed, reads as a *brise-soleil* thanks to its balconies, deeply set windows, and open colonnade at ground level. At the rear of this new building is a surprising little enclave of surviving nineteenth-century buildings, reminders of how this part of town looked before the McMillan Commission imposed its will on the city's core.

C ST

EAST CAPITOL ST

NORTH CAROLINA AVE

PENNSYLVANIA AVE

6th ST

1200 ft

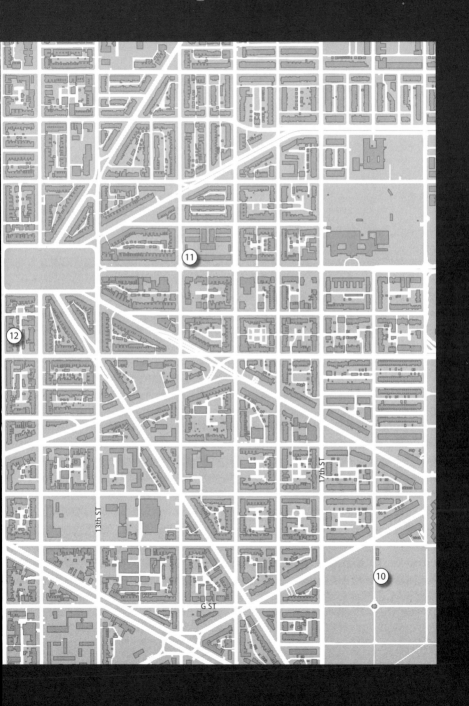

"Capitol Hill" is synonymous with the legislative branch of the U.S. government, but in local parlance, the term also refers to the adjacent neighborhood east of the Capitol, which comprises a diverse collection of institutional, commercial, and residential buildings. The juncture between the two faces of Capitol Hill can be strikingly abrupt, as along the unit block of Second Street, NE, where modest, privately owned row houses stand directly across from the seat of the highest court in the nation.

The city's founders assumed that the area to the east of the Capitol would become the primary locus of nongovernmental development, since it lay between the legislative building and the convenient port along the Anacostia River. Perhaps, however, they underestimated the attraction of executive authority, even in a democracy, because over time the White House, rather than the Capitol, became the center of gravity for Washington real estate. Ultimately, the city's commercial and residential development surged in the Northwest quadrant, leaving the residential part of Capitol Hill a surprisingly quiet enclave despite its proximity to many of the nation's most important institutions.

Although the neighborhood suffered a disheartening period of high

This 1992 aerial view of Stanton Park looking toward the northwest shows the dense texture of the Capitol Hill neighborhood.

crime rates and partial abandonment, as did many urban areas in the United States in the mid- to late twentieth century, Capitol Hill never lost its sense of community. For decades it has been beloved by residents for its ethnic diversity. Today, even as rising housing prices have led to demographic homogenization, "the Hill" remains a vibrant and highly sought-after place to live.

B1   518 C Street, NW

1990 Weinstein Associates Architects

Amy Weinstein reintroduced Washington to brick polychromy—the use of several colors of masonry forming decorative patterns—which she viewed as an economical means of lending visual texture to projects such as this small speculative office building. The primary façade, with its implied tower (the tower is not actually a discrete element in plan), has a civic—even church-like—character, while the projecting bays along 6th Street clearly relate to the rhythm of row houses on that block and throughout the neighborhood.

The building faces Stanton Park, one of several squares that lend a small-town quality to the residential part of Capitol Hill. The peripheral buildings are notably diverse, including a historic school, small commercial structures, and single-family residences.

B2   Saint Mark's Episcopal Church

3rd and A streets, SE

1889 T. Buckler Ghequier
1894, 1930 Additions: Architects unknown
1926 Addition: Delos Smith
1965 Interior alterations: Kent Cooper & Associates

This eclectic church, which from 1896 to 1902 served as the "pro-cathedral" —in effect, an acting cathedral—for the Episcopal Diocese of Washington, blends neo-Romanesque and neo-Gothic motifs. The interior derives warmth and visual richness from a range of materials, from the timber roof structure to the rounded masonry arches supported by skinny cast iron columns. The stained glass in the main baptistery window came from the studio of Louis Comfort Tiffany. Fixed pews were removed in the 1960s in favor of flexible seating in the round, better to accommodate the parish's progressive style of services, as well as its ambitious arts programming.

B3 Eastern Market

7th and C streets, SE

1873 South Hall: Adolf Cluss
1908 Center and North Halls:
Snowden Ashford

Washington once boasted several of these airy markets offering fresh produce, flowers, and other goods. The Georgetown Market [see K17] still exists, but has been gussied up as a branch of a high-end retail food chain. Eastern Market is the only survivor still functioning as a municipal market in the traditional sense. Many Capitol Hill residents consider it to be the unofficial center of their neighborhood.

A cast iron shed, intended to shelter vendors, runs along the 7th Street edge of the site. Behind it stands the enclosed main structure, marked by an unusual pattern of arched and bull's-eye windows that provide light for the stalls inside. The interior is essentially one vast space whose roof is supported by exposed iron trusses. The building was designed by the German-born Adolf Cluss, one of the city's most prolific mid-nineteenth-century architects. From 1862 to 1876 his office designed or supervised construction of nearly every public building erected by the District government, along with a number of private projects.

B4 The Penn Theater Project

650 Pennsylvania Avenue, SE

1935 John Eberson
1986 David M. Schwarz/
Architectural Services

The 1980s brought a wave of nostalgia for Art Deco and Art Moderne, styles that had been dismissed as frivolous by post–World War II academic modernists. Neo-Deco skyscrapers and other commercial structures began to spring up, many of them characterized by hollow appliqués that only hinted at the exuberant complexity of original Deco works.

In this project, a rather small remnant of an Art Moderne theater served as the centerpiece for a mixed-use development. The new structure fronting Pennsylvania Avenue employs Moderne-inspired motifs that are relatively convincing largely because they are appropriately modest (the old theater was built during the Depression, after all, when the lavish ornament common to earlier Art Deco buildings had given way to the simpler, streamlined aesthetic of Art Moderne). The building shares a courtyard with the red brick apartment house at 649 C Street, which was part of the same redevelopment project but completely different in architectural expression.

B5   660 Pennsylvania Avenue, SE

1939 Architect unknown
1943 Addition: Architect unknown
1991 Renovation and addition: Weinstein Associates Architects

A one-story, Art Moderne, former Kresge store was the foundation for a 1991 development that included rebuilding the old storefront and adding three stories of speculative office space. The distinctive decorative panels, executed in fiber-reinforced concrete, and the pattern of glazed and unglazed bricks were all inspired by textile designs of the era in which the original store was built. The office entrance lobby on 7th Street elegantly continues this decorative program and is worth a special look.

B6   Friendship House (The Maples)

619 D Street, SE

1796 William Lovering, architect-builder
1858, 1871 Additions: Architect unknown
1936 Restoration: Horace W. Peaslee

"This fine house in the woods between Capitol Hill and the Navy Yard," as George Washington is said to have described it, has been expanded several times, used for a variety of purposes (including a hospital), and had a lengthy list of owners, yet still manages to retain a modicum of its eighteenth-century character. Lovering, one of early Washington's best-known master craftsmen, built the place for William Mayne Duncanson, a rich planter who made and lost a fortune in District real estate, though according to *The WPA Guide to Washington, D.C.*, it was not poor investments but "Lavish entertainment [that] brought Duncanson to poverty." Later owners included Francis Scott Key.

B7   Christ Church Washington Parish

620 G Street, SE

1807 Robert Alexander
1824, 1849, 1874, 1891 Additions and renovations: Architects unknown
1877 Renovation: William H. Hoffman
1921 Interior alterations: Delos Smith
1954 Interior alterations: Horace W. Peaslee

The myriad expansions, renovations, and reversals of previous alterations that mark the history of this Gothic Revival church—among the earliest structures in that style in the United States—are typical of the changes that prominent buildings tend to undergo over time. The original church was a simple brick box designed by Robert Alexander, a builder who worked with Benjamin Henry Latrobe on the Washington Navy Yard. In 1824 came a small expansion at the rear, and in 1849, the narthex and the bell tower were added at the front. The 1870s brought an interior renovation intended to make the church more fashionably Victorian, and then in 1891, the tower was enlarged and a new entry vestibule appended. In the 1950s, Horace Peaslee set out to undo the then-fussy interiors and return the building to its rational and coherent beginnings. After all that, the little stucco building still stands serenely in its modest churchyard, looking only slightly weary from two centuries of tinkering.

B8 Town Houses on Capitol Hill (Ellen Wilson Complex)

I Street and Ellen Wilson Place, between 6th and 7th streets, SE

2000 Weinstein Associates Architects

The U.S. Department of Housing and Urban Development's HOPE VI program has been praised for bringing about the demolition of failed high-rise housing projects in cities across the country, though some activists have criticized the smaller-scale developments that replaced them because they often house fewer residents. In this instance, however, an abandoned, low-rise, garden-apartment complex was replaced by a new town house development that actually accommodates *more* families.

The project, on the former site of the Ellen Wilson Dwellings, was obviously designed to fit into the historic fabric of Capitol Hill. It is composed solely of separate row houses, each with its own direct entry from the street. Given a predictably modest budget, the architect chose to concentrate funds on creating a wide range of different façades, using a kit of parts to produce varied effects (these elements included an inexpensive but versatile bracket of an uncertain material that the architect jokingly calls "mystery meat"). The result looks a bit like a stage set, thanks in part to the thin, vertical extensions of many of the façades that are evident from certain angles, but certainly yields a strong sense of place and communal identity.

Ellen Wilson Place, a newly created street in the middle of the block, harks back to the alleys of Capitol Hill that were once lined with working-class housing—some of it quite squalid—surrounded by higher-quality housing on the main streets. There is no such distinction in quality here, of course, but the contrasting house styles and distinct spatial character of the mid-block street hint at this historical difference. Ellen Wilson, by the way, was the first wife of President Woodrow Wilson. On her deathbed, she is said to have urged her husband to push for the passage of the first federal public housing legislation, which was ultimately enacted in 1917.

B9 Marine Barracks and Commandant's House

8th and I streets, SE

1806 Home of the Commandants: George Hadfield
1840, 1891, 1934 Additions: Various architects
1906 Barracks, officers' housing, and Band Hall: Hornblower & Marshall
2004 Annex and band facility, renovation of southern part of complex: Brennan Beer Gorman Monk

This site, which housed the Marine Corps's headquarters for a century beginning in 1801, is also the nation's oldest continuously occupied Corps facility. Framed by simple arcaded brick barracks and with the drill field stretching out as a mall, the Home of the Commandants forms the focal point of this cloistered block. The residence of every Marine Corps chief since 1806, its many remodelings bear witness to the shifting tastes of successive generations.

B10 Congressional Cemetery

18th and E streets, SE

Established in 1807

TEL: (202) 543-0539

Although this was once the official congressional burial ground, architects Thornton, Hadfield, and Mills managed to squeeze their way in along with other private citizens. Many politicians who were buried elsewhere are also commemorated here in more than eighty official cenotaphs. Use of the cenotaphs, designed by Benjamin Henry Latrobe and paid for by Congress, began in 1816 but abruptly ended in 1877, when Senator George Hoar of Massachusetts remarked on the floor of the Senate that the ungainly structures added "a new terror to death."

Among those actually interred here are John Philip Sousa, Commodore John Rodgers, Push-Ma-Ta-Ha (a Choctaw chief who died while in

Washington negotiating a treaty), Marion Kahlert (killed at age ten in 1904, the city's first automobile accident victim), J. Edgar Hoover, photographer Mathew Brady, and George Watterson (first Librarian of Congress). Elbridge Gerry is also buried here: a signer of the Declaration of Independence, governor of Massachusetts, and vice president under Madison, he is undoubtedly best known for giving rise to the term *gerrymander*.

B11 East Capitol Street Car Barn

1400 East Capitol Street, NE

1896 Waddy B. Wood
1983 Renovation and additions: Martin and Jones

Like the Car Barn in Georgetown [see K11], the original complex here was built as an administrative, storage, and repair facility for electric streetcars. The long, low structure facing East Capitol Street housed offices, while the storage and repair sheds were located at the northern side of the block. In the early 1980s, when this part of Capitol Hill was terra incognita to most real estate agents, a developer saw the potential of the old car barn to become a residential complex of unique character. The office wing was largely preserved, while only remnants of the other structures were kept and incorporated into new apartments.

B12 Philadelphia Row

132–154 11th Street, SE

1867 George Gessford

According to oral tradition (supported by the name historically attached to this group of buildings), Gessford built these side hall–plan row houses to assuage the homesickness of his Philadelphia-born wife. The style is clearly evocative of the Federal houses in that city, with their flat, chaste brick façades, arched doors, and simple stone sills and lintels, though Victorian brackets and unusual window patterns betray the houses' anachronism.

INDEPENDENCE AVE

7th ST

I-395

P ST

2400 ft

Once the site of the new capital city had been selected, land speculators flocked to the banks of the Anacostia River, hoping to cash in on the development potential along what was then a readily navigable waterway. John Greenleaf, who gave his name to the point of land at the convergence of the Anacostia and the Potomac, struck a particularly advantageous deal with Congress: he was allowed to purchase three thousand city lots on the cheap, in exchange for lending the municipal government funds to be used for public improvements. Wheat Row resulted from this cozy arrangement, but little else did, since Greenleaf went bankrupt in 1797. Other developers active in the area included William Duncanson, whose mansion has been incorporated into the Harbour Square complex, and Thomas Law, whose house still stands at 6th and N streets, SW.

The initial burst of development along the Anacostia never turned into a sustained boom, partially because the river silted up and was heavily polluted by the late nineteenth century. Conditions in the near Southwest quadrant, in particular, deteriorated rapidly in the early twentieth century—by World War II it had degenerated into the city's most notori-

The Navy Yard along the Anacostia River figures prominently in this 1837 engraving by Louis Clover. The White House and Capitol, in the left and right background, respectively, appear isolated from the bustle of the waterfront. The large flag in the right middle ground marks the Marine Barracks just beyond the Navy Yard.

ous slum, in which half the dwellings lacked plumbing. In the 1950s, the District and federal governments finally took action, embarking on a vast campaign resulting in the demolition of over six thousand dwellings.

"Urban renewal" was a national buzz phrase during that period, as America's struggling cities went under the knife for experimental surgery intended to cure a variety of social maladies. Decades later, many cities are still recuperating from these generally well-intentioned initiatives, and that once-optimistic term—urban *renewal*—has come to symbolize indiscriminate destruction of neighborhoods (squalid though they may have been) in favor of drab, soulless superblocks. Fortunately for Washington, however, much of the redevelopment in the Southwest quadrant was of unusually high quality, avoiding the pitfalls that plagued many such projects elsewhere. Notwithstanding the sensitive social issues surrounding the genesis of such endeavors, several of the housing developments in Southwest are among the best works of large-scale urban architecture of their era.

Today, the future of the Anacostia waterfront looks bright. The District of Columbia Office of Planning has developed an ambitious plan to transform both banks of the river through substantial new residential, commercial, and recreational development. Massive construction is already under way in the area known as the Southeast Federal Center, which will house a new headquarters for the Department of Transportation and other agencies. If successful, the Anacostia initiative could bring economic opportunities and civic amenities to parts of the city that, despite being close to the monumental core, have not yet enjoyed the real estate boom so evident elsewhere in the District.

C1 L'Enfant Plaza

10th Street and Independence
Avenue, SW

1968 I. M. Pei & Partners;
Landscape architect for
Banneker Circle: Dan Kiley
1970 Forrestal Building:
Curtis and Davis Architects
and Planners; Fordyce &
Hamby Associates; Frank Grad and Sons
1973 Hotel and west office building: Vlastimil Koubek
1987 370 L'Enfant Promenade: Eisenman Robertson

L'Enfant Plaza was designed during an era in which heroically scaled, monumental buildings were in vogue, and governmental authorities commanded wholesale reconstruction of large urban precincts without a quiver of doubt about the wisdom of such initiatives. The grand intentions for the complex are evident not only in its lofty name, honoring the city's creator, but also in its enormous scale and the knot of Metro lines that meet below. Although it was conceived as a cultural center of a vibrant new Southwest Washington, however, the result was a sterile precinct that has never achieved the vitality its designers envisioned.

The hollowness of the project is most evident in the barren swath running down the middle of the 10th Street spine, and at Banneker Circle, named for the eighteenth-century African American surveyor of the District of Columbia, which terminates the axis. Intended as a belvedere, but in reality a place offering no amenity to reward the pedestrian (or motorist, for that matter), the circle is nothing more than an empty cul-de-sac. At the center of the complex, in front of the hotel, is a broad plaza that is only slightly less desolate. Fortunately, help may be on the way for this space, as plans are currently being developed for a glassy, sculptural building to occupy the plaza, a portion of which will accommodate the new home of the National Children's Museum.

The existing buildings in this precinct, though bombastic, are generally well composed and detailed. The least successful from an aesthetic standpoint is Curtis and Davis's Forrestal Building, which houses the U.S. Department of Energy. Its primary component is a bulky bar that spans 10th Street, thereby creating a grudging gateway to the complex. Despite the arrogance of L'Enfant Plaza's architecture and the vapidity of its urban spaces, however, one can imagine a future in which the complex is lined with shops and restaurants drawing hordes of tourists from nearby Smithsonian museums. The property's current owners envision the new children's museum as a catalyst for such an ambitious but welcome redevelopment.

C2 Central Heating Plant

13th and C streets, SW

1934 Paul Philippe Cret

Although it cannot compete with, say, London's Battersea Power Station for awesome industrial beauty, Cret's Art Deco–inspired heating plant is remarkably elegant considering its mundane purpose. The facility, which supplies heat to all of the federal buildings along the Mall, bears sculptural limestone panels depicting the machinery of power production.

C3   **Robert C. Weaver Federal
      Building (Department
      of Housing and Urban
      Development)**

451 7th Street, SW

1968 Marcel Breuer and
Associates (Marcel Breuer and
Herbert Beckhard); Architects
of record: Nolen-Swinburne &
Associates
1998 Plaza landscape: Martha Schwartz

The word *Brutalism* derives from the French term *béton brut,* meaning
"raw concrete," but you can't tell that to the movement's many detractors, for whom the term aptly describes what they consider to be the
inhumanity of buildings in this style. Nonetheless, Brutalism could be
done well or badly, and Marcel Breuer was certainly among its most
skillful exponents.

Breuer's design for the HUD building was immediately newsworthy
as a departure from the plain, boxy structures that had become standard
for mid-twentieth-century government offices. In plan, HUD is a giant
X (Breuer's UNESCO Headquarters complex in Paris is its Y-shaped
counterpart), with a long spine and four bilaterally symmetrical, gently
curving appendages. The muscular columns at the base of the building
provide an angular counterpoint to the sweeping curves. The ends of the
wings are sheathed in dark stone to contrast with the lighter concrete of
the main façades.

The spaces between the arms of the X are exterior plazas. In the
1990s, HUD commissioned Martha Schwartz to make the primary
plaza more attractive as an urban space. The solution is only partially
successful. While the hovering translucent doughnuts are jaunty at
first glance, for instance, they are disengaged from the seating areas,
rendering them almost useless as shading devices in warm weather.
The landscape architect had originally planned to introduce bright colors into the composition, which would have helped to give it life, but
sadly the National Capital Planning Commission vetoed that aspect of
the proposal.

C4 Washington Design Center

300 D Street, SW

1920s Original structure:
Architect unknown
1983 Keyes Condon Florance
Architects; Associated
architects: Bryant & Bryant
Architects
1994 Office addition: Keyes
Condon Florance Architects

Originally a refrigerated warehouse, this building was adapted to house the Washington Design Center, the first expansion of Chicago's Merchandise Mart outside that city. One of the big questions in the minds of the architects during the renovation was what would happen to the old building's structure as it thawed. The answer: nothing.

C5 Capitol Park

Between 1st and 4th and G and I
streets, SW

1958–63 Satterlee & Smith;
Chloethiel Woodard Smith and
Associates; Landscape architect:
Dan Kiley

The first of the major modern housing
developments in Southwest, Capitol
Park is a complex of apartment towers
and town houses, creating a community that is typologically diverse but aesthetically cohesive. While the apartment blocks are unusually varied in texture, it is the town house clusters that make this project extraordinary, thanks to their intricate networks of courtyards, pathways, and gardens. Although thoroughly modern in their materials and architectural expression, these buildings and spaces evoke the mysterious qualities typical of streetscapes in medieval European towns—quiet and modestly scaled, but richly layered and full of small surprises.

This project is also noteworthy as one of the earliest major American urban-scale projects designed by a woman. Chloethiel Woodard Smith was a pioneer not just by virtue of her sex, but also in the inventiveness and finesse of her work.

C6 Arena Stage

6th and M streets, SW

1961 Harry Weese & Associates
1970 Kreeger Theater: Harry Weese & Associates

The architecture of this complex vividly expresses the bold approach to performance that made Arena Stage an early leader in American regional theater (and the first such theater to win a Tony award). The building is noteworthy in its clear differentiation of functions, the highly choreographed sequence of spaces leading to the theaters, and the layouts of the stages themselves. Though it looks dated now—a victim of facile comparison to numerous more clumsily designed buildings of the same era—the structure remains a remarkable example of a thoughtful integration of form and function.

As of this writing, Arena Stage is raising funds for an ambitious renovation and addition by Canadian architect Bing Thom, which would encapsulate the existing structure in a glass box under a broad, thin roof.

C7 Town Center Plaza

1100 block of 3rd Street, SW, and 1100 block of 6th Street, SW

1962 I. M. Pei & Partners

Pei's apartment complex, unlike most others in the area, included neither town houses nor balconies. These buildings were conceived as slick towers with taut glass façades and pure, rectilinear forms. Single columns at the base split into pairs above ground level, thereby introducing a tartan grid in elevation that adds a bit of visual texture.

C8 Law House

6th and N streets, SW

c. 1796 Attributed to William
Lovering
c. 1938 Addition: Architect unknown
1964 Restoration: Keyes, Lethbridge
& Condon; Chloethiel Woodard
Smith & Associates

Congressional authorization of the new
federal city in 1790 set off a spate of
speculative building. Thomas Law, an
influential businessman who had made a fortune in the East India trade,
was among the major speculators. He put up this elegant, center hall,
piano nobile house for himself and his bride, née Eliza Parke Custis, a
granddaughter of Martha Washington. In 1797 Law optimistically built
a sugar refinery nearby, the District's first heavy industry, but he overex-
tended himself and, notwithstanding his rich wife, promptly went bankrupt. The Law house has survived these and other vicissitudes and now
serves as the Tiber Island Center for Cultural and Community Activities.

C9 Tiber Island/Carrollsburg Square

M and N streets, SW, between
Delaware Avenue and the
Waterfront

1965 Keyes, Lethbridge &
Condon
1993 Concrete restoration:
architrave, p.c., architects

The design for these complexes
by Keyes, Lethbridge & Condon
was selected in a competition conducted by the Redevelopment Land
Agency. In several respects, such as the inclusion of both towers and
town houses, and the incorporation of a web of small outdoor spaces,
these projects draw on the design of Capitol Park. These buildings have
a very different character, though, especially evident in the brick-and-
precast concrete town houses, which draw more directly from the local
domestic vernacular than does the highly abstract Capitol Park.

C10 River Park

Between 4th Street and
Delaware Avenue, and N and
O streets, SW

1963 Charles M. Goodman
Associates

Quietly sitting in Southwest
Washington is one of the most
innovative modernist urban
developments anywhere in the country—an enclave of apartments and
town houses in which aluminum is featured as a structural and ornamental material. Most notable are the town houses, many of which are
improbably and entertainingly capped with wafer-thin barrel vaults. The
use of aluminum in such structures was highly unusual, but was no mere
whim on the part of the architect. Rather, it reflects the role of the developer—none other than the Reynolds Aluminum Service Corporation,
eager to promote the use of its parent company's products in the many
urban redevelopment projects then under way across the country.

　　Charles Goodman helped pioneer modernist architecture in Washington, but his national reputation was limited, probably because aspects of his work—such as those rather whimsical barrel vaults—did not
always fit comfortably with International-style orthodoxy. His greatest
work is arguably Hollin Hills, an entire neighborhood of sleek, single-
family houses in nearby Virginia.

C11 Harbour Square–Wheat Row

1313–1321 4th Street, SW

c. 1794 Wheat Row: Attributed to
William Lovering
1966 Harbour Square and renovation
of Wheat Row: Chloethiel Woodard
Smith & Associates; Landscape
architect: Dan Kiley

Wheat Row is an example of the speculative housing ventures that were common early in the capital's history. This
row, named for John Wheat (who lived at 1315) and erected by wheeler-
dealer John Greenleaf, was among the best of these projects. Saved and
renovated when most of the neighborhood was destroyed during the

urban renewal era, these Federal houses (with the Duncanson-Cranch House and the Washington-Lewis House around the corner of N Street) were incorporated into the new Harbour Square complex, the centerpiece of which is a large and elegant pool with fountains.

C12 National War College

Fort Lesley J. McNair
4th and P streets, SW

1907 Theodore Roosevelt Hall: McKim, Mead & White
2000 Renovation: Ellerbe Becket

Fort McNair, established in 1791, is the second oldest military reservation in the country, after West Point. The fort (which acquired its current name after World War II) was damaged by the British in 1814, but rebuilt shortly thereafter. It was later the site of the District's federal penitentiary, where the convicted Lincoln assassins were hanged.

In 1901, President Theodore Roosevelt and Secretary of War Elihu Root established the Army (now National) War College as part of an initiative to modernize the nation's military in the wake of the Spanish-American War, and in 1907, the institution moved into its permanent home here at the apex of Greenleaf Point. The domed college building itself, solidly executed in brick with granite trim, presides at the end of a grand lawn, much like Thomas Jefferson's library at the University of Virginia. In this case, the sides of the lawn are lined with houses for officers (on the water side) and noncommissioned officers (opposite), surely among the most genteel military housing anywhere in the country.

C13 King Greenleaf Recreation Center

201 N Street, SW

2005 Devrouax & Purnell Architects-Planners

The curving and angled forms of this public recreation center are in sharp contrast to the rectilin-

earity that was typical of the mid-twentieth-century modern architecture in the Southwest urban renewal area. Glass walls allow views from the park into the basketball court and other interior spaces; in the evenings, the glow emanating from the building advertises its role as a gathering place for the neighborhood.

C14 Washington Navy Yard

8th and M streets, SE

c. 1804 Commandant's House (Tingey House): Attributed to William Lovering
1806 Latrobe Gate: Benjamin Henry Latrobe
Numerous other buildings, additions, and alterations: Various architects

The Washington Navy Yard, established in 1799, is America's oldest such facility. Early construction on the base was spotty until 1803, when Benjamin Henry Latrobe assumed supervision of the facility's development in his new capacity as surveyor of public buildings. (Latrobe's earlier, unexecuted design for an innovative dry dock at the Navy Yard had impressed President Jefferson, who appointed him to the powerful position.) Sadly, of all Latrobe's works at the Navy Yard, only the stucco-covered brick entrance gate remains—and it has been heavily altered. Still, what is left of the gate deserves note as one of the earliest examples of Greek Revival building in America.

The Commandant's House, made of brick with trim of Aquia Creek stone, is the only other substantial survivor of the original naval complex, the British having torched most of the rest when they stormed into town in 1814 (though it may have been the Americans who burned the base in order to keep it out of the enemy's hands). Much of the house's interior—mantels, staircase, and so on—dates from a mid-nineteenth-century renovation, but the Federal era's clean lines remain discernible on the exterior. The government built the house for Captain Thomas Tingey, first commandant of the yard.

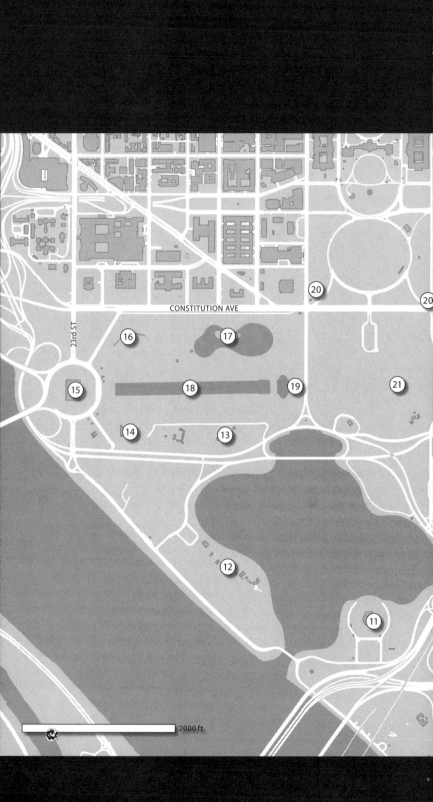

CONSTITUTION AVE

23rd ST

2000 ft

The Mall

The Mall is both the oldest federal park in the nation and the most ambitious single gesture in the plan of Washington, D.C. L'Enfant conceived it as a grand, axial sweep running from the Capitol to a large equestrian statue of George Washington, but for most of the city's history the space fell far short of his vision. In the mid- to late nineteenth century, trains chugged in and out of a railroad station near the center of the Mall, generating smoke that frequently obscured the view of the Capitol. An open sewer, built as a canal, crossed the Mall, while down at the Potomac end, the largest marsh in the city emitted noxious vapors. Some of the leftover space was landscaped in a "romantic" manner, with winding paths and what A. J. Downing intended as a "public museum of living trees and shrubs," but this picturesque layout contributed to the perception of disorder. The ruddy turrets of the Smithsonian "Castle," then starkly isolated in the middle of the Mall, added a somber touch, and for a considerable interval, the incomplete shaft of the Washington Monument loomed near the terminus of the Mall's western axis, as if to mock the chaos of it all.

In 1901–2, the Senate Park Commission, often called the McMillan Commission after the Michigan senator who formed it, launched a campaign to change the Mall from a civic embarrassment into a national treasure. The commissioners resurrected L'Enfant's plans, up-

Although titled "View of Washington," this engraving published by Baltimore's E. Sachse & Co. in 1852 mostly conveyed wishful thinking. The Mall is inaccurately depicted as a clean, grassy swath, and in the distance the Washington Monument, which at this time was nowhere near finished, is shown full height, surrounded by the circular temple-like base that was never built.

dated them to reflect the spirit of the time, and produced a majestic, classically inspired plan for Washington's monumental core. Over time, Downing's serpentine paths were obliterated, the railroad agreed to relocate (and received the new Union Station for being so public-spirited), the marshes and canals were drained and filled in, and the Lincoln and Jefferson memorials rose in marble splendor in the reclaimed marshlands. The commission's quasi-imperial plan was never fully realized—the decidedly nonclassical Smithsonian Castle successfully held its ground, for instance, and the broad, imposing terrace proposed for the base of the Washington Monument was not built—but the essence of the 1902 plan has largely come to fruition.

The present, two-mile-long Mall is almost incomprehensively grand; it is also one of the most audaciously designed landscapes in the world, an impressive rebuke to the *horror vacui* that has engendered so many overwrought public spaces in America. Christopher Knight of the *Los Angeles Times* praised the Mall's "sublime emptiness," which he defends as an important symbol of the nation's democratic, open society. Interestingly, his comments appeared in an article decrying a great threat to this important space—a proliferation of new monuments and memorials, with countless additional advocates clamoring for their own causes to be recognized on this highly symbolic tract. The Mall is thus in danger of becoming a victim of its own civic success. As the capital's various design review agencies actively work to address this dilemma, for now the Mall can safely be enjoyed for its myriad museums, its often inspiring monuments, and, above all, its gloriously improbable openness.

D1 **National Museum of the American Indian**

4th Street and Independence Avenue, SW

2004 Architect and project designer: Douglas Cardinal; Design architects: GBQC Architects and Johnpaul Jones; Project architects: Jones & Jones Architects and Landscape Architects, and SmithGroup, in association with Lou Weller and the Native American Design Collaborative, and Polshek Partnership Architects; Landscape architects: Jones & Jones Architects and Landscape Architects, and EDAW

TEL: (202) 633-1000   www.nmai.si.edu

The first new museum on the Mall proper in nearly two decades, the National Museum of the American Indian (NMAI) stands out both for its organic form and for its rich symbolism. The museum's curvilinear façades, covered in rough-hewn Kasota limestone, were conceived to suggest natural rock formations sculpted by wind and rain over millennia—an evocative design strategy that speaks to Native Americans' respect and affinity for the natural landscape, while also establishing a dramatic contrast to the intensely angular, impeccably honed East Building of the National Gallery of Art directly across the Mall. The landscape immediately surrounding the new building is equally extraordinary—in effect, it successfully captures a portion of the vast and largely undifferentiated Mall, gently appropriating it for the museum's own identity and programmatic purposes. The informal arrangement of indigenous plants in the museum's garden is another nod to naturalism; the garden also shelters several paved outdoor areas designed to accommodate Native American rituals and ceremonies.

The original design for the building was by Douglas Cardinal, a Native North American (he is Canadian) whose substantial portfolio contains many equally sculptural buildings. Cardinal was removed from the project, however, following a dispute with the Smithsonian, of which the museum is a part. Polshek Partnership then took over, working with many of the original team members, but not without controversy. Cardinal claims that his design was hijacked, though the exterior as executed seems generally true to his intentions. The interior is less successful—the domed atrium space, called simply the Potomac, is vacuous and a little disorienting, while the galleries and peripheral spaces are generally unmemorable. The initial exhibitions seem to be more about quantity than quality, but even so, the museum boasts a wealth of historical artifacts, complemented by contemporary art and crafts.

D2 National Air and Space Museum

Between Jefferson Drive and Independence Avenue, and 4th and 7th streets, SW

1976 Hellmuth, Obata + Kassabaum
1988 Addition: Hellmuth, Obata + Kassabaum

TEL: (202) 633-1000
www.nasm.si.edu

Behold the most popular museum in the entire world, drawing up to 9 million visitors per year. The building, while reasonably dignified and certainly imposing, is laudable mostly for staying out of the way and allowing the museum's awe-inspiring artifacts to speak for themselves. From the Wright Brothers' "Flyer" of 1903, to Charles Lindbergh's *Spirit of St. Louis*, to the *Apollo 11* command module, the hangar-like halls brim with historic airplanes, spacecraft, and related objects filling more than 160,000 square feet of exhibition space. The idea of hanging many of the airplanes from the trusses now seems obvious, but it was an innovative design move when employed here for the first time at a significant scale.

The museum's exterior subtly plays off of nearby buildings. For example, architect Gyo Obata designed the north façade as a series of projecting and recessed bays, geometrically complementing the pattern of bays on the National Gallery of Art's south façade across the Mall—a kind of abstracted version of the yin and yang. The two buildings also share a distinctive, pinkish Tennessee marble. Meanwhile, the dark, horizontal recesses near the tops of the Air and Space Museum's stone-faced blocks recall the similar slit in the Hirshhorn next door.

In 1988, a glassy restaurant was appended to the east end of the building, with a sloping, stepped roof that offsets the insistently chunky quality of the main structure. In 2003, the Smithsonian opened a branch of the museum—if "branch" is the right word, since it is large enough to swallow the "home" museum whole—adjacent to Dulles airport. Named the Steven F. Udvar-Hazy Center, the new facility holds some of the institution's largest items, including the space shuttle prototype *Enterprise* and the eerily beautiful SR-71 Blackbird spy plane.

D3 Hirshhorn Museum and Sculpture Garden

Independence Avenue at 7th Street, SW

1974 Skidmore, Owings & Merrill
1981 Redesign of sculpture garden: Lester Collins
1993 Redesign of plaza: James Urban
2005 Restoration of fountain and conversion of tunnel to program space: architrave, p.c., architects

TEL: (202) 633-1000   www.hirshhorn.si.edu

At the opening of the Hirshhorn Museum, the legendary S. Dillon Ripley, secretary of the Smithsonian, declared that if the building "were not controversial in almost every way, it would hardly qualify as a place to house contemporary art." While it is easy to dismiss the Hirshhorn as a glorified bunker—especially considering the dark, horizontal slit on the Mall side that looks as though it might produce sixteen-inch gun barrels at any moment—the building has proved to be a hospitable place for the display of art.

Designed by SOM principal Gordon Bunshaft, the building is actually a doughnut in plan, with a central courtyard focused on an eccentrically placed bronze fountain. In contrast to the almost completely solid perimeter, the internal façade is a grid of windows, which bring natural light to corridor-like galleries—mostly for sculpture—that hug the inside of the doughnut. The windowless perimeter galleries are well suited to paintings and other artwork that is sensitive to light—these galleries are the primary venues for the museum's changing exhibitions.

Across Jefferson Drive is the Hirshhorn's sunken garden for large-scale modern sculptures, one of the finest such collections in the United States. The garden was originally conceived to span the Mall, but was scaled back in response to opposition by design review agencies and political leaders.

D4   Arts and Industries Building

900 Jefferson Drive, SW

1881 Adolf Cluss and Paul Schulze, with Montgomery C. Meigs; Sculptor: Caspar Buberl
1897–1903 Modifications: Hornblower & Marshall
1976 Restoration: Hugh Newell Jacobsen
1985 Exterior roof, masonry, and window restoration: MMM Design Group/PUDI—Oehrlein & Associates Architects

TEL: (202) 633-1000   www.si.edu/ai

Covering more than two acres, the Arts and Industries Building is one of the largest extant Victorian-era structures in Washington. Initially known simply as the National Museum building (not to be confused with the National *Building Museum* [see E2], especially since Montgomery Meigs played a role in the design of both buildings), it was built to house the Smithsonian's growing collection, which had recently expanded with the addition of artifacts from the 1876 Centennial Exposition in Philadelphia.

Meigs prepared a conceptual plan for the building, calling for a large square structure with a central rotunda. Cluss and Schulze subsequently won a competition for the actual commission. Their plan was similar to Meigs's, but with an overlay of a Greek cross that divided the building into quadrants, which were in turn subdivided into smaller spaces. Both schemes were likely inspired by a well-known ideal museum plan developed in the early 1800s by J.-N.-L. Durand, a teacher of architecture at the École Polytechnique in Paris. Meigs served as a consultant to Cluss and Schulze during the construction.

The polychrome brick building was touted as the least expensive major structure erected by the federal government to date—it cost less than $3 per square foot—though, as architectural historian Cynthia Field points out, this figure ignored the costs of mechanical systems and marble floors that were pushed into the following year's budget. Work began in April 1879, some offices were occupied by the end of 1880, and the building was sufficiently finished to host President Garfield's Inaugural Ball in March 1881, though temporary floors and furniture had to be installed for the occasion.

Inside, the great trusses, meandering iron balconies, and complex roofing system have a character that is simultaneously industrial and nostalgic. Cluss, the quintessential late-Victorian progressive, had a limitless faith in the possibilities of technology, which may help to explain why so many aspects of the building suggest settings from a Jules Verne novel. As of this writing, the building is closed for a major renovation—its reopening date and ultimate use remain uncertain.

D5   The Smithsonian Institution Building ("The Castle")

1000 Jefferson Drive, SW

1855 James Renwick Jr.
1867 Alterations: Adolf Cluss
1872, 1884, 1887 Remodelings:
Various architects
1970 Restoration: Chatelain,
Samperton and Nolan Architects
1999 Exterior masonry restoration
and window replacement: Oehrlein &
Associates Architects

TEL: (202) 633-1000   www.si.edu/visit/infocenter/sicastle.htm

When James Smithson, a British scientist and illegitimate son of the eccentric first Duke of Northumberland, died in 1829, he left his estate to his nephew. Smithson's will, however, included a surprising stipulation: if the nephew should die without heirs, which he did in 1835, then the bulk of the fortune would go instead to the United States of America—a country Smithson had never visited—for the purpose of founding in Washington "an Establishment for the increase & diffusion of knowledge among men."

In some respects, the bequest should not have been so surprising, since Smithson was something of a political radical, who had dismissed the British monarchy as a "contemptible encumbrance" and publicly predicted that the future lay with the new democracy across the Atlantic. Nonetheless, American politicians were not only surprised by Smithson's gift, but also highly suspicious of it. After a good deal of debate and anti-British posturing, Congress finally accepted Smithson's largesse in 1836, and in 1838, the American government received the funds totaling more than $500,000, an enormous sum at the time. The Smithsonian Institution—the exact name was also stipulated in the benefactor's will—was formally established in 1846.

The young James Renwick was soon chosen over more established architects to design the new institution's home. Renwick produced a picturesque, asymmetrical, "Norman"-style castle that is now widely regarded as one of the greatest mid-nineteenth-century works of American architecture. Originally, the Castle, as it came to be called, held the entire institution, including the residence of the secretary, the title given to the Smithsonian's chief executive. It now houses the institution's central administration and information center.

Like many of its stylistic siblings, however, the venerable Castle almost fell victim to changing tastes when the McMillan Commission proposed its plan for the Mall in 1901–2. The plan called for both the Castle and the Arts and Industries Building to be razed in favor of Beaux-Arts classical buildings that would toe a rigid line in terms of architectural style and the physical boundaries of the Mall. Both survived, though, and are now beloved for their exceptional (in the true sense of the word) character—bastions of the old brick Washington that survived the marble, classical onslaught.

D6 Quadrangle Museums Project (Arthur M. Sackler Gallery, National Museum of African Art, Enid A. Haupt Garden, and S. Dillon Ripley Center)

Independence Avenue between the Arts and Industries Building and the Freer Gallery of Art

1987 Shepley, Bulfinch, Richardson & Abbott, based on initial concept by Junzo Yoshimura; Landscape architect: Lester Collins

TEL: (202) 633-1000   www.asia.si.edu   www.nmafa.si.edu

Designing a new museum complex immediately adjacent to the revered Smithsonian Castle and nestled between the Victorian Arts and Industries Building and the classical Freer Gallery of Art would be a challenge under any circumstances. Given that the project also entailed three quite distinct programmatic components, including new galleries for Asian and African art and the multifunction Ripley Center, this was surely one of the most difficult architectural commissions of the late twentieth century.

The conceptual design, by Japanese architect Junzo Yoshimura, understandably called for placing the bulk of the new facilities underground. After Yoshimura became ill, the venerable Boston firm of Shepley, Bulfinch, Richardson & Abbott, which had initially been brought on in an associate role, assumed full control of the project. For the above-ground structures, lead architect Jean-Paul Carlhian responded to the blizzard of competing styles and functions he faced by using a kind of generic, classically inspired vocabulary. Unfortunately, as executed, these elements seem uncomfortably stiff and self-conscious. Blocky granite trim, awkwardly large spherical finials, and a profusion of pyramidal and domed roofs yield buildings that appear comparatively crude on such a star-studded stage, though the garden itself succeeds as a pleasant public space thanks to its changing flora, elegant fountains, and a few relatively engaging works of sculpture.

The most intriguing architectural elements of the complex are the two vertiginous atria, with spiraling stairs, which connect the ground-level pavilions to the facilities below. Once inside the bowels of the museums, however, the visitor is likely to feel a bit claustrophobic and disoriented, faced with a labyrinth of corridors, galleries, and shops. To add to the confusion, the Sackler Gallery is connected underground to the Freer, as the two museums share a single administrative structure.

D7   Freer Gallery of Art

Between Independence
Avenue and Jefferson Drive at
12th Street, SW

1923 Charles Adams Platt
1990 Interior renovations:
Shepley, Bulfinch, Richardson
& Abbott; E. Verner Johnson
and Associates; Smithsonian
staff architects
1993 Renovations of interiors and courtyards: Cole & Denny/BVH
TEL: (202) 633-1000   www.asia.si.edu

Charles Lang Freer made a fortune manufacturing railroad cars, but his real interest always lay in art. In fact, one Detroit industrialist complained that Freer "would rather discuss the tariffs on early Italian art than the price of pig iron." Freer's collecting focused on the work of contemporary Americans, particularly James McNeill Whistler, and on the painting and sculpture of ancient Asia. Once he had assembled his collection, he donated it to the Smithsonian, along with money to build a museum to house it. Freer personally hired Platt, one of the giants of American classicism, to create the building, and worked closely with him throughout the design process.

The result is a low-rise, neo-Italian Renaissance palazzo, whose bold façade and vigorous rustication bring to mind the work of the sixteenth-century Mannerist period. At its core is a rather intimate courtyard, surrounded by an open loggia. Inside, art and architecture come together in the Peacock Room, an interior designed by Whistler for London shipbuilder F. R. Leyland, which was dismantled and reconstructed in the Freer's galleries.

D8 Jamie L. Whitten Federal Building (Department of Agriculture)

14th Street and Independence Avenue, SW

1908 Wings: Rankin, Kellogg & Crane
1930 Central section: Rankin, Kellogg & Crane

This huge federal office building was the first project designed for the south side of the Mall in accordance with the dicta of the McMillan Plan of 1901–2. Controversy raged as to the best location for the building—it took the direct intervention of President Theodore Roosevelt to stop the department from building smack in the middle of the Mall—but the cornerstone was eventually laid here in 1905, on a site previously occupied by greenhouses. Funding problems regularly halted construction, and by the time the structure was completed in 1930, the Mall was already quite a different place, with a new Lincoln Memorial standing at its western terminus and the vast Federal Triangle under way across Constitution Avenue.

The building's mammoth façades contain a few flashes of wit: note particularly the sculptures of oddly muscular children holding escutcheons labeled, variously, "Forests," "Cereals," "Flowers," and "Fruits."

D9 Sidney R. Yates Federal Building (Auditors Main Building)

201 14th Street, SW, at Independence Avenue

1880 James G. Hill
1902 Addition: James Knox Taylor
1915 Renovation: Architect unknown
1989 Renovation: Notter Finegold + Alexander Inc./Mariani, Architects

Along with the Smithsonian Castle, the Arts and Industries Building, and the National Building Museum, this is one of the remnants of the red-brick era in federal architecture. Like its few remaining siblings, the building survived even though its quirkiness, asymmetry, and dark cragginess soon fell out of favor with the advent of the City Beautiful movement. Built for the Bureau of Engraving and Printing, it now houses offices of the Department of Agriculture.

D10 U.S. Holocaust Memorial Museum

Raoul Wallenberg Place (between 14th and 15th streets, SW)

1993 Pei Cobb Freed & Partners; Associated architects: Notter Finegold + Alexander

TEL: (202) 488-0400
www.ushmm.org

This haunting structure is America's living memorial to the millions of Jews, homosexuals, prisoners of war, and others murdered by the Nazis in the 1930s and 1940s. The brilliance of the design lies in its evocation of the veneer of normalcy that obscured so many aspects of the Holocaust. The exterior of the museum, by virtue of its materials, scale, and simple geometric forms, is disarmingly harmonious with the governmental buildings surrounding it, as if to remind visitors of the insidious integration of the Holocaust's administrative mechanisms into broader society. The interior is more strongly allusive, with blank brick walls, steel bridges, and stark lighting suggesting the mundane industrial architecture of concentration camps. Beneath the ostensible banality, however, lurks a sinister quality that powerfully frames some of the most troubling and affecting exhibitions to be found in any museum.

"You cannot deal with the Holocaust as a reasonable thing," explained architect James Ingo Freed; this "wholly un-American subject" can only be treated in "an emotional dimension." In designing this building, he successfully created an environment in which visitors are inexorably drawn into the personal stories of Holocaust victims, and engaged in an intensely emotional experience from which few emerge unmoved.

D11 Thomas Jefferson Memorial

The Tidal Basin

1938–43 John Russell Pope;
Sculptor: Rudolph Evans
1996 Restoration first phase:
Einhorn Yaffee Prescott
2000 Restoration second
phase: Hartman-Cox
Architects
2006 Security upgrades and stone restoration: McKissack &
McKissack; Preservation consultants: John Milner Associates

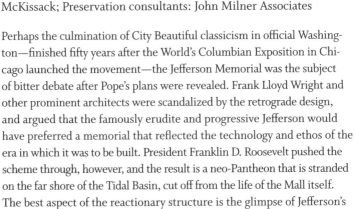

Perhaps the culmination of City Beautiful classicism in official Washington—finished fifty years after the World's Columbian Exposition in Chicago launched the movement—the Jefferson Memorial was the subject of bitter debate after Pope's plans were revealed. Frank Lloyd Wright and other prominent architects were scandalized by the retrograde design, and argued that the famously erudite and progressive Jefferson would have preferred a memorial that reflected the technology and ethos of the era in which it was to be built. President Franklin D. Roosevelt pushed the scheme through, however, and the result is a neo-Pantheon that is stranded on the far shore of the Tidal Basin, cut off from the life of the Mall itself. The best aspect of the reactionary structure is the glimpse of Jefferson's statue through one of the side openings, silhouetted against the sky.

D12 Franklin Delano Roosevelt Memorial

West Potomac Park

1997 (based on design of
1974) Lawrence Halprin;
Sculptors: Leonard Baskin, Neil
Estern, Robert Graham, Thomas
Hardy, George Segal

www.nps.gov/fdrm

Franklin Delano Roosevelt allegedly once directed that, if the nation ever wished to erect a monument to him, it should be no larger than his desk. He got that—a modest monument that now stands on the Pennsylvania Avenue side of the National Archives—but his fans found that inadequate, and in 1955, a commission was established to bring about a larger memorial on a site near the Mall. A design by landscape architect Lawrence Halprin was approved in 1974, but the scheme sat around gathering dust for two decades before construction finally began. In 1997, the new memorial was dedicated, and in addition to his requested desk-sized monument, the revered president is now honored by means of this seven-and-a-half-acre landscape.

Considering the time that elapsed between the design and its execution, the project turned out remarkably well. The memorial is organized as a series of four outdoor "rooms," representing Roosevelt's four terms as president. What could have devolved into a clichéd 1970s abstract landscape of vast slabs of stone and a few fastidiously planted trees is greatly enlivened by an engaging sculptural program. Examples include the timeless, all-white George Segal piece representing a breadline during the Depression. One particularly clever work is the sculpture that shows Roosevelt seated in what appears to be a simple wooden chair, but his cape subtly parts to reveal the small casters on the chair's legs—an accurate depiction of one of the disabled president's preferred mobility devices. Unfortunately, some vocal protestors claimed that the president's disability was nowhere portrayed overtly, and an uninspiring sculpture of Roosevelt in a wheelchair was added as an obvious afterthought.

Several of the fountains rely too heavily on pretentiously composed giant stone blocks, but overall the memorial is both a pleasant and a dignified place. In retrospect, though FDR himself opposed a memorial of such scale, his legacy clearly warrants the acreage.

D13 District of Columbia World War Memorial

West Potomac Park between the Reflecting Pool and Independence Avenue, SE

1931 Frederick H. Brooke; Associated architects: Nathan C. Wyeth and Horace W. Peaslee

Easily overlooked amid the much larger and more famous memorials that line the Mall, this classical *tempietto* honors the citizens of the District of Columbia who served in what the inscription calls simply "the World War," that is, World War I. Designed to double as a stand for commemorative performances by the U.S. Marine Band, it was the first memorial on the Mall to list the names of African Americans and women alongside those of white men.

D14 Korean War Veterans Memorial

The Mall, near Independence Avenue, SW

1995 Cooper-Lecky Architects; Sculptor: Frank Gaylord

www.nps.gov/kowa

The Korean War Veterans Memorial is based on a competition-winning design by a team of faculty members from Pennsylvania State University, but due to a controversy that arose during the design development phase, it was actually executed without their direct involvement. The memorial seems to be derivative of several more famous projects, and suffers by comparison. The black granite wall, for instance, obviously evokes the Vietnam Veterans Memorial across the Mall, but is used to lesser effect here. Meanwhile, the bland literalness of the over-scaled statues, which are deliberately antiheroic depictions of soldiers on a routine march, inadvertently trivializes the subject matter.

D15 Lincoln Memorial

West Potomac Park (west end of the Mall)

1913–22 Henry Bacon; Sculptor: Daniel Chester French; Muralist: Jules Guerin
1996 Restoration first phase: Einhorn Yaffee Prescott
2000 Restoration second phase: Hartman-Cox Architects

2006 Security upgrades and stone restoration: McKissack & McKissack; Preservation consultants: John Milner Associates

www.nps.gov/linc

Built on land that did not exist when L'Enfant devised his plan for Washington, the Lincoln Memorial is a worthy counterpoint to the Capitol at the other end of the Mall. To some extent, the memorial's dignity defies analysis, but probably relates as much to Americans' continuing reverence for Lincoln and the structure's incomparable site as it does to the architecture itself.

A movement to erect some sort of monument to the sixteenth president began almost immediately after his assassination. Congress, however, waited until 1911 to initiate the project, and by then there were nearly as many concepts for the memorial as there had been for the Washington Monument. Some people favored an obelisk to echo Washington's and to respect the Egyptian tradition of building such structures in pairs; others wanted a pyramid; and the new but already powerful automobile lobby pushed instead for a seventy-mile parkway to link Washington and Gettysburg. The site selection itself was controversial: Illinois Congressman Joseph Cannon balked at this marshy spot ("I'll never let a memorial to Abraham Lincoln be erected in that God-damned swamp," he insisted) and pressed for a site on the high ground across the Potomac. The idea of building a memorial to Lincoln on Robert E. Lee's former turf did not seem quite right, however, so the congressman backed down and this location prevailed.

Henry Bacon's design was loosely based on the Parthenon, but different in two key respects: he replaced the classic pedimented roof with a flattened and recessed attic, and he moved the entrance from the short end to the long façade. Bacon gave the memorial thirty-six columns, the number of states in the Union when Lincoln was elected president, and forty-eight festoons, the number when the memorial was completed.

Much of the memorial's emotional power derives from Daniel Chester French's iconic statue of the seated Lincoln, which compellingly portrays the president's anguished resolve. The lateral walls on either side of the sculpture are engraved with the text of two of Lincoln's most eloquent speeches: those from Gettysburg and his second inaugural. Light enters the space from above through panels made not of glass but of marble soaked in beeswax in order to enhance its translucence (to understand the rationale for this technique, think of a piece of paper stained with oil, and how much more light passes through the greasy spot—the concept behind the beeswax bath is essentially the same). Beneath the memorial is a fascinating, crypt-like space where visitors can examine the memorial's foundations and substructure.

The memorial, like Lincoln himself, is a symbol of freedom, and has therefore become a popular place for public demonstrations in favor of civil rights and related causes. It was here that Marian Anderson sang after she was turned away from Constitution Hall [see I7], and it was on the steps in front of the memorial that Martin Luther King Jr. matched Lincoln's eloquence with his "I Have a Dream" speech.

D16 Vietnam Veterans Memorial

The Mall, near 21st Street, NW

1982 Designer: Maya Ying Lin; Architects of record: Cooper-Lecky
Partnership

One of the most beautiful and moving memorials anywhere, this black
granite slash in the Mall is inscribed with the names of the Americans
killed or missing in the undeclared war in Southeast Asia. Lin, who was
still an architecture student when she won the international competition
for the memorial, said she envisioned it as a symbol of regeneration: "Take
a knife and cut open the earth," she explained, "and with time the grass
will heal it."

The experience of this memorial is unlike any other, and it is powerfully evocative. The egalitarian listing of the names of casualties, arranged chronologically by the date of death rather than alphabetically
or by rank, instantly humanizes the story of the war. The texture of the
inscribed names compels most visitors to touch the wall, while the re-
flectivity of the black granite turns each visitor's own image into a virtual
part of the surface. (The two wings of the memorial are aligned with the
Washington Monument and Lincoln Memorial, respectively, and from
certain vantage points, the reflections of those two white structures can
be seen in the stone, too.) The procession from one end to the other—
standing at the top edge of the wall, descending to a point where it is
over one's head, and then ascending again to ground level—serves as a
poignant metaphor for so many aspects of war, grief, and remembrance.

The wall's brilliant minimalism confounded many critics after the design was revealed, and even once it was completed. Various proposals to "heroify" the memorial with more traditional sculptural installations were, fortunately, either dismissed or relegated to a nearby spot out of immediate view. So far, the original has survived intact.

D17   Constitution Gardens/Signers Memorial

The Mall, near 19th Street, NW

1976 Constitution Gardens: Skidmore, Owings & Merrill
1982 Signers Memorial: EDAW

The elements used in this landscape—a six-acre lake, meadows, clumps of trees, hillocks, and serpentine paths—are remarkably like what A. J. Downing and Calvert Vaux had planned for the entire Mall 120 years earlier and precisely what the classically inclined McMillan Plan swept away. For much of the nineteenth century the Department of Agriculture used a tract nearby as a garden and nursery. During World War I much of this end of the Mall was filled with dozens of "temporary" structures to house government offices and workers. The buildings lingered (causing some to remark that nothing is so permanent in Washington as a temporary building), until the "tempos" were finally removed in the late 1960s and early 1970s to make way for these gardens.

Built on a little island in a lake in Constitution Gardens is Washington's only monument to the signers of the Declaration of Independence. Each signer is represented by a block of red marble, and each block is incised with an enlarged replica of that man's signature. EDAW arranged the blocks in a semicircle to suggest the composition of figures in John Trumbull's famous painting of the signing.

D18 Reflecting Pool

The Mall

1922 Henry Bacon and others

The McMillan Plan called for a cruciform pool between the Washington and Lincoln memorials, but World War I came and brought with it the "temporary" Navy and Munitions Buildings along Constitution Avenue. The "tempos" encroached upon the area set aside for the pool's north arm, so the cruciform was abandoned in favor of the current two thousand-foot-long rectangular basin with a hint of a transverse axis at the eastern end. In an astonishingly elaborate ceremony in 1923, architect Henry Bacon rode a decorated barge the length of the Reflecting Pool on his way to receive the Gold Medal of the American Institute of Architects from President Warren Harding on the steps of the Lincoln Memorial.

D19 World War II Memorial

17th Street between Constitution and Independence avenues

2004 Friedrich St. Florian; Architects of record: Leo A Daly; Associated architect: George Hartman; Landscape architects: Oehme, van Sweden & Associates; Sculptor: Ray Kaskey

The World War II Memorial was mired in controversy as soon as it was proposed for this location. Some argued that no new structures of any kind should go here and risk interrupting the views between the Washington Monument and the Lincoln Memorial; others felt that an appropriate memorial was possible on the site, but that the competition-winning design was not it. After the winner was selected, federal design review agencies insisted that the scope of the project be reduced—eliminating, for example, interior exhibition spaces that had been included in the original program. Now that the pared-down project is completed, it seems that the fears about compromising views were largely, if not wholly, unjustified. The center of the memorial is a void—a rebuilt version of the shallow "Rainbow Pool" that was already there—and the most prominent constructed elements are kept well off of the main axis. Thus, the view corridor is essentially preserved.

The lingering questions now are ones of architectural expression. The stele-like piers, arranged in two opposing semicircles, hark back to the severe classical architecture popular in various countries—including both the United States and Germany—in the 1930s and 1940s. To some critics, there is a particularly strong association with the work of Hitler's architect, Albert Speer. St. Florian presumably had no intention to evoke fascist architecture in this memorial, but such reactions underscore the difficulties that can arise from the use of forms and motifs that are so strongly rooted in a particular historical era.

Then there is the problem of the memorial's iconography. The names of individual states are called out on separate piers, for instance, and each pier stands in a hemicycle labeled either "Atlantic" or "Pacific." This scheme not only suggests an inaccurate connection between each state and a particular theater of war, but also implies that state identity was especially prominent in the public consciousness during a period that was in fact marked by remarkable national unity.

Ultimately, in its stiff classicism and its lack of compelling expressive gestures, the World War II Memorial's impression is not so much fascist as it is merely generic.

D20 Capitol Gatehouses

Constitution Avenue at 15th and 17th streets, NW

1828 Charles Bulfinch
1874 Dismantled
1880 Installed in current location
1940 Restoration: Architect unknown

The observant reader will notice that these are the *Capitol,* not *Capital,* Gatehouses. That is because they formerly guarded the Capitol and are made of the same soft sandstone found in the original building. They were dismantled in 1874 and moved here in 1880. For a time, they were used ignominiously as storage bins for National Park Service lawnmowers and such.

D21 The Washington Monument

The Mall

1848–56, 1876–84 Robert Mills and others
1962 Exterior restoration: Don Myer/ National Park Service
2000 Preservation architects for exterior restoration and interior renovation: Oehrlein & Associates Architects; Interior renovation: Michael Graves & Associates
2005 Landscape perimeter security improvements: Olin Partnership

TEL: (202) 426-6841 www.nps.gov/wamo/home.htm

At 555 feet, 5-1/8 inches, the Washington Monument was the tallest structure in the world when completed, and remains the tallest made of masonry. It now seems so obvious, so perfect, so timeless, that it is hard to imagine when this symbol of Washington—both the president and the city—was far from a certainty.

The monument's tumultuous history goes back to 1783, when the Continental Congress voted to build a statue of General Washington on horseback "at the place where the residence of Congress shall be established." The District of Columbia was created in 1790 and soon President Washington and Pierre L'Enfant agreed on a site for the statue. But then Washington died, and in 1800 Congress jettisoned the original plan in favor of a "mausoleum of American granite and marble, in pyramidal form." The Senate failed to approve funds for this scheme, however, and several subsequent plans faced opposition from Washington's family and others.

In 1832, the centenary of Washington's birth sparked renewed interest in creating some sort of monument to

Ostensibly showing the construction of the Washington Monument, this drawing actually depicts how the perpetually unfinished monument looked for much of the nineteenth century.

One of the many fanciful proposals from the 1870s for a redesign of the incomplete Washington Monument.

him. The Washington National Monument Society was formed in 1833, and in 1836 its members launched a national design competition, which was won by architect Robert Mills. His design called for a circular, Greek-inspired peristyle temple at the base and an obelisk slightly taller (at six hundred feet) and blunter than the present shaft. Lack of funds caused more delay, but ground was finally broken for this design on July 4, 1848.

The site for the construction was not exactly where L'Enfant had intended. Soil tests indicated that the planned position, at the apex of a perfect right triangle with the White House and the Capitol, was too marshy, so the foundation was instead placed well east, and slightly south, of the original spot. This decision had major ramifications for the Mall, forcing a slight southward kink in the axis emanating from the west portico of the Capitol, and leaving its obvious intersection with the cross-axis through the White House hauntingly vacant.

Construction sputtered along despite a near-farcical series of delays and complications: the records of the monument society were purloined, members of the anti-Catholic Know-Nothing Party stole a stone donated by Pope Pius IX, and the Civil War halted progress altogether. Then, during the 1870s, a spate of revisionism nearly derailed the whole effort: someone suggested that the monument be redesigned as a twelfth-century Italian campanile; someone else suggested one of "the better Hindu pagodas." Each proposal was given due (or excessive) consideration, but, after heated discussion, eventually all were tossed aside, and the simple shaft continued its fitful rise. A slight shift in the color of the marble about a third of the way up indicates the height at which construction was halted for nearly two decades. On December 6, 1884, the aluminum capstone was finally set and the monument was dedicated. It remains one of the noblest memorials ever erected.

D22 National Museum of American History, Behring Center

Between Constitution Avenue and Madison Drive, and 12th and 14th streets, NW

1964 Steinman, Cain & White (successor to McKim, Mead & White); Associated architects: Mills, Petticord & Mills

TEL: (202) 633-1000   www.americanhistory.si.edu

Opened in 1964 as the Museum of History and Technology and later renamed the National Museum of American History, this institution also could be considered the National Closet. And a huge closet it is, housing diverse artifacts ranging from Judy Garland's ruby slippers, to the trite but still irresistible collection of First Ladies' gowns, to cars, locomotives, and even a substantial chunk of a suspension bridge.

If only the building erected for the display of these curious objects were equally intriguing. After seeing the museum, columnist Russell Baker lamented, "Our own generation is unable to build a shelter worthy of housing what the old people left us." Fortunately, architectural improvements are afoot, as the firm of Skidmore, Owings & Merrill is now in the midst of a very long-term project to rationalize and upgrade the interior of the infamous warren of a building. Eventually, if all goes according to plan, a large new central space will facilitate orientation and circulation, and a few new additions may even bring some grandeur and excitement to the exterior.

D23 National Museum of Natural History

Between Constitution Avenue and
Madison Drive, and 9th and 12th
streets, NW

1911 Hornblower & Marshall
1964, 1965 Additions: Mills,
Petticord & Mills
1990 Upgrades: HSMM
1994 Enclosure of East Court:
Mariani & Associates
1999 Renovations (including new
Discovery Center, theater, and restaurant): Hammel, Green and
Abrahamson (HGA); SmithGroup
2000 Renovations: architrave, p.c., architects
2003 West Hall restoration: HSMM

TEL: (202) 633-1000   www.mnh.si.edu

The Department of Agriculture was the first building on the south side
of the Mall erected in accordance with the Senate Park Commission's
classical plan, and this rather academic-looking Beaux-Arts building was
the first on the north. Part of the Smithsonian, the museum contains
a hodgepodge of artifacts that might be taken as a microcosm of the
parent institution. Highlights include the "striding" bull elephant that
greets visitors in the building's rotunda, an enormous array of shells and
sponges, the Hope Diamond, and what must be the world's largest ant
farm.

Recent enclosures of the two courtyards have introduced some airy,
modern spaces to the building. Of particular note is the new staircase in
the west court, the design of which was allegedly inspired by the anat-
omy of vertebrate animals.

D24 National Gallery of Art Sculpture Garden

Between Constitution Avenue and Madison Drive, and 7th and 9th streets, NW

1988 Pavilion: Skidmore, Owings & Merrill
1999 Sculpture garden: Olin Partnership

TEL: (202) 737-4215   www.nga.gov

A national sculpture garden was first formally proposed for this site in 1966. In 1974, an ice skating rink was built here, and then the little green pavilion—a modern take on Art Nouveau motifs—was completed in 1988. The full sculpture garden finally came to fruition in 1999, when the original skating rink was removed and reconstructed. The somewhat staid landscape design, incorporating cast iron and steel fences, as well as the same marble used on the National Gallery's two buildings, is offset by the very lively and entertaining modern sculptures. Standing near Claes Oldenburg's huge rendition of a typewriter eraser, one may often hear adults attempting to explain to their computer-oriented children and grandchildren just what it represents.

D25 National Gallery of Art (West Building)

Between Constitution Avenue and Madison Drive, and 4th and 7th streets, NW

1941 John Russell Pope/Eggers & Higgins
1998 Reorganization and renovation: Keyes Condon Florance Architects
2002 Renovation of Sculpture Gallery: HSMM

TEL: (202) 737-4215   www.nga.gov

Founded in 1937, the National Gallery of Art owes its existence to Andrew Mellon, who donated both his own collection of Old Master paintings and a sizeable endowment to establish the institution. Visitors unaware of the late date of the gallery's construction generally assume that the building is much older than it is—the architect, of course, was an unapologetic classicist who had spent his entire career refining his execution of the style. While the large blank areas on the façade and the general restraint in ornamentation may suggest the influence of modern minimalism, for the most part, Pope's museum is a pure homage to classical antiquity and the Renaissance.

Conservative though the design may be, the building incorporates some subtle gestures that add interest. Note, for instance, the very shallow pilasters, barely articulated against the apparently blank walls near the central portico of the north façade. Also, look closely at the color of the pink Tennessee marble—in just the right light, one can see that it is not monochromatic, but graduated from a somewhat darker color at the bottom of the façade to a lighter shade at the top.

The galleries themselves provide handsome places for the display of art. A 1980s reorganization, which was prompted by the addition of the new East Wing, vastly improved how the entire gallery works, both for museum staff and for the visiting public.

D26 National Gallery of Art (East Building)

Constitution Avenue and 4th Street, NW

1978 I. M. Pei & Partners; Landscape architect: Dan Kiley

TEL: (202) 737-4215
www.nga.gov

The East Building of the National Gallery of Art is widely regarded as the pinnacle of high modern architecture in Washington, and arguably one of the finest such works anywhere in the country, despite its slavish reliance on a geometrical regimen that may have caused as many problems as it solved. Pei's signature strategy was to split a potentially awkward trapezoidal site into two triangles: the larger, isosceles triangle contains gallery space, while the smaller, right triangle contains offices and the Center for Advanced Study in the Visual Arts. Slivers of space have been excised from these two basic forms; the resulting voids visually lighten the structure and introduce shadows that create additional, animated geometrical patterns (while they also create some obviously useless nooks and crannies). At the core of the building is a brightly skylit atrium, which appears in plan as a second isosceles triangle, offset from, and slightly smaller than, the main block. The triangular theme is carried through obsessively at various scales, including the shape of the floor tiles in the atrium.

Pei related the building to its architectural and urban context without stooping to imitation. In elevation, for example, the building's main forms are of two quite different heights, which mediate between the scale of the West Building and the more bureaucratic structures across Pennsylvania and Constitution avenues. The new building is physically connected to its sibling by a tunnel whose design now seems dated, though still rather amusing in a 1970s, space-age way. At the other end of the tunnel awaits a more archetypal modern restaurant, fronting a glass wall improbably holding back a torrential cascading fountain.

Judiciary Square / Gallery Place

The name *Judiciary Square* refers to a multiblock area spanning from D to G streets and from 4th to 5th streets, NW. In the late nineteenth and early twentieth centuries, the full square was easily perceived as such, since it was a cohesively landscaped park containing just two discrete, though monumental, structures—the Old City Hall and what was then the Pension Building. Several other structures were added in the 1930s to house various judicial functions, and today, with E and F streets continuing straight through the site and miscellaneous parking lots lining its edges, the larger historic square is illegible in person, though it is still evident on most maps.

L'Enfant and Washington envisioned Judiciary Square and the area immediately to its west (now called Gallery Place) as the civic hub of the District: the site of the post office, the city hall, the court buildings, the jail, the hospital, and so on. At first, the area seemed destined to fulfill that vision, boasting some of the nation's earliest and finest Greek Revival public buildings. Soon, however, a mishmash of hotels, houses, and shops insinuated themselves among the governmental grandeur. The innkeepers and homeowners were drawn here in part by a powerful stream that began at a spring near 5th and L streets and raced southward to join the Tiber Creek near the Mall (sometimes, according to the *Evening Star,* the water in the canal was

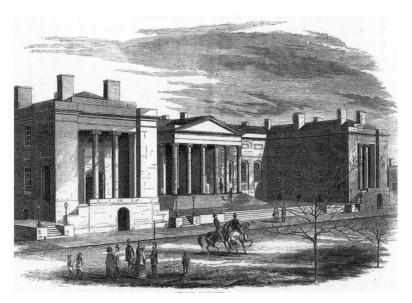

View of the Old City Hall (now part of the Superior Court of the District of Columbia), around 1853, when the building had a much more immediate relationship to the street than it does today.

"deep enough for canoeing," but more often it was simply a fast-moving sewer). Italian, Jewish, and Chinese enclaves emerged at different times in the vicinity.

The neighborhood declined gradually in the mid-twentieth century as commercial investment became focused on the area northwest of the White House. Since the 1990s, however, substantial new commercial and residential development has brought life to the Gallery Place and Judiciary Square areas and especially to the 7th Street corridor, which is now a vibrant spine of restaurants, cultural institutions, and nightlife.

E1   National Law Enforcement Officers Memorial

Between E and F streets, NW, across from the National Building Museum

1991 Davis Buckley, Architects and Planners; Sculptor: Ray Kaskey

The public space at the heart of Judiciary Square is now occupied by a memorial to law enforcement officers killed in the line of duty, whose names are inscribed in the low marble walls that trace broad arcs at the east and west sides of the site. The memorial is organized around an open plaza with a distinctive paving pattern inspired by that of Michelangelo's Campidoglio in Rome. The plaza has a subtle camber, with a medallion at the center marking the crown.

The site presented a design challenge in the form of two preexisting Metro elevator structures set at an angle reflecting the diagonal path of the station below. The architect cleverly restored symmetry by using the elevators as the compositional anchors for two complementary curving pergolas. Because the trellises stand directly over the Metro tunnel, they were constructed of aluminum to minimize their weight.

E2 National Building Museum (Pension Building)

4th and F streets, NW

1887 Montgomery C. Meigs;
Sculptor: Caspar Buberl
1985 Renovation: Keyes Condon
Florance Architects; Associated
architect: Giorgio Cavaglieri
1991–2003 Various alterations: Karn
Charuhas Chapman & Twohey

TEL: (202) 272-2448   www.nbm.org

Built, improbably enough, as a government office building, and now serving as the home of the world's most-visited museum of architecture and engineering, this is one of Washington's largest, quirkiest, and most beloved landmarks. Supposedly built of 15.5 million bricks, the imposing structure was designed by Montgomery C. Meigs, who had served as quartermaster general of the Union army during the Civil War. Meigs, an inventive and multitalented engineer, is credited by author David Miller as having been "second only to Grant" in terms of his importance to the Union victory. Before and after the war, he was involved in several major Washington building projects, including the expansion of the Capitol.

This building was constructed for the federal Bureau of Pensions, which needed a large new facility to process payments to Civil War veterans, widows, and orphans (at one point, nearly one-quarter of the entire federal budget was administered here). Meigs was a logical choice as architect, given his army background and substantial engineering experience, but his design was not well received at first. Many politicians derided the building as "Meigs's Old Red Barn," and William Tecumseh Sherman supposedly scoffed, "The worst of it is, it is fireproof." After the Pension Bureau moved out in the early twentieth century, the building was occupied by various federal agencies and even served as a courthouse. In 1980, a group of avid preservationists successfully lobbied Congress to save the structure, which had come to be regarded as a white elephant, and set it aside for use as a private, nonprofit museum of the building arts. Following extensive renovations, the museum opened its doors to the public in 1985.

The exterior of the building owes a debt to the sixteenth-century Palazzo Farnese, designed by Antonio da Sangallo the Younger and later modified by Michelangelo, which Meigs had admired while visiting Rome. The comparison goes only so far, however—the principal façade of the museum is much longer than that of its Renaissance counterpart,

Teddy Roosevelt's 1901 inaugural ball in what was then known as the Pension Building.

it is rendered in red brick rather than buff brick and stone, and it is crowned by a pedimented roof structure while the Palazzo Farnese ends with a flat cornice. Also, the window surrounds on Meigs's structure are of red brick, rather than contrasting stone, making the building appear almost as if it were carved out of a single block of clay.

The relentless "brickiness" is relieved by the building's most remarkable exterior feature—a three-foot-tall terra cotta sculptural band between the first and second floors, depicting scenes of Union military forces. Spanning the entire perimeter of the 400-by-200-foot structure, the frieze is thus nearly a quarter of a mile in total length. The sculptor, Caspar Buberl, was a Bohemian—back when that was a geographical term rather than a comment on his lifestyle—who immigrated to the United States in 1854. Buberl's other works include the sculptures over the entry to the Smithsonian's Arts and Industries Building and numerous commemorative statues of soldiers, firemen, and other heroic figures in cities across the country.

Impressive as the exterior is, it pales in comparison to the building's big surprise—the main interior space known as the Great Hall, which is larger than a football field and soars to 159 feet at its highest point. This space—in effect, an early version of the modern atrium—was partially inspired by the courtyard of Bramante's Palazzo della Cancelleria, not far from the Palazzo Farnese in Rome. The Great Hall is divided into three courts by two rows of colossal Corinthian columns—among the tallest such columns in the world—which are made of seventy thousand bricks each, covered in plaster, and painted to look like solid blocks of marble. Surrounding the hall is a double arcade with terra cotta columns on the first floor and cast iron columns above. The cast iron–trussed roof, reminiscent of a Victorian train shed, contrasts sharply with the space's predominant classicism. The hall has been the site of presidential inaugural balls going back to Grover Cleveland's in 1885 (before the building was even finished), and now provides a place for the museum's educational programs, special events, and occasional exhibitions.

The building is also remarkable as one of the earliest works of architecture to employ deliberate design strategies to enhance the health of occupants. Small openings under each window allowed fresh air to enter the perimeter office spaces. Warmed during the winter over radiators along the exterior walls, the air then passed through the arched openings into the Great Hall. Clerestory windows at the crest of the roof vented the space, resulting in a remarkably efficient ventilation system that Meigs later claimed had dramatically reduced absenteeism among Pension Bureau employees. Now, of course, the building is air-conditioned and the exterior openings are sealed off, but the "Old Red Barn" survives as a testament to Meigs's ingenuity and a handsome venue for exhibitions and educational programs about architecture, engineering, and construction.

E3   Lillian and Albert Small Jewish Museum/Jewish Historical Society of Greater Washington (Adas Israel Synagogue)

701 3rd Street, NW

1876   Architect unknown; Draftsman: Max Kleinman
1969   Moved to present site

TEL: (202) 789-0900
www.jhsgw.org

The Adas Israel Synagogue was established in 1876 by thirty-five traditionalist families that broke off from the increasingly liberal Washington Hebrew Congregation (founded in 1852). The design of their new building reflected the seceding group's more conservative bent. Exterior decoration was restricted to simple wooden fans over the windows and doors, while inside, a second-floor women's gallery allowed segregation of the sexes during services.

Most, but not all, of this building originally stood at 600 5th Street, NW. Adas Israel left in 1908 for new quarters and the structure fell into a succession of uses, including a grocery. With demolition looming in the 1960s, the District government—the building's owner at the time—donated it to the Jewish Historical Society of Greater Washington, which pledged to move it to a new location for conversion into a museum. In 1969, the upper portion of the old synagogue was sheared off and moved in one piece to the current site, where it was carefully placed atop newly constructed base walls. Subtle differences in the color and proportions of the brick and mortar reveal the juncture between the original structure and the new base.

E4 Metropolitan Community Church of Washington, D.C.

474 Ridge Street, NW

1992 Suzanne Reatig Architecture

One of the first entirely new structures in the country built expressly for a gay and lesbian religious congregation, the Metropolitan Community Church of Washington, D.C., was a harbinger of gentrification in this rapidly changing neighborhood. The church's auxiliary functions are housed in an L-shaped band along the two street façades, sheathed in split-face concrete block that recalls the texture of nearby masonry row houses. These wings shield a bright and airy sanctuary of steel and glass, which is covered with a shallow barrel vault supported by delicate bowstring trusses. From the inside, at certain times of day, the sanctuary appears to be twice as long as it really is thanks to the architect's clever use of reflective glass.

E5 Washington Convention Center

801 Mount Vernon Place, NW

2003 Thompson, Ventulett, Stainback & Associates; Devrouax and Purnell Architects-Planners; Mariani Architects-Engineers

Washington's new, 2.3-million-square-foot convention center is a rhapsody in beige: relentlessly bland in color, but nonetheless skillfully chiseled, tucked, and squeezed to fit relatively unobtrusively into a low-rise residential and commercial context. To preserve as much of the existing street pattern as possible, the architects placed the primary exhibit hall underground, with secondary halls, ballrooms, meeting rooms, and other smaller spaces above ground, connected by wide bridges spanning L and M streets. Although this unusual arrangement results in a rather confusing and inconvenient internal circulation pattern, the trade-off seems worthwhile.

The center's most engaging features are the lounge spaces cantilevered over the sidewalks along 7th and 9th streets, near the southern end of the building, which suggest lookout platforms projecting from the bridge of a giant cruise ship. Also noteworthy are the tall pylons bracketing the main entrance on Mount Vernon Square, which incorporate stacks of flat glass strips—modern totem poles welcoming the hordes of badge-bedecked conventioneers, while also marking the corners where 8th Street originally met the square.

E6   Historical Society of Washington, D.C. (Central Library)

Mount Vernon Square (8th and K streets, NW)

1903 Ackerman & Ross
1980 Partial renovation: Architects unknown
2003 Renovation: Devrouax & Purnell Architects-Planners, with RKK&G Museum and Cultural Facilities Consultants

One of scores of library buildings across the nation built with funds donated by Andrew Carnegie, this was the District's central public library for nearly seventy years, until it was replaced by its own aesthetic foil—the Mies van der Rohe–designed, dark steel-and-glass Martin Luther King Library at 9th and G streets, NW. Following nearly a decade of disuse, the old Carnegie building was partially renovated and turned over to the University of the District of Columbia, which simply did not have the necessary resources to care for the structure properly. Then, in 1999, the Historical Society of Washington, D.C., proposed that the building be turned into a museum dedicated to the civic history of the nation's capital. Congress provided funding to assist in establishing the institution, the District government granted the Historical Society a long-term lease on the building for one dollar per year, and in May 2003, the City Museum of Washington, D.C., opened to the public.

Alas, the enterprise was short-lived. Projections for income and visitorship proved to be overly optimistic, and the museum was forced to cease operations in late 2004, little more than a year after its inauguration. As of this writing, numerous proposals for the building's future use are floating about.

E7 PEPCO Headquarters

701 9th Street, NW

2001 Devrouax & Purnell Architects-Planners

For the pedestrian or driver approaching along 9th Street from the north, the curving glass curtain wall of the new headquarters for the city's electrical utility gradually reveals views of the historic Patent Office Building across G Street. The bold gesture of this broad, curving wall is offset by a simple, delicate trellis that simultaneously reinforces the street edge and lends a human scale to the building's base. Amazingly, given how recently it was built, this was the first major building in downtown Washington designed by an African American–owned architecture firm.

E8 National Portrait Gallery and Smithsonian American Art Museum/Donald W. Reynolds Center for American Art and Portraiture (Old Patent Office Building)

Between 7th, 9th, F, and G streets, NW

1836–68 Ithiel Town, William P. Elliot Jr., Robert Mills, Thomas U. Walter, Edward Clark, Alexander Jackson Davis
1878–85 Interior alterations: Cluss & Schulze
1936 South portico steps removed
1968 Renovation: Faulkner, Kingsbury & Stenhouse/Faulkner, Fryer & Faulkner; Bayard Underwood
2006 Renovation and restoration: Hartman-Cox Architects

TEL: (202) 633-1000   www.npg.si.edu   www.americanart.si.edu

L'Enfant's plan reserved this site for a "shrine to American heroes," but it was never used for that purpose. After the government's first Patent

Office burned, this largely vacant lot was selected as the site for its fire-proof replacement. Another of Washington's innumerable design competitions ensued, which was won by William Elliot, who had worked in association with Ithiel Town. The construction of Town and Elliot's design was to be supervised, however, by Robert Mills, whom President Andrew Jackson appointed as the official architect of federal buildings in 1836. Mills is widely considered to have been the first great American-born professional architect (Latrobe was born in England; Jefferson was an amateur). Unfortunately, he and Elliot later ended up in a highly public dispute regarding credit for specific aspects of the Patent Office's design, making a clear assessment of authorship difficult.

It was probably Mills who designed the building's quintessential south portico, comprising eight beefy Doric columns rendered in fragile Aquia sandstone. Mills was also the lead architect for the expansion of the building beginning in 1849, and here he switched to sturdier marble as the finish material for the new wings. Mills was ousted from the job in 1851, however, and replaced by Thomas U. Walter, who worked with Edward Clark to complete what Mills had begun. When work was finally finished, the result was the largest office building in Washington. It was a busy place; over the years clerks here issued five hundred thousand patents to the likes of Alexander Graham Bell, Cyrus McCormick, and Thomas Edison. During the Civil War the building served as a hospital; one of the ministering nurses was Walt Whitman, who based his poem "The Wound Dresser" on his experiences. Whitman returned to the building in 1865, working briefly as a clerk for the Indian Bureau, which, like the Patent Office at the time, was a division of the Interior Department. A puritanical new secretary of the interior soon discovered a copy of *Leaves of Grass* in Whitman's desk, however, and immediately fired him, declaring, "I will not have the author of that book in this department."

A fire in 1877 seriously damaged the west and north wings of the building, leading to a major reconstruction that included several of the most important interior spaces, such as the display halls for models of inventions submitted for patents. Executed in a style that E. J. Applewhite called "Victorian Psychedelic," these fantastically ornate rooms contrast dramatically with the building's severe exterior.

The Patent Office moved out in 1932, and the Civil Service Commission occupied the building until 1963. By the 1950s, however, the elderly structure was already considered thoroughly obsolete for governmental offices, and demolition loomed as a possibility. President Eisenhower intervened in 1955 and offered the building to the Smithsonian, which eventually assumed control and adapted it to museum use. Now known as the Donald W. Reynolds Center for American Art and Portraiture, the building actually houses two separate institutions—the National Portrait Gallery and the Smithsonian American Art Museum—and has just emerged from a comprehensive restoration by Hartman-Cox Architects. As of this writing, construction is proceeding on a controversial project by the British superstar architect Lord Norman Foster to enclose the building's long underutilized courtyard, making it available for public functions throughout the year. The signature element of the project is an undulating, metal-and-glass roof, supported on slender columns, which will add a striking, twenty-first-century crown to an already majestic, nineteenth-century landmark.

E9 International Spy Museum

8th and F streets, NW

1875 LeDroit Building (800–810 F Street): James H. McGill
1875–81 Other buildings in 800 block of F Street: Architects unknown (possibly by James McGill)
2003 Renovation and addition: Shalom Baranes Associates

The historic block that is now part of the International Spy Museum is a rare extant example of late nineteenth-century commercial architecture in Washington's central business district. The Victorian buildings, with their ornamental brackets and distinctive tripartite windows, still seem more likely to hold shoe repair shops and milliners rather than a for-profit museum of espionage. The modern addition, including some museum facilities as well as leasable office space, is designed to be compatible with, but clearly different from, the existing structures.

E10 Hotel Monaco (General Post Office/Tariff Commission)

7th and 8th streets between E and F streets, NW

1829–44 Robert Mills
1855–66 Thomas U. Walter; Superintendent of construction: Montgomery C. Meigs

2002 Renovation: Michael Stanton Architects; Preservation
architects: Oehrlein & Associates Architects; Restaurant: Adamstein
& Demetriou

Three office buildings by Robert Mills are extant in Washington: the
Patent Office, the Treasury, and this former General Post Office, later
occupied by the Tariff Commission. Standing at the southeast corner of
7th and F streets and facing west, one can simultaneously see all three
buildings, and note that they cover the three basic Greek orders—Doric
on the Patent Office, Ionic on the Treasury, and Corinthian on the Tariff
Building. Perhaps the least known of the trio, the Tariff Building occupies the former site of Blodget's Hotel (c. 1793), which burned to the
ground in 1836. The fate of the hotel helped make fire protection a para-
mount concern as the design of the new post office developed, and Mills
therefore gave the building masonry vaults and thick marble walls. The
solid structure is well proportioned and, though more ornate than its
cousin across the street, still beautifully restrained.

   Like so many of the city's large early structures, however, the Tariff
Building fell on hard times when the East End of downtown grew unfash-
ionable, and when its highly compartmentalized floor plan proved in-
imical to modern governmental office use. In 1997, the General Services
Administration—newly invigorated by dedicated, forward-looking staff
with an appreciation for high-quality design—decided to issue a request
for proposals, seeking the best possible use for the building. The winning idea was a hotel, which made sense because the relentless march of
vaulted structural bays around the perimeter implied relatively easy conversion into discrete guest rooms, requiring no significant modifications
to the historic building fabric. The Kimpton Group, a hospitality chain
known for its funky hostelries, took a sixty-year lease on the building, and
oversaw conversion into a surprisingly hip hotel. The former mail-sort-
ing room, occupying a peninsular structure in the central courtyard, was
converted into a restaurant. The slick glass addition, which is structurally
independent of the historic building, serves as a beacon when lit at night,
drawing patrons through the carriageway off of 8th Street.

E11 The Lansburgh

420–424 7th Street, NW
425 8th Street, NW

1890–1918 Various architects
1991 Renovations and
additions: Graham Gund
Architects (now GUND
Partnership); Associated
architects: Bryant & Bryant;
Preservation architects:
Oehrlein & Associates Architects

The Lansburgh complex, which gets its name from a venerable department store that once occupied part of this block, is a quilt of many patterns. Incorporating the rescued shells of several adjacent structures, including Kresge's (the corner of 7th and E streets) and the Busch Building (710 E Street), the development entails commercial, retail, and residential uses, and is the home of Washington's Shakespeare Theatre, renowned for its resident actors and inventive reinterpretations of plays by Shakespeare and others. A raised, open courtyard occupies the center of the block and serves the complex's residents.

E12 Gallery Row

401–413 7th Street, NW

1877–83 Original buildings:
R. D. Fleming, Germond
Crandell, J. A. Michiels
1986 Hartman-Cox
Architects; Preservation
architects: Oehrlein &
Associates Architects

In the nineteenth century, this part of town was filled with a diverse assemblage of commercial uses and residences. Architect Thomas U. Walter lived at 614 F Street; the *National Era* (an abolitionist newspaper) was published at 427 F Street; the improbably named Mr. Croissant led the city's temperance drive from his Holly Tree Hotel at 518 9th Street; and Samuel F. B. Morse tinkered with his new-fangled telegraph in a since-demolished building that stood on 7th Street between E and F. The twentieth-century architects of this art gallery complex captured that lively history in 409 7th

Street's Mannerist exterior; inside, the new unit's four-story rotunda acts as a lobby and a pivot for the entire project.

E13 Terrell Place (Old Hecht Company Building)

575 7th Street, NW

1924 Jarvis Hunt
2003 Renovation and addition: SmithGroup;
Preservation architects: Oehrlein & Associates Architects

The former Hecht's department store was designed by a nephew of Richard Morris Hunt, architect of the Biltmore House in Asheville, North Carolina, and other opulent works of the Gilded Age. With white, glazed terra cotta façades, intricate iron detailing, and an ornate clock suspended above the street corner, the Hecht Company Building exudes a subdued classiness that evokes the heyday of urban retail in the early twentieth century.

After Hecht's moved to a new flagship store in the 1980s, the old structure sat idle for many years until it was adapted for office use during the renaissance of the East End of downtown. Much of the exterior ornament had been removed but preserved inside the building, and was put back in place during the renovation. The project also entailed weaving together parts of several smaller structures on the same block of 7th Street (three of which were even earlier Hecht Company properties), plus an entirely new structure immediately to the east on F Street.

E14 Verizon Center

F Street between 6th and 7th
streets, NW

1997 Ellerbe Becket;
Associate architects: KCF-
SHG Architects, Devrouax &
Purnell Architects-Planners

Squeezing a major sports facility
into an existing urban neighborhood is never an easy task,
and it was especially difficult
to accommodate a new basketball, hockey, and concert venue in one
of L'Enfant's city blocks. In fact, it proved impossible—the plan for this
arena could fit only if the 600 block of G Street, NW, were obliterated.
After much controversy, all of the necessary governmental authorities
agreed to the closure of the street. Soon thereafter, however, the District
government decided to reopen several nearby blocks, including the 900
block of G Street, which had been turned into useless "pedestrian plazas" in the 1970s. Restoring these blocks to vehicular traffic has clearly
facilitated redevelopment in the East End of downtown, so the trade-off
may have been worth it in the long run, especially because the Verizon
Center itself is also widely credited with sparking the renaissance of its
immediate neighborhood.

Because the center abuts the Chinatown historic district, the architectural team had the unusual additional challenge of incorporating Chi-
nese-inspired motifs into the design of the sports arena—an odd fusion,
to say the least. To achieve this, the designers relied primarily on graphic
devices and a few architectural elements, such as the wavy canopy on the
northwest corner of the building, that vaguely suggest Asian architectural forms. By contrast, the main entry on F Street, with its tall columns
and slanted canopy, clearly alludes to the Neoclassical porticoes that
mark the Old Patent Office Building next door. The rest of the façades
are cleanly generic. The result is a slightly haphazard building, but one
that manages to seem modest and neighborly, belying its true scale.

E15 Jackson Graham Building (Washington Metropolitan Area Transit Authority Headquarters)

600 5th Street, NW

1974 Keyes, Lethbridge & Condon, Architects

Extended floor slabs and a parade of widely spaced, cylindrical concrete columns give this office building visual depth, while changing shadows throughout the day animate what might otherwise be a severely plain work of architecture. The building was designed so that a Metro car could stop directly beneath it to drop off money collected throughout the system each day.

E16 National Academies Building

500 5th Street, NW

2003 SmithGroup

The new headquarters of the National Academies, an umbrella organization that includes the National Academy of Sciences, the National Academy of Engineering, the Institute of Medicine, and the National Research Council, was carefully inserted into a block containing some of the last extant historic row houses in Washington's commercial downtown. Although these buildings were not landmarked at the time that the building was conceived, the architects anticipated strong objections to any proposal that involved tearing them down, and therefore worked with preservation organizations to devise a scheme that would save the historic buildings while allowing substantial new construction on the site. Perhaps as a result, the restored buildings still read as discrete, substantive structures, rather than just pickled façades, even though their interiors have been greatly altered in order to weave them into the larger complex.

E17 Superior Court of the District of Columbia (Old City Hall)

451 Indiana Avenue, NW

1820–49 George Hadfield
1883 Expansion: Edward Clark
1919 Renovation: Elliott Woods
2003 Master plan: Karn Charuhas Chapman & Twohey

Emphatically terminating the axis of lower 4th Street, NW, this was the first public building erected by and for the District's municipal government. After the seemingly obligatory funding crises (a "grand National Lottery" was one of several unsuccessful schemes to raise the cash), the mayor laid the cornerstone in August 1820 for "the seat of legislation and of the administration of justice for this metropolis." The central part of the Greek Revival structure is the oldest and simplest. The modest but well-proportioned Ionic portico that marks the main entry was finished in 1849. The east and west wings, added in 1826 and 1849, respectively, are a little more adventurous— their southern ends have porches with paired columns *in antis*, meaning that they are bracketed by extensions of the side walls, with arched openings behind and steps leading to ground level. Originally, these wings directly abutted the sidewalk along Indiana Avenue, but the street itself was later regraded and lowered, resulting in a somewhat nebulous front yard that only somewhat diminishes the building's urbane dignity.

Elliott Woods established the present form of the building in a major renovation of 1917–19. The work included constructing an entirely new interior, strengthening the walls with steel beams, encasing the original brick-and-stucco exterior in Indiana limestone, and replacing the original sandstone columns with limestone replicas. As of this writing, the firm of Beyer Blinder Belle is overseeing a renovation of, and addition to, the historic structure.

E18   Henry J. Daly Building (Municipal Building)

300 Indiana Avenue, NW

1941   Nathan C. Wyeth

One of a number of District government buildings in this vicinity designed by Nathan Wyeth, who served as the city's municipal architect from 1934 to 1946, this is the headquarters of the Metropolitan Police Department—as well as the lair of the vicious hydra known as the Department of Motor Vehicles (which, in fairness, is not as scary as it used to be). The building is typical of Wyeth's stripped classicism—note the mere hint of classical pilasters inscribed into the stone on either side of each of the major window openings. Be sure to see the ceramic tile friezes that grace the building's two courtyards, illustrating *Democracy in Action* (by Waylande Gregory) in the west courtyard, and *Health and Welfare* (by Hildreth Meiere) in the east.

E19   U.S. Tax Court Building

400 2nd Street, NW

1974   Victor A. Lundy; Associated architects: Lyles Bissett/Carlisle & Wolff

The fashion for public buildings in the late 1960s and 1970s tended toward abstraction and extreme monumentality. In the case of the U.S. Tax Court, the result was a forbidding, space-age grandeur exuding power and authority. The building does have a certain minimalist magnificence, best appreciated from the plaza over the freeway immediately east of the site (which has obviously never attracted people as the architect hoped it would). Along the 2nd Street façade, an absurdly wide staircase leads visitors into an inky void that obscures the original main entrance, which has been closed for security reasons for much of the building's history. Suspended above is a huge, windowless, cantilevered slab clad in granite, which holds courtrooms and offices.

Pennsylvania Avenue has long been dubbed "America's Main Street." According to lore, the avenue got its name as a sop to politicians from the Keystone State, who became disgruntled when Congress decided to build a national capital from scratch instead of giving Philadelphia that honor. If true, the gesture was probably not appreciated—one early nineteenth-century congressman described Pennsylvania Avenue as "a deep morass covered with elder bushes," and, despite Thomas Jefferson's attempts to beautify the thoroughfare by planting flanking rows of Lombardy poplars, that description remained valid for much of the first half of the century. While fretting about the street's appearance, Jefferson, perhaps unwittingly, began an honored tradition when he walked down Pennsylvania Avenue for his inauguration in March 1801. Since then, except perhaps for New York's Fifth Avenue, Pennsylvania Avenue has witnessed more parades for more different organizations and causes than any other thoroughfare in the nation.

During the Civil War, Pennsylvania Avenue, especially between 7th Street and 14th Street, became the favorite haunt of the countless prostitutes who were drawn to Washington, in venerable tradition, by the city's hundreds of thousands of soldiers. According to one story, General Joseph Hooker tried to get the prostitutes to confine their activities to a small zone, but the women refused and taunted the general by starting

Aerial view of the Federal Triangle still under construction in the 1930s.

to call themselves "Hooker's Army," later shortened to "hookers" (though there are other stories about the origin of both terms). That phase of the avenue's history ended when the District outlawed brothels in 1914, and not long thereafter the southern side of Pennsylvania was transformed by the gargantuan Federal Triangle project.

By the 1960s, the northern side of the ceremonial stretch of Pennsylvania Avenue, despite its historic and symbolic importance, was thoroughly decrepit. President Kennedy, riding down the avenue after his inauguration, expressed shock over what appeared to be a "slum" between the nation's two most prominent public buildings. Kennedy appointed a temporary commission to study possible remedies, and in 1972, Congress established the Pennsylvania Avenue Development Corporation (PADC), a unique independent agency of the federal government that was given broad powers to redevelop the area. Over the next two decades or so, the corporation was extremely successful in acquiring, rehabilitating, selling, and leasing property. The PADC used its design oversight authority to guide renovations and new construction, and largely as a result of the agency's work, the once shabby thoroughfare is now a truly grand, if not especially vibrant, boulevard worthy of the national landmarks that it connects.

F1   E. Barrett Prettyman Courthouse

333 Constitution Avenue, NW

1952 Louis Justement
2005 Addition and
renovation: Michael Graves
Associates; Preservation
architects: Oehrlein &
Associates Architects;
Associated architects:
SmithGroup; Courthouse
consultants: Ricci Architects &
Planners

In the realm of stripped classicism, the original Prettyman Courthouse is the Full Monty—as bare as bare can be. Designed and built not long after World War II, it reflects official Washington's continued unwillingness to accept truly modern architecture for major public buildings, even as full-fledged classicism had come to seem untenable, if not absolutely absurd, at the dawn of the 1950s. The result is a building that looks as if it is trying very hard to be nothing at all.

In contrast, the recent addition by Michael Graves seems to be trying desperately to be *something*, though what, precisely, is unclear. Oddly reminiscent of the architect's various projects for the Walt Disney Company, the addition exhibits little of the stateliness one would expect of a federal court facility. Instead, it comes off as an overly teased, fluffy tail wagging a shaved and slightly embarrassed dog.

Immediately west of the original courthouse is John Marshall Park, designed by Carol R. Johnson Associates and completed in 1983. The park's honoree, Chief Justice John Marshall, once lived in a rooming house that, ironically, was one of dozens of structures demolished to make way for this green space.

F2　Canadian Chancery

501 Pennsylvania Avenue, NW

1989　Arthur Erickson
Architects

Thanks to Washington's building height limit and other stringent zoning restrictions, many of the city's commercial structures are designed to squeeze in as much square footage as possible, and often look as if they were ready to burst beyond the maximum buildable volume allowed by law. In contrast, the Canadian Embassy seems not quite big enough to fill its site, and in fact, that is the case. Guidelines established by the Pennsylvania Avenue Development Corporation dictated the cornice line and basic footprint for any building to go on this prominent plot, and the Canadian Embassy simply did not need all of the space that the prescribed building envelope would have allowed. As a result, the embassy building is a little hollow, with a profusion of columns that do not support much substance. On the positive side, however, the resulting open courtyard is publicly accessible—a rarity in an era of draconian security measures at so many diplomatic facilities.

The most prominent corner of the site, facing the Capitol, is marked by an outdoor rotunda defined by twelve columns, one for each of Canada's provinces and territories at the time the building was completed (such numerological tributes in architecture can quickly become dated—a thirteenth jurisdiction, Nunavut, was carved out of the Northwest Territories in 1999). Just inside the courtyard is a row of six huge, eighty-foot-tall aluminum columns, fluted in a nod to classicism, which incongruously hold up an obviously lightweight glass canopy. The strongest exterior architectural element is the cascading, lushly planted west wall of the courtyard, which recalls similar stepped forms on several of Erickson's governmental and academic projects in Vancouver. The embassy's interior public spaces are serene and elegantly understated.

F3   The Federal Triangle

Between Pennsylvania and Constitution avenues, and 6th and 15th streets, NW

The most ambitious architectural undertaking in the history of Washington, the Federal Triangle in many ways represents the culmination of the City Beautiful movement. Conceived in the Roaring Twenties and largely executed during the Great Depression, the vast complex is remarkable for its conceptual and visual cohesion, even as the individual buildings reflect sometimes surprisingly varied attitudes toward ornament and architectural form. The Triangle's buildings were, in fact, designed by many different architects, but they were conceived as a single monumental composition and were guided to completion by a coordinating committee headed by Edward Bennett, architectural advisor to Andrew Mellon.

F3A Federal Trade Commission

Between 6th and 7th streets, and Constitution and Pennsylvania avenues, NW

1937 Bennett, Parsons & Frost; Sculptors: Michael Lantz et al.

Forming the apex of the Federal Triangle is the last of the buildings completed during the 1930s. Not surprisingly, given its construction late in the Depression, the Federal Trade Commission is the plainest of the Triangle's original structures. The chastity of the building design contrasts with the exaggerated muscularity of Michael Lantz's freestanding sculptures depicting, believe it or not, "Man Controlling Trade."

F3B National Archives Building

700 Pennsylvania Avenue, NW (Exhibit Hall Entrance on Constitution Avenue)

1935 John Russell Pope; Sculptors: Adolph A. Weinman, James Earle Fraser, and Robert Aitken

2003 Renovation: Hartman-Cox Architects

www.archives.gov

Of all the buildings in the Federal Triangle, this one achieves the greatest individual architectural distinction; what success the others enjoy is largely dependent on their cumulative effect. As with Pope's design for the Scottish Rite Temple on 16th Street [see L26], the National Archives Building seems to have been inspired by a mausoleum—an appropriate reference, really, since it was conceived as a permanent repository for the nation's most important documents. The Declaration of Independence, the Constitution, and other documents are on view in the Rotunda, which was recently restored to allow greater accessibility and visibility without compromising the James Bond–like security measures that protect these invaluable items from every imaginable threat.

F3C Robert F. Kennedy Federal Building (Department of Justice)

Between 9th and 10th streets, and Pennsylvania and Constitution avenues, NW

1934 Zantzinger, Borie & Medary
2004 Renovation: Burt Hill Kosar Rittelmann Associates; Preservation architects: Oehrlein & Associates Architects

The Justice Department is an interesting hybrid—a clearly classical building with Art Deco motifs sprinkled throughout. On the exterior, most of the Art Deco influences are subtle—notice, for instance, the Ionic column capitals, whose scrolls have unorthodox, bulging tops—though the exuberant light fixtures unabashedly reflect the glamour and audacity so closely associated with the style. Most of the Deco elements, however, are inside, where, sadly, the average citizen will never get to see them. These include stunning murals, as well as elaborate mosaics by local artisan John Joseph Earley. The mosaic ceilings over the driveways are partially visible from the sidewalk.

F3D   Internal Revenue Service

1111 Constitution Avenue, NW

1936   Louis A. Simon
1993   Façade completion: Karn Charuhas Chapman & Twohey
2005   Renovation: Swanke Hayden Connell

The purpose of this building is evident in Oliver Wendell Holmes's sober maxim, carved over the Constitution Avenue entrance, that "taxes are what we pay for a civilized society." The northwestern corner of the site was obviously truncated to accommodate the Old Post Office, which stubbornly lingered to the consternation of the classicist crusaders (a raw end at the western end of the Pennsylvania Avenue façade was finally finished in 1993, recognizing that the Post Office simply is not going anywhere).

F3E   Environmental Protection Agency & Andrew W. Mellon Auditorium

Constitution Avenue between 12th and 14th streets, NW

1934   Arthur Brown Jr.
2000   Renovation: RTKL Associates

Brown, best known as the architect of San Francisco's elegant City Hall, originally designed this three-unit behemoth to house the Interstate Commerce Commission and the Labor Department. Sandwiched between the two office blocks is a spectacularly ornate and impeccably proportioned auditorium now named for Andrew Mellon, who, as secretary of the treasury, was instrumental in the planning of the Federal Triangle. The auditorium is a multipurpose public assembly facility for important lectures, receptions, banquets, and other fancy social affairs, not to mention the occasional treaty signing. Few spaces in Washington can compete with it for sheer grandeur.

F3F Ariel Rios Building

Pennsylvania Avenue and 12th Street, NW

1935 Delano & Aldrich
1998 Façade completion: Karn Charuhas Chapman & Twohey
2000 Renovation: RTKL Associates

Two broad concave arcs, back to back, lend a Baroque quality to the structure originally known as the Post Office Building (housing the headquarters of the U.S. Postal Service, not to be confused with local post office facilities such as those at Postal Square [see A11] and the old Tariff Building [see E10]). Projecting bays extend all the way to the 12th Street line, providing pedestrian archways over the sidewalk—welcome anomalies in a city where public and commercial buildings rarely engage the streetscape so boldly. The Internal Revenue Service building across the street was intended to incorporate a complementary arc, creating a full circle. Meanwhile, the western façade of the Ariel Rios Building was conceived as the apse of a "Grand Plaza," which was instead relegated to use as a parking lot for decades until the Ronald Reagan Building filled the site.

F3G Ronald Reagan Building and International Trade Center

1300 Pennsylvania Avenue, NW

1998 Pei Cobb Freed & Partners; Associated architects: Ellerbe Becket Architects and Engineers

2001 Center for Association Leadership at the Marriott Learning Complex: VOA Associates

Washington is full of architectural anachronisms, but this may be the most anachronistic of them all. Conceived as the very belated completion of the Federal Triangle, it is ponderously and stodgily classical. Its formalism is so relentless that—unconscionably in a modern office building—the architects actually omitted exterior windows from a significant portion of one floor so as not to interfere with the composition of the façades. Strangely, though, given the conservatism and formality of the overall design, the eastern façade and the resulting outdoor plaza between it and the Ariel Rios Building are unexpectedly asymmetrical and dynamic. More curious is the stark contrast between the Mannerist classical exterior (note how each individual block of stone at the base of the façades is chamfered on two sides to create an impression of shadow and, thus, of greater depth) and the futuristic main atrium space. The conference and event facilities inside the complex fall somewhere in between—relatively straightforward, cleanly modern, and warm.

F3H Herbert Clark Hoover Federal Building (Department of Commerce)

Between 14th and 15th streets, and E Street and Constitution Avenue, NW

1932 Louis Ayres
1989 Law Library restoration: Einhorn Yaffee Prescott

Scored walls and a range of pedimented windows lend an Italianate character to this thousand-foot-long building. When new, this was the largest office building in the country, with over one million square feet of floor space.

F4   Sears House (Apex, Brady, and Gilman Buildings)

625–633 Pennsylvania Avenue, NW

c. 1840–65 Architects unknown
1888 Apex/Central National Bank Building addition: Alfred B. Mullett
1984 New structure: Geier Brown Renfrow Architects; Restoration: Hartman-Cox Architects; Preservation consultants: John Milner Associates

Three buildings were combined to make the current Sears House. Mathew Brady, the great Civil War photographer, kept his studio and office in the back building for more than twenty years. The combined structures are currently painted a ghastly shade of pink that diminishes their dignity and blurs their architectural details.

F5   Argentine Naval Attaché Building (National Bank of Washington, later Riggs Bank)

630 Indiana Avenue, NW

1889 James G. Hill
1979 Interior renovation: P. T. Astore
1982 Renovation: Vlastimil Koubek

One of the most elegant works of Romanesque Revival architecture in the city, the Argentine Naval Attaché's building is made of rough-faced granite ashlar with smooth trim. The balance of textures, the rhythm of the windows, and the intricate but modest details all serve to distinguish the building. A large trompe-l'oeil mural adorns the eastern façade.

In the plaza just west of the Argentine Naval Building stands the Temperance Fountain of 1882. The fountain, which was presented to the city by temperance crusader Henry D. Cogswell, a San Francisco dentist, is now—perhaps more appropriately—dry. Dr. Cogswell picked a good site from which to launch his local antivice crusade, since for most of the nineteenth century this block marked the eastern boundary of the city's large red light district.

F6 The Pennsylvania/Pennsylvania Plaza

601 Pennsylvania Avenue, NW, North Building

1990 Hartman-Cox Architects

The address is a stretch, of course—an effort to capture some Pennsylvania Avenue prestige for a complex that is clearly on Indiana Avenue. The residential portion, known as The Pennsylvania, is an unassuming brick-and-precast-concrete structure replete with balconies. The office block, called Pennsylvania Plaza, is designed to evoke the cast iron façades common among late nineteenth-century commercial buildings. The two structures blend together at the top, revealing that they are part of a single project. The plaza between this complex and the south building, designed by the firm of Eisenman Robertson, is a pleasantly scaled urban space.

F7 Market Square

Pennsylvania Avenue between 7th and 9th streets, NW

1990 Hartman-Cox Architects; Associated architects: Morris*Architects

The team that planned the rebirth of Pennsylvania Avenue in the 1960s, during the heyday of the heroic period of modernism, could scarcely have imagined that, just a couple of decades later, this prominent site would be occupied by two buildings boasting a phalanx of five-story classical columns. Taking its name from the Center Market that once stood across the street from this site, Market Square is a mixed-use complex with residential units over offices and retail space. The late Senator Daniel Patrick Moynihan, a vocal advocate for the avenue's revitalization, put his money where his mouth was and bought one of the apartments boasting spectacular views of the city's monumental core. Nestled in the embrace of Market Square is the Navy Memorial, by the firm of Conklin Rossant, with sculptures by Stanley Bleifeld.

F8　J. Edgar Hoover Building (FBI Headquarters)

Pennsylvania Avenue between 9th and 10th streets, NW

1974　C. F. Murphy & Associates

The swaggering bully of the neighborhood, the FBI headquarters is ungainly, ill-mannered, and seemingly looking for trouble. A cynic could argue that it is all too successful as a piece of architecture to the extent that the building's form so starkly reflects the clandestine work of the agency it houses: the impenetrable base, shadowy courtyard, and looming upper stories bespeak security and surveillance. The prototype for the Pennsylvania Avenue redevelopment plan devised under the direction of Nathaniel Owings, it helped to ensure that the full plan would never be realized.

F9　1001 Pennsylvania Avenue, NW

1987　Hartman-Cox Architects; Associated architects: Smith Segreti Tepper, Architects/Planners; Preservation architects: Oehrlein & Associates Architects

This full-city-block commercial building is most interesting where it defers to the remnants of the small-scale, historic structures that were preserved as part of the project, creating a layered composition. Compare this to Lincoln Square across E Street, a later effort by the same firm executed with greater finesse.

F10 Evening Star Building

1101 Pennsylvania Avenue, NW

1899 Marsh and Peter
1919 Addition: Architect unknown
1989 Renovation and addition:
Skidmore, Owings & Merrill;
Preservation architects: Oehrlein &
Associates Architects

When this Beaux-Arts building first
opened, the *Evening Star,* pleased with
its new digs, ran a full-page story to
announce its "architectural triumph." Continuing, the article stated that
the paper's publisher had decided to make the District "notable in an artistic sense" and thus chose to erect "such a building as would be harmonious with that future and an inspiration to its speedy attainments." The
Star pursued many crusades from this building until 1955 (it published
from a different location for another generation before its demise). The
building's future was uncertain until the Pennsylvania Avenue Development Corporation redeveloped and expanded it for modern office use.

F11 Nancy Hanks Center/Old Post Office Building

12th Street and Pennsylvania Avenue,
NW

1899 Willoughby J. Edbrooke
1983 Adaptive reuse: Arthur Cotton
Moore/Associates; Associated
architects: McGaughy, Marshall &
McMillan
1991 Addition: Karn Charuhas
Chapman & Twohey

This Romanesque Revival building,
with its 315-foot tower, stands out
dramatically amid the otherwise exclusively, and perhaps oppressively,
classical Federal Triangle. Controversy swirled around this former post
office, the first major steel-framed structure in town, since its completion, when the *New York Times* sniffed that the new building looked like
"a cross between a cathedral and a cotton mill."

The Postal Service abandoned the building in the 1930s for its new headquarters nearby, and threats of demolition hung over the place for a half century simply because it was deemed out of step with its neighbors. Finally, in the early 1970s, preservationists prevailed and the building was saved in a widely publicized case of adaptive reuse. Upper levels were restored for government offices, and the lower levels of the atrium were turned into an early version of a food court. Two decades hence, the building looks tired, and the government offices within are accommodated quite uncomfortably. Rumors swirl that the structure will eventually become a luxury hotel, where the atrium could actually become a logical amenity rather than merely an unusually copious lightwell.

F12 Warner Theatre/Office Building (Earle Theatre)

1299 Pennsylvania Avenue, NW

1924 C. Howard Crane and Kenneth Franzheim
1927 Addition of top floor: Zink, Atkins and Craycroft
1993 Renovation: Shalom Baranes Associates; Addition: Pei Cobb Freed & Partners Architects

The original building, which is actually at the corner of 13th and E streets despite its Pennsylvania Avenue address, is a classic 1920s theater, with finely honed ornament and an enticing marquee. The location of the stage is expressed on the E Street elevation by windowless panels carrying a decorative diamond pattern. The large addition is articulated along E Street as if it were two buildings—the easternmost part of the façade is a modern recapitulation of the theater façade, while the central part is designed as a slightly different but compatible composition, lending a basic, tripartite symmetry to the entire block.

F13 John Wilson Building (District Building)

1350 Pennsylvania Avenue, NW

1908 Cope & Stewardson; Sculptor: Adolfo De Nesti
2003 Renovation and addition: Shalom Baranes Associates; Exterior preservation architects: Oehrlein & Associates Architects; Architects of record: Kendall Heaton Associates

Elegant in a way, but also ungainly in comparison to many of its Beaux-Arts siblings, the John Wilson Building houses the offices of the mayor and Council of the District of Columbia. The building was in such bad shape in the early 1990s that city officials actually decamped for leased space in a bland commercial structure on Judiciary Square. The District government later entered into a complicated and rather mysterious deal with the federal government and a private developer by which the structure was renovated, the U-shaped courtyard was filled in with a glassy addition, and the city officials were eventually able to move back into the historic, de facto city hall. According to the preservation architect, the exterior of the building was so heavily caked in pigeon droppings that it took two years of restoration before the exterior marble approximated its original color.

F14 Freedom Plaza/Pershing Park (Western Plaza)

Pennsylvania Avenue between 13th and 15th streets, NW

1980 Freedom Plaza: Venturi, Rauch & Scott Brown; Landscape architect: George E. Patton
1981 Pershing Park: M. Paul Friedberg; Associated architect: Jerome Lindsay

It is ironic that a firm known for its advocacy of "popular" architecture should have created such a desolate and cheerless public space as Freedom Plaza. Laid out on a large, raised terrace, the plaza renders L'Enfant's plan in black and white stone, framing the giant map with paving stones inscribed with quotes about the District—some serious, some less so. In typical fashion, the architects filled the site with complexities and hidden meanings. They once stated that the plaza's form is, like the city's, controlled by two "orders"—not the conventional Doric and Ionic but the "giant," or diagonal, and "minor," or rectangular grid. All of this is lost on the typical visitor, who just scurries across the plaza as quickly as possible or avoids it altogether. In fairness, it should be noted that the architects' original design included tall pylons and large-scale models of the White House and Capitol, which would have brought some three-dimensional interest to the design, but would have done little to relieve its wind- and sun-swept barrenness.

Just to the west is the lushly landscaped Pershing Park. With its sense of enclosure and intimacy, this park is a pleasant foil to Freedom Plaza.

F15 National Place/J. W. Marriott Hotel

Between E, F, 13th, and 14th streets, NW

1984 Hotel: Mitchell/Giurgola Architects; National Place: Frank Schlesinger Associates
2005 Renovation of National Place food court: Brian G. Thornton Designs; Exterior canopy at National Place: Soe Lin & Associates

The Marriott chain's flagship hotel and the adjoining, mixed-use National Place complex were among the earliest developments in the renaissance of Washington's former commercial core. The new structures were woven into a block that includes a small remnant of the Capitol Theater (1927—Rapp & Rapp), marked by an apse-like, concave façade on F Street.

F16 Willard Hotel

14th Street and Pennsylvania Avenue, NW

1901–4 Henry Hardenbergh
1926 Addition: Walter G. Peter
1986 Renovation and addition conceptual design: Hardy Holzman Pfeiffer Associates; Executive architect: Vlastimil Koubek; Restoration: Stuart Golding

Without doubt the most fabled hostelry in town, the present Willard is the last in a succession of hotels that have stood on this site since about 1816. In that year, John Tayloe, builder of the Octagon [see I3], built six houses on this lot and leased them to Joshua Tennison, who established Tennison's Hotel. In 1847 Tayloe's son, Benjamin Ogle Tayloe, paid to have the hotel refurbished and hired twenty-five-year-old Henry Willard to run it. Willard and his brother Joseph bought the structure outright in 1853 and renamed it Willard's, and the name stuck though it eventually lost the possessive form.

During the Civil War, Julia Ward Howe wrote the "Battle Hymn of the Republic" in her room at the Willard and the building played host to so many luminaries that Nathaniel Hawthorne, covering the war for *The Atlantic,* observed, "This hotel . . . may be more justly called the center of Washington and the Union than either the Capitol, the White House, or the State Department." On a less exalted level, the Willard also gave rise to the term *lobbyist,* which referred to any of the men who prowled the lobby, peering through cigar smoke and potted palms in search of political figures to accost.

The present building was the work of Henry Hardenbergh, who also designed the Plaza Hotel in New York. Good times and the Willard remained synonymous until after World War II, when the entire neighborhood suffered an extended, grueling decline. (One of the hotel's few bright postwar moments came in 1963, when Martin Luther King Jr. penned his "I Have a Dream" speech in a room upstairs.) Boarded up and threatened with demolition, the Willard was finally saved through the intervention of the Pennsylvania Avenue Development Corporation and, after a lengthy restoration, reopened its opulent doors in 1986 as the Willard InterContinental Hotel. Its public rooms—the main lobby, with its thirty-five different types of marble; Peacock Alley, a block-long promenade of ritzy shops; and Round Robin Bar, which boasted a sign during Carrie Nation's heyday proclaiming "All Nations Welcome Except Carrie"—rank among the grandest such spaces in the city.

The addition, designed by Hardy Holzman Pfeiffer Associates and executed by Vlastimil Koubek, reflects a concerted effort to replicate the basic forms of the existing building while still deferring to it—a challenging task. The architects' solution entailed the use of multiple setbacks, diminishing the apparent scale of new construction.

F17   Hotel Washington

15th Street and Pennsylvania Avenue, NW

1918 Carrère & Hastings
1985 Renovation: Mariani and Associates; Materials conservator: Ivan Valtchev

Washington's oldest hotel in continuous use, the Hotel Washington is best known for its roof deck, which, though far from being a design landmark, boasts some of the best views in the city. Carrère and Hastings, architects of such masterpieces as the main New York Public Library on Fifth Avenue, sheathed this steel-frame structure in veneers of pale, smooth stone below the third story and in similar-hued brick above, with liver-colored *sgraffito* decorations (in which designs are scratched into layered plaster, revealing colors beneath the surface) around the upper floors' windows and in the building's main frieze incorporating images of American presidents.

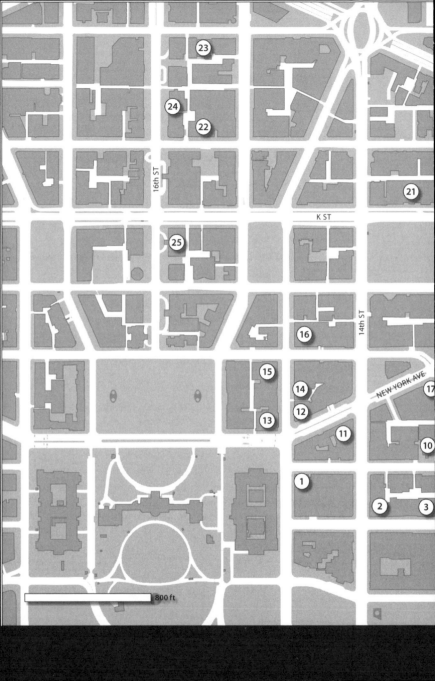

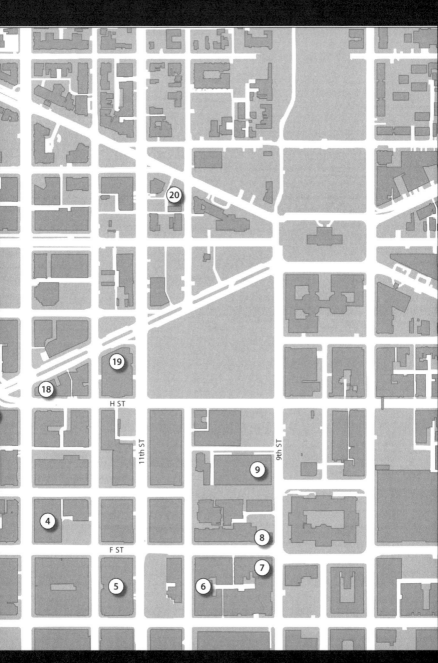

The early twentieth century was the heyday of the American downtown, when shoppers flocked to department stores and streetcars plied their routes amid the throngs of pedestrians. The area east of the White House and above Pennsylvania Avenue was Washington's true downtown during that period, with F Street as its principal retail strip. After World War II, however, the thriving district declined rapidly, as did so many similar areas in cities across the country, leaving dozens of grand works of architecture to decay. New development in the postwar era focused instead on K Street, particularly to the west of 16th Street.

By the 1980s, as developable sites in the West End were growing rarer, commercial interests began to reconsider the old East End. A booming real estate market, interrupted only briefly by a couple of recessions, has subsequently driven a phenomenally rapid rejuvenation of this area. Though only one department store remains in the old center, smaller retailers have moved back in, and residential development is increasingly common. Local political leaders and developers are now hopeful that a truly vibrant downtown is once again on the horizon.

Washington's old downtown was once full of small to medium-scale commercial structures, such as this one at 7th and G streets, NW. Most such buildings were demolished in the late twentieth century to make way for much larger office buildings.

G1 Metropolitan Square

655 15th Street, NW

1986 Vlastimil Koubek; Consulting
architects: Skidmore, Owings &
Merrill

For nearly 185 years, the northeast
corner of 15th and F streets was
occupied by the unassuming but ultra-
historic Rhodes Tavern. Opened in
1801, the tavern had served, in effect, as
Washington's first town hall, providing a venue for numerous meetings
that helped to shape the nascent capital. Shortly thereafter it housed
the rather optimistically named Bank of the Metropolis and, much
later, the National Press Club. Having survived the British invasion
in 1814 and numerous construction booms in the late nineteenth and
twentieth centuries, the tavern ultimately succumbed in 1984 to make
way for the Metropolitan Square project despite fierce opposition from
local preservationists. Though the Rhodes was lost, the mixed-use
mega-building erected on the site does incorporate façades of several
much younger historic structures, including the National Metropolitan
Bank (1907—B. Stanley Simmons; Gordon, Tracy and Swartout) and
the Keith-Albee Building (1912—Jules Henri de Sibour), which once
contained a 1,838-seat theater, shops, and Turkish baths.

G2 Westory

607 14th Street, NW

1908 Henry L. A. Jeckel
1990 Renovation and addition:
Shalom Baranes Associates;
Preservation architects: Oehrlein &
Associates Architects
2003 Addition: Shalom Baranes
Associates

The new part of this complex facing
14th Street was originally conceived
as an addition to the National Bank of
Washington at the corner of 14th and G, and was intended to serve as
the bank's headquarters, but the institution declared bankruptcy before

the project got under way. At that point, it morphed into a speculative commercial development, executed in two phases, which are clearly legible along the F Street façade—at the corner of 14th and F is the original building (with a one-story addition on top); immediately to its east is part of the 1991 addition, designed as an abstraction of the older structure; and following that is the newest addition, which is an abstraction of the abstraction.

G3 The Sun Building

1317 F Street, NW

1887 Alfred B. Mullett
1983 Restoration: Abel & Weinstein

Surprisingly, some guidebooks tout this building—in the heart of famously low-rise Washington—as the oldest skyscraper still standing. In truth, the designations of "first" and "oldest" skyscraper are disputable, and while this building has a metal structure (iron rather than steel), it does not truly have a skeletal frame or curtain walls, making the aptness of the term *skyscraper* suspect. None of that takes away from the fact that it was an ambitiously tall pioneer when built, especially with the small spire that originally sprang from the top but was later removed.

Built for Baltimore's newspaper, *The Sun*, the mid-block building has a single major façade of rough-hewn granite, with windows, dormers, and projecting bays framed by simple blocks of smooth stone. It was designed by Alfred B. Mullett after he left his position as supervising architect of the Treasury.

G4 Homer Building

601 13th Street, NW

1914 Appleton P. Clark Jr.
1990 Shalom Baranes
Associates; Preservation
architects: Oehrlein &
Associates Architects

Appleton Clark anticipated that his original four-story, terra cotta–faced building would eventually be expanded vertically, and so he designed the structure to support the weight of additional stories. As it turned out, however, when the addition was finally commissioned, the Metro ran beneath the building, posing unanticipated engineering challenges. As a result, an entirely new structural system was required and only the façades of the original building were retained.

G5   555 12th Street, NW

1995 Florance Eichbaum Esocoff
King Architects

Architects of commercial buildings in Washington have long grappled with the question of how to introduce ornament without resorting to cutesiness or anachronism. In the case of 555 12th Street, the results of that effort are quite convincing, even when viewed at close range (where modern attempts at pure decoration are often revealed to be crudely conceived and executed). Here, all of the decorative elements—including spandrel panels, grilles, canopies, colonnettes resting on the black granite base, and even the door hardware—appear to be holistically conceived, carefully detailed, and well made. As with some roughly contemporaneous buildings by this architecture firm (previously Keyes Condon Florance, and now part of SmithGroup), the effect is reminiscent of the work of the Viennese Secession, which makes some sense, as that movement produced buildings that represented a comfortably ornamented modernism.

G6 Ford's Theatre

511 10th Street, NW

1863 James J. Gifford
1894 Alterations: Architect unknown
1968 Macomber & Peter;
Restoration: William Haussman

TEL: (202) 426-6924
www.fordstheatre.org

Impresario John T. Ford arrived in town
in 1861, flush from a string of successes
at Baltimore's Holliday Street Theater.
He began building this theater in 1863 and seemed destined to repeat
his Baltimore triumphs until April 14, 1865, when John Wilkes Booth
shot President Lincoln in one of the theater's boxes. After the tragedy,
the federal government leased the building and converted it to offices
and the Army Medical Museum, and later used it as a storage facility. It
was transferred to the National Park Service in 1932, and was finally restored to its original condition several decades later. Although the stage
lights now glow once again, it is difficult to watch a play there without
frequently glancing at the box where Booth's bullet changed history. The
government still owns the theater and maintains, through the National
Park Service, a small museum in the basement. It also maintains the
Peterson House, directly across 10th Street at number 516, where the
wounded president was carried and soon died.

The block of 10th Street on which the theater stands is noteworthy as
one of the most eclectic ensembles remaining in downtown Washington,
including, on the east side of the street, a small Second Empire commercial structure and a stolid, early twentieth-century office building, and,
on the west side, everything from a former 1950s waffle shop, to a sleek
Art Moderne building, to a brand-new glass-and-steel tour bus facility by
Shalom Baranes Associates.

G7 Courtyard by Marriott (Riggs National Bank)

900 F Street, NW

1891 James G. Hill
1912 Interior renovation: Architect unknown
1927 Addition: Arthur Heaton
1998 Renovation: Gordon & Greenberg Architects

The robust, arcuated granite façades of this former bank building recall those of Louis Sullivan's Auditorium Building and H. H. Richardson's Marshall Field store in Chicago. Notice the alternating courses of narrow and wide stones, a very subtle trick that manages to lend the façades a surprising degree of delicacy despite their heaviness. Along the F Street face, the vertical line between the original building and the addition is quite clear thanks to a noticeable change in color. The ornate banking hall and related spaces on the main floor have been respectably restored, though in their adaptation to new uses (as the dining room of a high-volume chain restaurant and common spaces for a very ordinary chain hotel), they have certainly lost much of their luster.

G8 Old Masonic Temple

9th and F streets, NW

1870 Cluss and Kammerhueber
c. 1921 Alterations: Architect unknown
1922 Restoration: Oehrlein & Associates Architects
2000 Renovation and new building: Martinez & Johnson; Interiors: VOA Associates
2001 Leadership Training Hall in original building: VOA Associates

President Andrew Johnson, a loyal Freemason, laid the cornerstone and led the parade that celebrated the start of construction of this Italian Renaissance–inspired Masonic Temple. In its prime the building accommodated much Gilded Age revelry: Washingtonians feted the prince of Wales here in 1876 at a U.S. centennial banquet, and for decades society matrons fought for the honor of having their daughters' debutante parties here. The Masons moved out in 1908, to be replaced in 1921 by Lansburgh's Furniture Store, which remained until the late 1970s. Then for years the elegant building stood abandoned, until it was restored in conjunction with the construction of the adjacent structure on 9th Street. The Gallup Organization now occupies both structures, and uses the grand Masonic hall on the second floor of the original building for meetings and ceremonial events.

G9 Martin Luther King Jr. Memorial Library

901 G Street, NW

1972 Office of Ludwig Mies van der Rohe

TEL: (202) 727-0321
www.dclibrary.org/mlk

Executed posthumously, Washington's central public library is the city's only work by modern master Ludwig Mies van der Rohe. The key elements are all classically Miesian, including a structural frame of dark steel, equally dark tinted windows, and large planes of buff brick. For decades, the building suffered from its adjacency to an unpleasant and ill-conceived "pedestrian mall" that occupied the 900 block of G Street. Now that vehicular traffic has been restored to the block, the library seems to have greater potential, though for what is not exactly clear. One could imagine that the cavernous and barren outdoor space at the base of the building might become an urban asset if only some attractive use could be found for it. Perhaps someday it will accommodate a busy sidewalk café, especially if some civic leaders get their wish, which entails building a new main library and adapting the Mies building for cultural, retail, or commercial functions yet to be determined.

G10 The Church of the Epiphany

1317 G Street, NW

1844 John C. Harkness
1857 Addition: Ammi Burnham Young
1874 Renovation: Henry Dudley
1890 Addition: Edward J. Neville-Stent
1911 Parish House: Frederick H. Brooke
1922 Tower: Frederick H. Brooke

Covered in an icing of white stucco, this church is interesting primarily as a reminder of the architectural scale and character that defined the center of antebellum Washington. The interior is a predictably picturesque affair in English Gothic Revival, notable for its hammer beam ceiling.

G11 Bond Building

14th Street and New York Avenue, NW

1901 George S. Cooper
1986 Addition and renovation: Shalom Baranes Associates

The renovation of the Bond Building was one of the harbingers of the renaissance of Washington's old downtown. It was also among the first commercial projects in the area to include the construction of a new "hat"—that is, the addition of several floors on top in order to fill out the maximum allowable built volume. The renovation also entailed two "bookend" additions, the design of which was inspired by that of a slender building at number 19 Lincoln's Inn Fields in London, which is depicted in a book that Baranes keeps in his library. Other downtown buildings that were expanded vertically during the 1980s and 1990s include the Army-Navy Building at the southeast corner of Farragut Square, also by Baranes, and the Colorado Building at the northeast corner of 14th and G, by KressCox Associates.

G12 Suntrust Bank (National Savings and Trust Company)

15th Street and New York Avenue, NW

1888 James T. Windrim
1916, 1925, 1985 Additions: Various architects

The intersection of 15th Street, New York Avenue, and Pennsylvania Avenue would be much less interesting without this building, with its dark red brick façades, florid Victorian ornament, and slender tower providing a foil to the more staid classical structures on the other three corners. A series of additions along New York Avenue remained true to the original building's aesthetic, despite shifts in building technology and performance expectations.

G13 Bank of America/PNC Bank

15th Street and Pennsylvania Avenue, NW

1902 1503 Pennsylvania: York & Sawyer
1905 1501 Pennsylvania: York & Sawyer
1924 Addition to 1503 Pennsylvania: Appleton P. Clark Jr.
1932 Renovation of 1501 Pennsylvania: Architect unknown
1986 Restoration of banking hall at 1503 Pennsylvania: John Blatteau

Though of modest size, these two adjoining bank buildings enjoy one of the most prestigious conceivable locations for such institutions. Although built for two different clients, they were designed by the same architects in such a harmonious fashion that they are often mistaken as one structure. The American Security Bank, which for decades occupied the building at the northwest corner of 15th and Pennsylvania before it was absorbed by another bank, used the slogan "When you need a bank for your money, bank with the bank that's *on* the money." The slogan referred to the fact that, on the back of the old $10 bill, the engraving of the Treasury Building included a glimpse of the private bank's flagship facility across the street.

G14 Folger Building and Playhouse Theater

725–727 15th Street, NW

1907 Folger Building: Jules Henri de Sibour; Playhouse Theater: Paul Pelz
1985 Addition: Mariani & Associates

Built for a brokerage firm, the Folger Building is small but quite lavish, with gleaming white marble and an exuberant Second Empire crown. Next to it stands the former entrance to the Playhouse Theater, which now serves as the base for a stark modern addition. Although the addition is quite plain in contrast to the historic remnants, its small scale and sympathetic materials are somehow just enough to make it fit reasonably comfortably into the streetscape.

G15 American Bar Association (Union Trust Building)

740 15th Street, NW

1907 Wood, Donn & Deming
1983 Renovation and expansion: Keyes Condon Florance Architects

The "UT" crests in the pediments over the ground floor windows are reminders of this building's original owner, the Union Trust Bank. It was designed by a firm headed by Waddy Wood, who on his own designed a number of smaller buildings such as the Alice Pike Barney Studio House [see P3].

G16 Southern Building

805 15th Street, NW

1914 Daniel Burnham and
Associates
1986 Restoration and
addition: Shalom Baranes
Associates; Preservation
architects: Oehrlein &
Associates Architects

Effusive terra cotta trim erupts
from the quite plain buff brick walls, and lions' heads poke out from the
spandrel panels of this elegant building by Daniel Burnham. In adding
another of his archetypal "hats," Shalom Baranes found justification for
the scale and detailing of the addition in several little-known drawings
of Burnham's showing designs for this and other buildings with their top
two stories above the main cornice line.

G17 Inter-American Development Bank

1300 New York Avenue, NW

1985 Skidmore, Owings &
Merrill

This project helped to define an
emerging Washington "school"
of architecture in the mid-
1980s, classical in spirit if not in
literal detail. The façades are ar-
ticulated in ways that indirectly evoke common classical motifs, though
expressed abstractly and at greatly enlarged scale—recessed bays on the
fourth through ninth floors are set behind paired columns that give the
impression of a colossal colonnade (compare this, for example, to the
façade of the American Bar Association Building [see G15]), the eighth-
floor windows are bracketed to suggest huge dentils, and the upper two
stories are finished in a darker material and a different fenestration pattern, creating a hint of a giant cornice. An enormous arch announces the
main entrance, which leads to a surprisingly large and lush atrium.

G18 National Museum of Women in the Arts (Masonic Temple)

New York Avenue and 13th Street, NW

1908 Wood, Donn & Deming
1987 Renovations: Keyes Condon
Florance Architects; Interiors: Carol
Lascaris

TEL: (202) 783-5000
www.nmwa.org

The Masons originally occupied a temple
at 9th and F streets [see G8], but when
their growing numbers rendered that building inadequate, they hired
Waddy Wood's firm to design this much larger structure. The building's
original purpose is evident in various decorative motifs, such as stone
calipers and other common Masonic symbols. After the Masons outgrew
this temple, it fell into an extended period of neglect until it was rescued
and adapted to museum use. Founded in 1981 through the largesse of
Wilhelmina and Wallace Holladay, the National Museum of Women in
the Arts settled into its new home six years later. The large lobby, which
feels a bit desolate except when the museum is hosting a special function, is lined with faux marble panels, suggesting an attempt to achieve
elegance on the cheap.

G19 1100 New York Avenue (Old Greyhound Bus Station)

1940 William S. Arrasmith/
Wischmeyer, Arrasmith &
Elswick
1991 Restoration: Vitetta
Group; New building:
Florance Eichbaum Esocoff
King Architects

The dozens of terminals built by the Greyhound Bus company in the
1930s and 1940s in cities across the country constituted one of the
greatest collections of Art Moderne architecture in the world. Many of
these stations, of which few remain, were designed by Louisville-based

architect William Arrasmith. For the Washington terminal, Arrasmith adapted the Art Moderne vocabulary to the capital city's conservative architectural culture, avoiding the striking asymmetry and bold colors that often characterized his work, and using such typical Washington materials as limestone and terra cotta for the façade.

The terminal, once known as the "Ellis Island of Washington" since it had welcomed so many African Americans moving from the South, was covered in cheap sheet metal in the mid-1970s, but fortunately, the original structure remained essentially undamaged beneath the crude cloak. It was restored to its sleek glory when the large office building, whose design is inspired by the Art Moderne terminal, was built behind it. The New York Avenue façade of the new building, like that of the terminal itself, initially appears to be symmetrical, but the eastern part of the façade curves away to follow the bend in the street. A close look reveals that the stone skin gradually gets lighter in color as the building rises.

G20 Cato Institute

1000 Massachusetts Avenue, NW

1993 Hellmuth, Obata + Kassabaum

One of the most purely geometrical responses to the irregular intersections characteristic of L'Enfant's plan, the Cato Institute building, which houses a libertarian think tank, suggests a three-dimensional puzzle. The atrium is, uniquely, outside the main body of the building, in a glassy, metal-frame structure that marks the angle of Massachusetts Avenue, while the office spaces are in a masonry box oriented to the rectilinear street grid. Subtle details add character—note the asymmetrical motifs at the intersections of the metal grid on the winter garden and the overlapping geometries in the window patterns of the main block.

G21 One Franklin Square

1301 K Street, NW

1990 Hartman-Cox
Architects; Associated
architects: Dewberry &
Davis/Habib; Preservation of
Almas Temple: Oehrlein &
Associates Architects

Washington's famous height limit has always allowed certain exceptions, such as "spires, towers, domes, pinnacles, or minarets" that are purely ornamental. One Franklin Square was among the first recent commercial buildings to take advantage of that loophole. Known colloquially as the "Twin Peaks" building, it recalls the stepped massing of 1920s New York skyscrapers. To make room for the new building, the historic Almas Temple (1930—Allen Hussell Potts) was dismantled and reconstructed slightly to the west, in a project supervised by Oehrlein & Associates. Only one piece out of more than seven thousand was lost in this move.

During the period of the old downtown's decrepitude, Franklin Square was the city's pornography and prostitution headquarters—one longtime porn shop in the area bore a sign that proudly proclaimed "Purveyors of Fine Smut." In the 1990s, however, commercial developers succeeded where the Metropolitan Police had consistently failed, and quickly supplanted the sex workers with lawyers and lobbyists.

Overlooking the square on the east is the Franklin School (1869—Adolf Cluss), which, in addition to being a widely admired educational facility, was the site of Alexander Graham Bell's first wireless message. A model of the school was displayed and much discussed at the World Exposition in Vienna in 1873, and helped to earn a Medal of Progress for the District of Columbia in education and school architecture.

G22 Old Washington Post Building (Lennox Building)

1515 L Street, NW

1951 Albert Kahn Associated
Architects and Engineers

Albert Kahn was a master of early twentieth-century industrial architecture,
such as the influential "daylight facto-
ries" he designed for Ford and other
automakers. This building was done by
his firm long after Kahn died, but it reflects his clean, functionalist aesthetic,
rendered elegant through carefully controlled composition.

G23 Metropolitan A.M.E. Church

1518 M Street, NW

1886 Samuel G. T. Morsell
1994, 1998 Renovations and
expansion: Baker Cooper &
Associates

Architecturally significant as a superior
example of red-brick Gothic Revival,
this granite-trimmed church, sometimes called the National Cathedral of
African Methodism, also played an important role in the American civil rights
movement. Organized in 1822 as the Union Bethel A.M.E. Church, it
was the largest nineteenth-century African American congregation in
the country.

G24 Russian Embassy (Pullman House)

1119–1125 16th Street, NW

1910 Nathan C. Wyeth
1933 Remodeling: Eugene Schoen and Sons
1977 Addition: Architect unknown

Harriet Sanger Pullman, wife of the inventor of the railroad sleeping car and one of the horde of wealthy midwesterners who flocked to town during Washington's belle époque, commissioned this mansion, but sold it shortly after its completion to the Russian government. Following the 1917 revolution, the house was occupied only by caretakers until the United States recognized the Soviet regime in 1933, at which point a modest remodeling of the building ensued. The Soviets moved most diplomatic operations to a huge new chancery complex on Wisconsin Avenue in the 1980s. Both properties passed to the new Russian government following the dissolution of the Soviet Union in 1991.

G25 St. Regis Hotel (Carlton Hotel)

923 16th Street, NW

1926 Mihran Mesrobian
1988 Renovation: Smith, Segreti, Tepper, McMahon & Harned

This elegant structure is indisputably one of the grandest hotels in the city. Designed in the manner of an Italian Renaissance palazzo, it reads as a freestanding block thanks to a garden that separates the building from its neighbor to the south. The relative austerity of the façades is relieved by a parade of arches along the ground floor and elaborate window surrounds on the third and seventh stories. A strong cornice line above the sixth story gives the impression that the building is shorter and more horizontal than it actually is.

Previously known as the Carlton, the hotel was designed by Mihran Mesrobian, a Turkish-born Armenian, who immigrated to the United States in 1921 and became the primary in-house architect for legendary Washington developer Harry Wardman. After Wardman declared bankruptcy in 1930, Mesrobian established his own practice, which produced a variety of residential and commercial work over the ensuing quarter century.

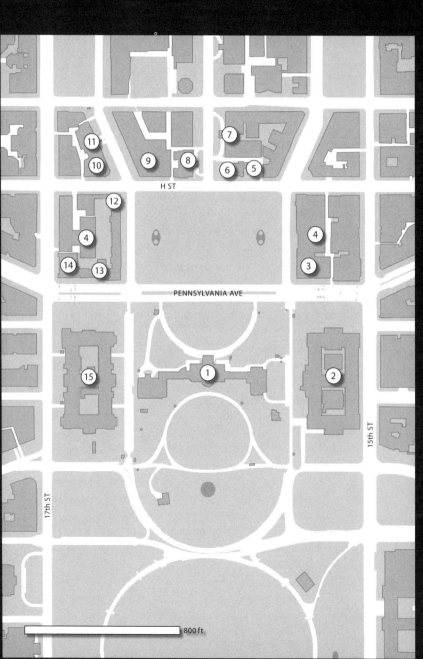

Henry Adams, who occupied a grand house overlooking Lafayette Square from 1885 until his death in 1918, wrote that in the neighborhood's early days, "Beyond the square, the country began." Adams also wrote that when he moved to the capital city, "no literary or scientific man, no artist, no gentleman without office or employment, had ever lived there. It was rural and its society was primitive . . . The happy village was innocent of a club . . . The value of real estate had not increased since 1800, and the pavements were more impassable than the mud."

Indeed, when L'Enfant selected the site for the President's House and the "President's Park" immediately to its north, the area was filled with a flourishing orchard. Construction on what came to be called the Executive Mansion began in 1792, and President and Mrs. John Adams (Henry's great-grandparents) moved into the semi-habitable dwelling in November 1800. Thomas Jefferson, who succeeded Adams in March of the following year, wrote, "we find this a very agreeable country residence . . . free from the noise, the heat, . . . and the bustle of a close-built town," which makes clear how undeveloped Washington was in 1801.

L'Enfant intended that the President's Park serve as an extension of the Executive Mansion grounds, but Jefferson and others with strongly democratic proclivities found such a large lawn uncomfortably imperial. Before long, a new stretch of Pennsylvania Avenue was laid down in front of the mansion, dividing the green space in two and creating the separate square, which was named (informally at first, and later officially) for Lafayette during his triumphant return to Washington in 1824. In 1829, after Andrew Jackson had defeated Henry Adams's grandfather for the presidency, he held boisterous, whiskey-fueled inauguration festivities in the square. During the Civil War, soldiers bivouacked in the park. In the 1870s, Ulysses S. Grant started a small zoo here. By the 1920s, improbably enough, the park—virtually in the shadow of the White House—was firmly established as a safe meeting place for closeted gay men. In the late twentieth century, for obvious reasons of visibility, the park had become a popular site for political protests of various kinds.

The Senate Park Commission plan of 1901–2 envisioned a wholesale reconstruction of Lafayette Square and its adjacent blocks to create a unified enclave of enormous, classical government office buildings, but only two buildings were eventually built in accordance with this plan. In the early 1960s, the character of the square was threatened again, and it was only through the personal and active intervention of Jacqueline Kennedy that the remaining town houses facing the square were saved. Sadly, security concerns following the bombing of the Oklahoma City federal building in 1995 led to the closure of Pennsylvania Avenue in

This isometric drawing shows the White House and Lafayette Square sometime before 1851, when the park was landscaped in accordance with plans by Andrew Jackson Downing. The drawing also shows idealized, symmetrical, E-shaped buildings for the War and Navy Departments at left and the Treasury at right.

front of the White House to vehicular traffic, and the once-busy thoroughfare suddenly became a rather desolate stretch disfigured by makeshift barriers. A serviceable if bland redesign of the block was finally completed in 2004, and while vehicular traffic is still banned, the appearance of the avenue now at least suggests the hope that it could once again become a vital urban street in some happier, more secure future.

H1 The White House

1600 Pennsylvania Avenue, NW

1792–1803 James Hoban
1803–14 Renovations and terrace additions: Benjamin Henry Latrobe
1814–17 Reconstruction after fire: James Hoban
1823, 1830 Portico additions: James Hoban, based on designs by Latrobe
1902 Addition of West Wing and renovation of interior and East Terrace: McKim, Mead & White

1909 Expansion of West Wing: Nathan C. Wyeth
1927 Addition of third floor: William Adams Delano
1934 Expansion of West Wing: Eric Gugler
1942 Addition of East Wing: Lorenzo S. Winslow
1948 South Portico balcony: Lorenzo S. Winslow and William Adams Delano
1949–52 Reconstruction of interior: Lorenzo S. Winslow
1970 Renovation of West Wing and North Portico: Architect unknown

TEL: (202) 456-7041   www.whitehouse.gov

"The white house"—rendered entirely in lowercase letters, the words could hardly be more generic or mundane. Capitalize the *w* and *h,* however, and suddenly the phrase connotes one of the world's most recognized symbols of governmental power. While the Capitol is the nucleus of L'Enfant's plan, the White House actually developed into the stronger architectural center of gravity for the District of Columbia.

Although the White House as it exists today seems both inevitable and immutable, in fact it is the result of more than two centuries of nearly constant alterations and additions, and even one comprehensive reconstruction. As with the Capitol, the basic design of the White House was selected through a competition (and, as with the Capitol, there is evidence that Thomas Jefferson entered and lost the competition under a gentlemanly pseudonym). The winning proposal was submitted by James Hoban, an Irish architect practicing in Charleston, South Carolina, whose somewhat conservative design was apparently inspired by Leinster House in Dublin, Ireland. Construction began in the fall of 1792, but the building was still unfinished when the government moved from Philadelphia in November 1800. The first residents, President and Mrs. John Adams, were not impressed by their new accommodations. Abigail wrote to her daughter, complaining, "There is not a single apartment finished . . . We had not the least fence, yard, or other convenience, without, and the great unfinished audience-room [the East Room] I make a drying room of, to hang up the clothes in."

Jefferson displaced the grumbling Adamses in 1801, but he wasn't enamored of the mansion, either, grousing that it was "big enough for two emperors, one Pope, and the grand Lama." A diligent amateur architect, Jefferson designed low pavilions for either side of the main building to moderate the structure's grandeur. He worked in association with the omnipresent Benjamin Henry Latrobe, who humored the president even while quietly dismissing Jefferson's proposals as "a litter of pigs worthy of the great sow it surrounds." Latrobe's own designs for the pavilions were

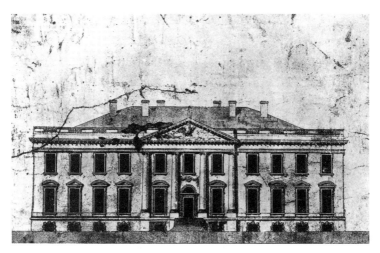

James Hoban's competition-winning design for the President's House, 1792.

actually built, and several of his other proposals inspired subsequent additions to the mansion.

Set ablaze by the British in August 1814, the Executive Mansion was saved from total destruction by a violent thunderstorm. After the fire, James and Dolley Madison rented the Octagon [see I3], and brought in Hoban to oversee the mansion's restoration. The building received a thick coat of white paint to cover charring from the fire (though it had been whitewashed before). It is not known who first called it the "White House," but when Theodore Roosevelt made the name official in 1901 he was merely giving formal sanction to longstanding common usage.

In 1824, Hoban, following Latrobe's plans, added the semicircular South Portico, thereby creating the house's signature façade, which is actually the rear of the building. The interior underwent frequent alterations, but in 1902, Theodore Roosevelt ordered an especially extensive renovation. He brought in McKim, Mead and White to remodel the original building, remove a run of Victorian conservatories, and add the West Wing. The famous Oval Office actually did not appear until the 1909 renovation by Nathan Wyeth, and even then it was not in its current location (it was relocated in 1934).

Investigations during Harry Truman's administration revealed that the aging mansion was on the verge of catastrophic structural failure. Although the exterior walls, which were, in Truman's memorable phrase, "standing up purely from habit," were salvaged, little else was as the building was gutted. Steel replaced the crumbling stone and wood structure, and while the original paneling and trim were removed, repaired, and reinstalled, many historic elements were, shockingly, simply discarded. While the rooms of the main house are thus largely replicas rather than true originals, this does not diminish the awe that these historic and venerable spaces inspire in general visitors, foreign dignitaries, and even the families afforded the temporary privilege of calling the White House home.

H2   Treasury Building

1500 Pennsylvania Avenue, NW

1836–69 Robert Mills, Thomas U. Walter, Ammi B. Young, Isaiah Rogers, Alfred B. Mullett
1910 Renovation and addition: York & Sawyer
1996–2005 Interior restoration: Shalom Baranes Associates; Preservation consultants: John Milner Associates; Project managers: McKissack & McKissack; Exterior restoration: Quinn Evans/Architects
1998 North plaza restoration: GMR; Preservation consultants: John Milner Associates

TEL: (202) 622-2000

The oldest Cabinet-level departmental headquarters, the Treasury Building also represents one of the earliest serious infringements upon L'Enfant's plan. According to legend, it was President Andrew Jackson who, tired of delays in determining the exact site of the building, stood at a spot on the diagonal axis of Pennsylvania Avenue and barked "Build it here!" thus dooming L'Enfant's intended clear line of sight between the White House and the Capitol.

The Treasury took more than three decades to build, and reflects the work of several of the country's most important nineteenth-century architects. Robert Mills was responsible for the original, Greek-inspired design, which incorporated his characteristic fireproof, brick-vaulted structural system. Mills also oversaw the initial phase of construction until 1842. Thomas U. Walter's design of 1855 expanded on Mills's plan; Ammi Young and Isaiah Rogers, each of whom served as supervising architect of the Treasury, executed Walter's scheme while making a variety of modifications of their own. Alfred Mullett was responsible for the north wing, the exterior of which respected the precedents set by Mills and Walter, though his interiors were designed in a much more elaborate, Renaissance Revival vein. The most notable of Mullett's interior spaces is the capacious Cash Room, which is lined with seven different types of marble.

The building's most distinguished exterior feature is the magnificent, 466-foot-long Ionic colonnade along 15th Street, originally built of Aquia sandstone but later reconstructed in more durable granite. Formerly, a grand staircase led to an entrance in the middle of the colonnade, but it was later removed due to subsequent regrading of the street.

H3   Treasury Annex

Madison Place and
Pennsylvania Avenue, NW

1919   Cass Gilbert

The 1901–2 McMillan Plan called for a series of office buildings that would have obliterated all of the row houses surrounding Lafayette Square, and in 1917, Cass Gilbert developed specific designs for the palatial marble structures the commission envisioned. Only this building and the Chamber of Commerce [see H9] were executed, however. Intended to alleviate the severe overcrowding that was plaguing the main Treasury building at the time, the annex exudes the sturdy rectitude one would expect given its purpose.

H4   Lafayette Square Federal Buildings

Blocks adjacent to Jackson
Place and Madison Place, NW

1969   John Carl Warnecke &
Associates

Lafayette Square, the pride of nineteenth-century Washington, lost several of its greatest treasures to twentieth-century wrecking balls. A scheme to raze nearly all of the remaining row houses on the square was still under consideration in 1961 when First Lady Jacqueline Kennedy intervened and asked Warnecke to devise a plan that would save what remained of the square. Warnecke's solution somehow seemed both radical and sensible at the time—the houses would be preserved while taller, "background" buildings would be built in what had been their back yards. The new buildings (the U.S. Court of Claims to the east and the New Executive Office Building to the west) were designed to be sympathetic to the context by means of their materials and motifs such as the mansard roofs. Unfortunately, as constructed, the buildings are still intrusive, with large, unrelieved, red brick walls, stingy windows, and awkwardly proportioned projecting bays. Still, the essential character of the square, as perceived from street level, was largely preserved. Such deference to existing architecture was virtually unheard of at the time, when abstract modernist ideology prevailed.

H5   St. John's Parish Building

1525 H Street, NW

1836 Architect unknown
1854 Renovation: Thomas U. Walter
1877 Addition and renovation:
Architect unknown
1955 Renovation: Horace Peaslee

Matthew St. Clair Clarke, clerk of the House of Representatives, began building this house in 1836, but he soon ran into financial trouble and was forced to sign over the property to his bankers. A number of distinguished people leased the house, and it served as the British Legation when diplomatic ministers Lord Ashburton and Sir Henry Bulwer lived there. Originally finished in brick, the house was given a coat of stucco in 1854, at the same time heavy window trim and other details were added. The oversized mansard roof was added in 1877. The AFL-CIO eventually bought the building and later sold it to St. John's for use as a parish hall.

H6 St. John's Church

16th and H streets, NW

1816 Benjamin Henry Latrobe
1820 Addition: George Bomford
1822 Steeple: Architect unknown
1842 Renovation: Architect unknown,
though possibly Robert Mills
1880s Alterations and addition: James
Renwick Jr.
1919 Renovation: McKim,
Mead & White

TEL: (202) 347-8766
www.stjohns-dc.org

Latrobe chose a Greek cross plan for this church, which he claimed, in characteristically immodest fashion, "made many Washingtonians religious who had not been religious before." His chaste little chapel, however, was profoundly altered by subsequent architects, who extended the nave toward 16th Street (creating a more typical, Latin cross plan), and added both a portico and a tall steeple. One can, however, sense the original plan while sitting in a pew under the central dome. Known as the "Church of the Presidents," it has hosted every chief executive since Madison. By tradition, pew 54 is reserved for the current president and First Family.

Rendering of St. John's Church in 1816, the year it was built, with the President's House in the background, still scarred from damage inflicted by the British in the War of 1812.

H7 AFL-CIO National Headquarters

815 16th Street, NW

1954 Voorhees Walker & Smith
1971 Addition: Mills Petticord & Mills
2002 Renovation: GGA. Ehrenkrantz Eckstut & Kuhn Architects

An organization hoping to influence federal policy could hardly find a more auspicious site for its headquarters, almost within shouting distance of the White House. The main body of the building is fairly typical of Washington's post–World War II commercial architecture—essentially a slightly modernized version of the stripped classicism that was so common before the war—but the top is unusual, with barrel vaulted mechanical penthouses perforated by concrete screens. With the top and bottom floors recessed behind simple colonnades, the effect is somewhat reminiscent of Mussolini-era government buildings in Rome. A skillful 2002 renovation moved the main entrance off center, providing space for conference facilities and a welcoming lobby featuring a stunning restored mosaic that is now visible to passersby. Site improvements yielded a pleasant front yard, with benches and other elements that both enhance building security and provide places for people to take a break or have lunch in nice weather.

H8 Hay-Adams Hotel

800 16th Street, NW

1927 Mihran Mesrobian
1983 Renovation: Leo A Daly
2002 Interior renovation:
Brennan Beer Gorman Monk;
Interior design: Thomas
Pheasant

The Hay-Adams Hotel derives
its name from two spectacular buildings that, unfortunately, were demolished to make way for it—adjoining houses for John Hay and Henry
Adams designed by H. H. Richardson and built in 1885. Mesrobian's hotel is a somewhat stolid but dignified structure, anchored by a slightly
rusticated base and heavy quoins at the corners and along the sides of
the projecting central bays. The exterior is loosely derived from Italian
Renaissance models, while the interior is more directly inspired by the
style of the English Renaissance.

H9 Chamber of Commerce Building

1615 H Street, NW

1924 Cass Gilbert

This and the Treasury Annex
[see H3] are the only completed
portions of the McMillan Commission's plan to unify the architecture of Lafayette Square in
the style of the older Treasury Building. This particular building replaced
a brace of houses owned by several prominent historical figures: Daniel
Webster lived at the corner of H Street and Connecticut Avenue, and the
adjacent house was home to John Slidell, antebellum congressman from
Louisiana, Confederate minister to France, and one-half of the Mason-
Slidell controversy, which nearly brought the British Empire into the
Civil War on the side of the South.

H10 800 Connecticut Avenue, NW

1993 Florance Eichbaum Esocoff King Architects

This commercial office building strongly evokes the architecture of the Viennese Secession in its basic forms, fenestration, and ornamental details. Given its location amid the centers of political power, the building was conceived with high-powered lobbyists in mind as potential tenants, and the architects therefore sought to provide as many "power perches" as possible, hence the profusion of corner offices and terraces. The upper levels are popular vantage points for television news cameras because of their clear views of the White House.

H11 816 Connecticut Avenue, NW

1987 Shalom Baranes Associates

This elegant, twenty-eight-foot-wide sliver evokes the bay-fronted row houses that characterize many of Washington's residential neighborhoods, but here the device is applied at a larger scale in a commercial building. The architect was able to obtain permission from zoning authorities for the projection over public space by arguing that the narrowness of the site created a unique aesthetic opportunity to accentuate the building's verticality. The advantage for the city is a slick exclamation mark that beautifully terminates the vista looking down 17th Street. Vertical slits lined with glass block and lit from behind emphasize the building's proportions.

H12 Stephen Decatur House Museum

748 Jackson Place, NW (visitor entrance
at 1610 H Street, NW)

1818 Benjamin Henry Latrobe
1876 Renovations: Architects unknown
1944 Restoration: Thomas T.
Waterman
2004 Restoration of original kitchen:
Davis Buckley Architects and Planners

TEL: (202) 842-0920
www.decaturhouse.org

The Decatur House was both the first and the last building on Lafayette
Square to be occupied as a private residence. Built for Commodore Stephen Decatur, scourge of the Barbary pirates, and his wife Susan, the
original house was a textbook example of Federal-style architecture, with
restrained details, a flat façade, and carefully controlled proportions. A
little over a year after the Decaturs moved in, however, Latrobe was dead
of yellow fever in New Orleans and the commodore was killed in a duel.
Susan Decatur decamped for a smaller house in Georgetown, and rented
the Lafayette Square property to a number of prominent residents, including several British, French, and Russian diplomats. The house was
the unofficial residence of secretaries of state from 1827 to 1833, as
Henry Clay, Martin Van Buren, and Edward Livingston all rented the
place during their tenures in that office.

John Gadsby, owner of the Washington Hotel and Gadsby's Tavern in
Virginia, bought the house in 1836, and then Western explorer Edward
Fitzgerald Beale and his wife, Mary, bought it from Gadsby's heirs in
1872. (It was Beale, then based near San Francisco, who in 1848 galloped
east to announce that gold had been discovered at Sutter's Mill.) The
Beales embarked on a thorough Victorianization of the chaste old Federal house, and proceeded to throw lavish parties that made it a nexus of
social life in the Gilded Age. They left the house to their son, Truxtun,
whose widow lived there until she bequeathed it to the National Trust
for Historic Preservation in 1956. The trust is currently conducting a
detailed historical analysis of the property, with plans to restore and in-
terpret it in a way that reflects the entire history of the structure.

H13 Blair-Lee House

1651–53 Pennsylvania Avenue, NW

1824 Blair House: Architect unknown
1859 Lee House: Architect unknown
1931 Blair House restoration: Waldron
Faulkner
1988 Restoration and addition:
Mendel Mesick Cohen Waite Hall
Architects, Allan Greenberg, Architect

Blair House was declared a National Historic Landmark by the Department of
the Interior in 1939, making it the first
building to be so designated. Three years later, as World War II was rag-
ing, the federal government bought the house to serve as guest quarters
for visiting heads of state, and then purchased Lee House next door for
the same purpose the following year. As the story is told by Franklin D.
Roosevelt Jr., his mother, Eleanor, enthusiastically supported the idea
of an official guesthouse after a late-night encounter with British Prime
Minister Winston Churchill, whom she found wandering the halls of the
White House in his nightshirt, carrying a cigar, and looking for the president in order to resume a discussion from earlier in the evening.

The original Blair House was built by Surgeon General Dr. Joseph
Lovell; its current name came after Francis Preston Blair, a newspaper
editor from Kentucky who helped shape American politics through his
influential publications *The Globe* and *The Congressional Globe*, bought it
in 1837. The house was later occupied by his son, Montgomery Blair, an
attorney who represented Dred Scott and served as postmaster general
under Lincoln. The adjacent house was built by the senior Blair for his
daughter and her husband, Samuel P. Lee, a cousin of Robert E. Lee.

From 1948 to 1952, President Harry Truman and his family lived here
while the White House underwent major structural renovations. During
this time, the Marshall Plan for the reconstruction of postwar Europe
was hatched in the Lee House dining room, which served as Truman's
cabinet room. In 1950, two Puerto Rican nationalists stormed Blair
House in an attempt to assassinate the president. One of the would-be
assassins and White House Police Officer Leslie Coffelt were killed in the
gunfight on the front sidewalk.

H14 Renwick Gallery of the Smithsonian American Art Museum (formerly Corcoran Gallery and U.S. Court of Claims)

Pennsylvania Avenue at 17th Street, NW

1861 James Renwick Jr.
1873 Restoration: Architect unknown
1972 Exterior restoration: John Carl Warnecke & Associates; Interior restoration and remodeling: Hugh Newell Jacobsen
2000 Renovation of Grand Salon: Ehrenkrantz Eckstut & Kuhn Architects

TEL: (202) 633-1000   www.americanart.si.edu

William Wilson Corcoran, cofounder of Washington's storied Riggs Bank, commissioned this building as a public gallery for his substantial art collection. Construction began in 1859, but when the Civil War broke out, the federal government appropriated the nearly completed building from its owner, a Southern sympathizer, and used it as a military ware-house and later as the headquarters of General Montgomery C. Meigs. The building was returned to Corcoran in 1869, and he finally opened his museum in 1873 following extensive renovations. The institution moved to a new facility in 1897 [see I5], and in 1899, the U.S. Court of Claims moved in and stayed for sixty-five years. Fortunately, the Smith-sonian then took possession of the building and returned it to museum use, as a branch of the Smithsonian American Art Museum focusing on crafts. It opened to the public in 1972.

The Renwick—probably the only museum named for its architect, rather than its benefactor—imitated the elaborate French Second Em-pire style, most notably in the characteristic mansard roof. The use of red brick as the primary finish material seems to be a distinctly American touch, however, as are the column capitals bearing ornamental motifs based on tobacco and corn (surely inspired by Latrobe's similar designs at the Capitol). Heavy, vermiculated quoins (with irregular, wormlike patterns etched into the stone) and swags bearing Corcoran's initials add to the liveliness of the façades. The interior is relatively intimate for a museum, though it does boast a quite grand staircase, leading to an equally grand salon with walls intended to be, in the words of E. J. Apple-white, "the color of crushed mulberries."

H15 Dwight D. Eisenhower Executive Office Building (Old Executive Office Building/State, War, and Navy Building)

Pennsylvania Avenue and 17th Street, NW

1871–88 Alfred B. Mullett, William Potter, Orville Babcock, Thomas Lincoln Casey; Interior engineering and design: Richard von Ezdorf

1987–2001 Various interior restoration projects: Kemnitzer, Reid & Haffler Architects; Quinn Evans/Architects; Einhorn Yaffee Prescott; SmithGroup
2006 Modernization of 17th Street Wing: HSMM

"The transitory taste for French neoclassicism, fostered by the École des Beaux Arts in Paris, has few more striking expressions." —*The WPA Guide to Washington, DC*, 1942

Washington's largest Second Empire-style building took seventeen years to build, and when finally finished, it was widely reviled as a symbol of Gilded Age excess. Its ornate style had fallen out of fashion, and the building's great cost—more than $10 million, an enormous sum in those days—was considered scandalous. Henry Adams infamously dubbed it "Mr. Mullett's architectural infant asylum," referring to the architect responsible for the design, who later committed suicide after unsuccessfully suing the federal government for additional compensation.

The building was repeatedly threatened with radical revisions that seemed almost punitive in spirit. In 1917, the U.S. Commission of Fine Arts asked John Russell Pope to cloak the hulking structure in more orthodox classical garb, and in 1929, after President Herbert Hoover groaned about the "architectural orgy" that loomed over the White House, Waddy Wood was given a similar assignment. Neither Pope's nor Wood's drastic proposal came to pass thanks to a lack of money, but the building's fate was still far from secure. In 1957, a presidential commission recommended total demolition, and it was not until the 1960s that general opinions of the building began to soften.

Built of dense, dark granite from Virginia and Maine, the structure is lined with some nine hundred columns, accented with dramatically projecting bays, and topped with a steep mansard roof and tall chimneys. Immense and undeniably eccentric, the building managed to survive decades of ignominy and is now, at long last, widely beloved as a welcome exception to the sedate architecture more typical of the nation's capital.

Foggy Bottom

There are various stories about the origins of this neighborhood's moniker, which suggests a dismal fen to be avoided at all costs. Some say the name commemorates the noxious fumes emanating from several now-defunct industries—the Heurich brewery, the city gas plant, and a glass factory—while others believe that it was simply an apt description of a low-lying, marshy area that was often shrouded in fog rolling off the Potomac. Then again, the name may have been a euphemistic reference to the fetid Tiber Canal, which emptied into the river near the neighborhood's southeast corner. By the time the Civil War broke out, the canal had degenerated into an open sewer, swarming with flies and mosquitoes.

Before the establishment of the District of Columbia, part of what is now Foggy Bottom was an inchoate town called Hamburgh, also known as Funkstown, conceived as a kind of suburb to the bustling port of Georgetown. Hamburgh never developed on its own, and its modest street grid was wiped out when L'Enfant's plan was imposed upon the landscape. Currently, Foggy Bottom is known primarily as the seat of the State Department and of George Washington University, a growing institution whose facilities requirements often lead to conflicts with neighbors fearful that what remains of the area's residential character is endangered.

Aerial view of Foggy Bottom, on the far side of the Potomac River, with Roosevelt Island and the Rosslyn area of Arlington, Virginia, in the foreground.

I1   Winder Building

604 17th Street, NW

1848 Richard A. Gilpin
1930–48 Various renovations:
Architects unknown
1975 Restoration: Max O.
Urbahn Associates
1990 Exterior restoration:
architrave, p.c., architects

It may not look like it now, but when new, the Winder Building was one of the most innovative structures in the city, the first to employ a central heating system and cast iron beams throughout. The building was also among the earliest examples of a now-ubiquitous Washington type—cheap, speculative office space built to be sold or leased to the federal government. When procured in 1854 by the government, it was the tallest (75 feet) and largest (130 rooms) office building in the nation's capital. For much of its history it was used by the Navy and War departments, and now houses staff from the U.S. trade representative's office.

I2   Office of Thrift Supervision/Liberty Plaza

1700 G Street, NW

1977 Max O. Urbahn
Associates; Courtyard: Sasaki
Associates

The present-day architecture buff, frustrated by the terrorism-inspired paranoia that has rendered many "public" buildings nearly inaccessible, may long for the comparatively halcyon days of 1976. In that year, Congress passed the Public Buildings Cooperative Use Act, which directed the head of the General Services Administration to "encourage the location of commercial, cultural, educational, and recreational facilities and activities within public buildings." This call for the integration of a mix of uses into governmental structures was part of a broader initiative intended to break down barriers between federal agencies and the citizens they serve, and to encourage true urban vitality around such facilities.

The building that now houses the Office of Thrift Supervision, which regulates savings banks, was among the first federal projects to reflect this new spirit of openness, accommodating shops and restaurants beneath bureaucratic office space while also meeting increasingly strict energy conservation standards. Architecturally, it is remarkable in its use of a very standard 1970s vocabulary—cylindrical concrete columns, thin concrete slabs, and dark tinted glass—to create façades of unusual depth and character. This spare vocabulary simultaneously alludes, in a highly abstract way, to the multicolumned façades of the Eisenhower Executive Office Building across the street. Perhaps reflecting a lesson learned from the nearby AIA headquarters, the new building wraps around, and is highly deferential to, the historic Winder Building. The courtyard that connects the two, while not exactly festive, is reasonably inviting and successfully draws pedestrians to the commercial establishments within.

I3   The Octagon

1799 New York Avenue, NW

1801 William Thornton
1817 Alterations: George Hadfield
1898 Interior restoration: Glenn Brown
1911, 1920s, 1940s, 1955, 1970 Miscellaneous restoration projects: Various architects
1989–94 Restoration: Mesick Cohen Waite Architects

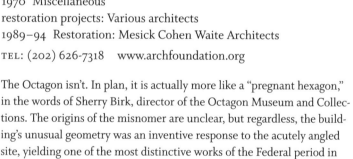

TEL: (202) 626-7318   www.archfoundation.org

The Octagon isn't. In plan, it is actually more like a "pregnant hexagon," in the words of Sherry Birk, director of the Octagon Museum and Collections. The origins of the misnomer are unclear, but regardless, the building's unusual geometry was an inventive response to the acutely angled site, yielding one of the most distinctive works of the Federal period in Washington. The plan also allowed for a number of atypical spaces inside the house, including a copious, circular entry hall and an oval stair hall that affords surprisingly vertiginous views between floors. Several doorways in the house are shaped to fit seamlessly within curved walls.

The house was designed by Dr. William Thornton for Colonel John Tayloe III, a scion of one of Virginia's most prominent families. Legend maintains that, on the whole, Tayloe would rather have been in Philadelphia, a much larger and more sophisticated city, but he settled in the new capital at the urging of his friend George Washington. During the War of 1812, Mrs. Tayloe prevailed upon the French minister to fly his country's flag from the house, which thus escaped the British torch. From 1814 to early 1815, James and Dolley Madison lived here while workmen repaired the charred Executive Mansion. The Tayloes were happy to accommodate the displaced president and First Lady, and just as happy to collect rent from the government for the time they spent here. In 1815, the Treaty of Ghent, formally ending hostilities with Great Britain, was signed in the Octagon's second-floor parlor.

For much of the nineteenth century, the building had a succession of occupants, including a Catholic girls' school, and gradually fell into disrepair. The American Institute of Architects leased the house as its headquarters beginning in 1898, and purchased it outright in 1902. The AIA eventually moved into a larger structure next door (which was torn down when the present headquarters was built), and in 1968, the AIA Foundation—now an independent organization known as the American Architectural Foundation—bought the Octagon and converted it into a historic house museum.

I4 American Institute of Architects Headquarters

1735 New York Avenue, NW

1973 The Architects Collaborative
1989 Interior renovation: Malesardi
+ Steiner/Architects
1993 Library expansion: The
Architects Collaborative; Malesardi +
Steiner/Architects

TEL: (202) 626-7300   www.aia.org

In the 1960s the AIA sponsored a competition for the design of a new headquarters building to be set behind the Octagon house. First place went to the entry by Mitchell/Giurgola Architects, which featured an expansive, concave, glass curtain wall stretching almost all the way across its primary façade. A revised version of this design, bolder and more complex, was rejected by the U.S. Commission of Fine Arts, which feared that it would overwhelm the historic house at the corner. Ultimately, Mitchell/Giurgola withdrew from the project, and the institute hired The Architects Collaborative (TAC) to devise a simpler solution, which ultimately won approval from the federal commission.

TAC's design, with its largely unrelieved ribbons of concrete and dark glass, might be overlooked among the many other 1970s-era structures based on a similar architectural language. The AIA building, however, offers greater visual interest than most of its contemporaries, thanks to the boomerang shape of its plan and the bold, projecting volume in the New York Avenue wing, which houses the boardroom. Originally, the area beneath this projection was a dark, disused corner of the otherwise pleasant courtyard between the new structure and the Octagon, but during the 1993 renovation, this space was enclosed as part of the expansion of the library. This change was a great improvement, alleviating the ominousness of the broad overhang and helping to direct visitors to the main entrance just to the left of the new space.

I5   **Corcoran Gallery of Art**

500 17th Street, NW

1897   Ernest Flagg
1915   Renovation: Waddy B. Wood
1928   Addition: Charles Adams Platt

TEL: (202) 639-1700
www.corcoran.org

Officially established in 1869, the Corcoran Gallery of Art is one of the nation's oldest art museums. It initially occupied the building that is now the Renwick Gallery [see H14], but moved to this location after outgrowing the original facility.

The main façade of the current gallery has great presence thanks to its closeness to the street, its mighty rusticated base, and the pair of lounging lions that guard the entrance. The façade's most audacious aspect is the broad, blank stone panel between the ground floor and the row of attic-level windows. Flagg skillfully controlled the panel's proportions and arranged the elements around it to create a powerful composition, reserved but supremely elegant. Unfortunately, this bold design was compromised in the 1990s, when a parade of banners was affixed to the blank panel.

The Corcoran's main lobby and adjacent grand staircase bring to mind the *gravitas* of the British Museum and similar venerable institutions. At the northeast corner of the building is a curved room known as the Hemicycle, which serves as a display space and as a knuckle connecting the museum to the wing that houses its affiliated art school. Another wing to the south was added in 1927 to accommodate a substantial bequest from Montana Senator William A. Clark that included paintings, sculptures, and even an entire room known as the Salon Doré. Originally part of an eighteenth-century private residence in Paris, the heavily gilded salon previously had been dismantled and reinstalled in Clark's mansion in New York.

The big architectural story at the Corcoran recently was the shelving of a much-anticipated addition designed by Frank Gehry, a casualty of an unsuccessful capital campaign. The institution has indicated that, should major donors come forward, the project might still proceed, but it seems that Gehry's signature billowy, metal-clad forms will not be coming to the Corcoran anytime soon.

I6 American National Red Cross

17th Street between D and E streets, NW

1917 A. Breck Trowbridge and Goodhue Livingston
1930, 1932 North and West Buildings: Trowbridge and Livingston

2005 Renovations: Shalom Baranes Associates; Preservation consultants: John Milner Associates

President Wilson laid the cornerstone in 1915 for what was to be a memorial "to the heroic women of the Civil War," and while subsequent additions yielded a rambling, full-block complex, the original building of Vermont marble remains dominant. Within the main structure are some eccentric treasures, including a trio of Tiffany windows depicting evocative figures such as St. Filomena, the patron saint of the sick, and, appropriately enough, the Redcrosse Knight from Edmund Spenser's *The Faerie Queene.*

I7 National Society Daughters of the American Revolution

1776 D Street, NW

1911 Memorial Continental Hall: Edward Pearce Casey
1923 Administration Building: Marsh and Peter
1929 Constitution Hall: John Russell Pope

1950 Addition to Administration Building: Eggers and Higgins
1994, 1997 Renovations of Constitution Hall: Blackburn and
Associates; KressCox Associates

TEL: (202) 628-1776   www.dar.org

Reputed to be the largest complex of buildings in the world owned
exclusively by women, this is also the seat of one of the nation's most
prominent patriotic organizations. Facing 17th Street is Memorial Continental Hall, an imposing structure marked by an unusual *porte cochere*—
its columns are set on tall pedestals, giving the false impression that
holes had been cut in a once solid base. Not surprisingly, the building
includes a number of elements that allude to the American Revolution,
such as the curving south porch with thirteen columns representing the
original colonies.

The organization's annual "Continental Congress" soon outgrew the
original building, necessitating the addition of a large auditorium, Constitution Hall, which became one of Washington's premier venues for
public concerts. The National Symphony was based here for more than
four decades, and the auditorium remains the largest such facility in
Washington. But this site is most famous for the concert that did *not* take
place here in 1939, when African American singer Marian Anderson was
denied the opportunity to perform because of her race, prompting First
Lady Eleanor Roosevelt to resign her DAR membership and help orches-
trate the outdoor concert by Anderson at the Lincoln Memorial (Anderson subsequently performed at the hall on several occasions).

Fortunately, the society is now a much more inclusive organization,
and its headquarters draws visitors both to its renowned genealogical library, and to its museum, incorporating period rooms that depict scenes
of early American life.

---

18   **Organization of American
     States (Pan-American
     Union)**
     17th Street and Constitution
     Avenue, NW

     1910 Albert Kelsey and Paul
     P. Cret
     1912 Annex: Kelsey and Cret
     2005 Renovation: John
     Milner Associates

TEL: (202) 458-3000   www.oas.org

Funded in part by a $750,000 gift from Andrew Carnegie, the headquarters of the oldest international organization of which the United States is a member was intended to symbolize the peaceful spirit pervading relations among the nations of North, South, and Central America. It occupies the former site of the Van Ness mansion, designed by Benjamin Henry Latrobe, which was built around 1816 and thought to be the most expensive residence in the United States in its day. The former stables of that estate, also by Latrobe, still stand at 18th and C streets, though their stucco finish is not original.

The exterior of Kelsey and Cret's building is classical, with a red tile roof and other details alluding to the Spanish Colonial architecture of Latin America. The sculptures flanking the entrance represent North America (by Gutzon Borglum, best known for his work on Mount Rushmore), and South America (by Isidor Konti). Other sculptural elements depict the eagle, associated with the north, and the condor, associated with the Andes and, thus, the south. Historical figures depicted include the great liberators George Washington, Simón Bolívar, and José de San Martín.

Inside, classical formality yields to tropical exoticism, as the building is organized around a lushly planted patio that was originally covered with a sliding glass roof, though modern air-conditioning now precludes the use of this feature. The centerpiece of the garden is Gertrude Vanderbilt Whitney's fountain representing Mayan, Aztec, and Zapotecan art. Behind the main building is another, originally known as the annex, which now houses the Art Museum of the Americas. Between the two buildings lies the Blue Aztec Garden, featuring a small reflecting pool. Presiding over the garden is a statue of Xochipilli, the Aztec god of flowers, which seems pleasant enough, though he was also associated with hallucinogenic drugs and human sacrifices.

I9   Department of the Interior

1849 C Street, NW

1936   Waddy B. Wood

TEL: (202) 208-4743
www.doi.gov

The first project undertaken by FDR's Public Works Administration, the Department of the Interior's headquarters is enormous and severe, but behind those forbidding façades await several entertaining surprises. Most noteworthy are the dozens of spectacular New

Deal murals and sculptures, many of them addressing Native American themes. There is also a small and slightly funky museum on the first floor, as well as an Indian Craft Shop (sadly, the Federal Duck Stamp Office, another longtime Interior Department oddity, has migrated to Arlington). The building's floor plan is unusual for its era—instead of the more typical courtyards to bring light to office spaces within a huge block, Wood organized the plan around a central, north-south spine, with six pairs of narrow wings projecting east and west. An ongoing renovation of the building by Shalom Baranes Associates is currently under way.

I10 Federal Reserve Building (Marriner S. Eccles Building)

Constitution Avenue between 20th and 21st streets, NW

1937 Paul Philippe Cret

TEL: (202) 452-3149
www.federalreserve.gov/
generalinfo/virtualtour

E. J. Applewhite called the Federal Reserve the "Valhalla of the dollar," and Paul Cret won an invited design competition to create an appropriately monumental temple for America's gods of economic policy. The exterior design may be the apotheosis of "starved classicism" in Washington, and with the eagle sculpture over its main doorway starkly lit at night, the building is perhaps uncomfortably reminiscent of the contemporary work of Albert Speer (suggesting that stylistic trends often trump ideology in architecture). The eagle motif is carried throughout the building, even appearing as an outline in the glass ceiling of the atrium, an elegant space lined with buttery marble and intricate railings by notable Philadelphia ironworker Samuel Yellin. The public may visit the Federal Reserve Building, which also hosts limited art exhibitions, but reservations are required.

I11 National Academy of Sciences

2101 Constitution Avenue, NW (2100 C Street, NW)

1924 Bertram Grosvenor Goodhue; Sculptor: Lee Lawrie
1962, 1965, 1970 West Wing, East Wing, and Auditorium additions: Harrison & Abramowitz
1979 Landscape design for Einstein statue: Oehme, van Sweden & Associates; Sculptor: Robert Berks

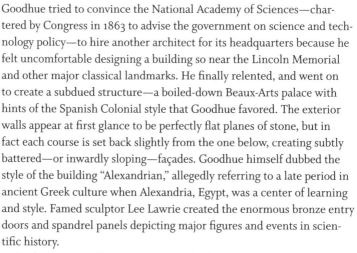

TEL: (202) 334-2436   www.nationalacademies.org/nas/nashome.nsf

Goodhue tried to convince the National Academy of Sciences—chartered by Congress in 1863 to advise the government on science and technology policy—to hire another architect for its headquarters because he felt uncomfortable designing a building so near the Lincoln Memorial and other major classical landmarks. He finally relented, and went on to create a subdued structure—a boiled-down Beaux-Arts palace with hints of the Spanish Colonial style that Goodhue favored. The exterior walls appear at first glance to be perfectly flat planes of stone, but in fact each course is set back slightly from the one below, creating subtly battered—or inwardly sloping—façades. Goodhue himself dubbed the style of the building "Alexandrian," allegedly referring to a late period in ancient Greek culture when Alexandria, Egypt, was a center of learning and style. Famed sculptor Lee Lawrie created the enormous bronze entry doors and spandrel panels depicting major figures and events in scientific history.

In the 1960s, Wallace K. Harrison, who had worked in Goodhue's office in his younger days, designed a trio of additions, the last of which houses a futuristic auditorium encased in a wildly faceted shell. In 1979, the endearingly frumpy Albert Einstein Memorial, by Robert Berks, was dedicated in the academy's front yard. The map at the base of the monument has more than 2,700 metal studs representing planets, stars, and other heavenly bodies in their relative positions as of the dedication date.

I12 American Pharmacists Association (American Pharmaceutical Association)

2215 Constitution Avenue, NW

1933 John Russell Pope
1962 Addition: Eggers & Higgins

The tourist coming upon this building for the first time would be excused for guessing that it is a shrine of some kind—a war memorial perhaps, or a dignified little museum dedicated to some archaic, vaguely remembered civic cause. In fact, it is the headquarters of a professional society, and for nearly seven decades, it was the only private building on Constitution Avenue, NW (the new private office building at 101 Constitution [see A17] now anchors the other end of this important thoroughfare). Pope's design for this structure was actually recycled—he originally created it as a shell for Abraham Lincoln's natal log cabin in Kentucky, but for various reasons he decided to use it here instead, and designed another classical reliquary for Lincoln's birthplace.

I13 Pan American Health Organization

525 23rd Street, NW

1965 Design architect: Román Fresnedo Siri; Architects of record: Justement, Elam, Callmer & Kidd
2001 Renovation: Ai

Like many Latin American architects of the mid-twentieth century, Román Fresnedo Siri, of Uruguay, was enthralled by Corbusian modernism. His competition-winning design for this complex reflects Le Corbusier's influence in the visual interplay between the cylindrical structure (housing a council chamber and related spaces) and the gently curved "secretariat" tower, the *brise-soleil* that shades the cylinder's glass curtain wall from the sun, and the *pilotis* that lift the main office block off the ground.

I14 John F. Kennedy Center for the Performing Arts

2700 F Street, NW

1971 Edward Durrell Stone Associates; Landscape architect: Edward Durrell Stone Jr.
1979 Terrace Theater: Philip C. Johnson
1997 Concert Hall renovation: Quinn Evans/Architects; Design architects: Hartman-Cox Architects
2003 Opera House renovation: Quinn Evans/Architects
2005 Family Theater: Richter Cornbrooks Gribble

TEL: (202) 416-8341   www.kennedy-center.org

If a Las Vegas developer were to open a casino under the theme of "Palace of the Soviets"—and unlikelier things happen hourly in Vegas—the result might look something like the Kennedy Center. Cut off from the adjacent neighborhood by a tangle of freeways, and from the Potomac riverfront by an enormous cantilevered balcony, the building is a gaudy concoction of vast marble planes, spindly bronze columns, overwrought chandeliers, and acres of bordello-red carpet. It brings to mind the work of Morris Lapidus, but without the sensuous curves (though Stone produced an earlier scheme with a curvilinear plan) and with, instead, a hefty dose of Stalinist bombast. Critic Ada Louise Huxtable decried the center as "a cross between a concrete candy box and a marble sarcophagus in which the art of architecture lies buried."

Some government officials had been calling for a major performing arts facility in central Washington since the 1930s, but the effort did not get under way in earnest until the Eisenhower administration. After Kennedy's assassination, the project was rechristened in his name as a "living memorial." It opened in 1971 with a requiem Mass in honor of the slain president. Since then, despite its architectural shortcomings, it has succeeded in becoming the musical and theatrical hub that the capital had so obviously lacked.

I15 The Watergate

2500–2700 Virginia Avenue,
NW, and 600–700 New
Hampshire Avenue, NW

1964–71 Luigi Moretti
with Mario di Valmarana;
Associated architects:
Corning, Moore, Elmore &
Fischer
1994 Renovation of office
building public spaces: Bass
Architects; Nora Fischer Designs

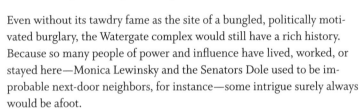

2000 Renovation of hotel: RJ Shirley & Associates Architects;
Interior designers: Hughes Design Associates

Even without its tawdry fame as the site of a bungled, politically moti-
vated burglary, the Watergate complex would still have a rich history.
Because so many people of power and influence have lived, worked, or
stayed here—Monica Lewinsky and the Senators Dole used to be improbable next-door neighbors, for instance—some intrigue surely always
would be afoot.

The Watergate's lead designer, Luigi Moretti, was once Benito Mussolini's favored architect, and never fully recanted his fascist sympathies.
He was hired to design this complex by a major Italian investment firm
that developed the project. Moretti consciously produced a design that
departed from what he saw as the rigid formality of official Washington
architecture. While much of the detailing is awkward—up close, for example, the chunky balcony railings look as if they were borrowed from
Fred Flintstone's house—overall the buildings succeed in bringing a welcome fluidity to an overwhelmingly linear and angular city. From certain
vantage points, in fact, the buildings almost suggest ocean liners, with
gentle curves and prow-like balconies.

The complex's curious name derives from the nearby Watergate
Steps, a curving structure providing access to the Potomac riverfront.
Completed in 1932, the steps were originally intended as a ceremonial
entrance to the city for dignitaries arriving by water, and as a docking
point for recreational boats. From 1935 to 1973, the steps served as an
amphitheater for musical performances, the stage for which was a barge
anchored at the structure's base.

As of this writing, the Watergate Hotel is about to be converted to
apartments in a project involving architecture firms ForrestPerkins,
Hickok Cole, and Yabu Pushelberg.

I16 St. Mary's Episcopal/ Anglican Church

730 23rd Street, NW

1881 Parish Hall: Architect unknown
1887 Church: Renwick, Aspinwall and Russell
1909 Parish House: Architect unknown
1913 Rectory: Architect unknown
2005 Restoration: Fetterman Associates

St. Mary's is the oldest African American Episcopal congregation in Washington. It held its first service on this site in 1867 in a reconstructed wooden chapel (later demolished) formerly attached to the Kalorama Hospital. The congregation prospered and grew, necessitating the new church by James Renwick Jr., built a couple of decades later. Above the altar in this structure are painted glass windows, made in France, depicting St. Cyprian, the African bishop and martyr, as well as St. Simon the Cyrenian and St. Tryphoena. Outside, between Renwick's church and the Sunday school building, is the tranquil Herbert Files Garden.

I17 George Washington University

Primarily between F Street and Pennsylvania Avenue, from 20th to 24th streets, NW

The most urban of Washington's major collegiate institutions, George Washington University does not enjoy a cohesive campus, and partially as a result, lacks a clear architectural identity. Nonetheless, the school includes a number of notable individual buildings. The Law School (1926—Albert Harris and Arthur Heaton; 1967–70—Mills, Petticord & Mills; 1984—Keyes Condon Florance Architects), at 20th and H streets, NW, is interesting as a mélange of quite different structures that seem to have grown together over time. The Lisner Auditorium (1940—Faulkner & Kingsbury) at 730 21st Street, NW, is a toned-down Art Moderne affair that was one of the primary performance venues in Washington before the opening of the Kennedy Center. The formerly undistinguished Marvin Center, at 800 21st Street, now boasts an inviting entrance (2002—SmithGroup) and provides a sense of place amid the otherwise generic campus.

I18   World Bank

1818 H Street, NW

1997 Kohn Pedersen Fox Associates; Associate architects: Nägele Hofmann Tiedemann und Partner, KressCox Associates

Kohn Pedersen Fox became famous in the 1980s for design-ing corporate office buildings that had one foot in the modern movement and the other in the turbid waters of postmodernism. The World Bank Headquarters was one of a series of buildings the firm de-signed in the 1990s that reflected a kind of retro-modernist approach. The complex takes up an entire city block, and actually incorporates two preexisting buildings along G Street. The cheerless gray concrete wall that ties the old and new structures together at ground level is the most unfortunate aspect of the design. Above that level, however, things get much livelier, especially along the north façade, facing Pennsylvania Av-enue, which is dynamically canted outward and emphatically articulated by horizontal mullions. At several points, distinct volumes break from the main building envelope, providing visual relief from the insistent ge-ometry and, in some cases, marking especially important spaces inside, such as the boardroom high up on the northeast corner of the building, which is capped by a swooping, upturned roof.

Downtown / West End

Strategically located between the White House and the elegant neighborhoods of Georgetown and Dupont Circle, the West End was the primary focus of Washington's commercial development during the major post–World War II economic booms. Although development in the old, eastern part of downtown took off again beginning in the 1980s, the area west of 16th Street and north of Pennsylvania Avenue continues to be a prestigious precinct of nonprofit organizations and other businesses. The area also contains the most consequential stretch of K Street, a thoroughfare synonymous with high-powered law firms and lobbyists. The streetscapes in this neighborhood tend to be rather bland, but they do contain a number of architecturally noteworthy individual buildings.

The Demonet Building, built in the 1880s at the corner of M Street and Connecticut Avenue, with a 1980s addition by Skidmore, Owings & Merrill behind it. The west end of downtown was the first area in central Washington to benefit from the boom in commercial real estate in the late twentieth century.

J1 Third Church of Christ, Scientist/ Christian Science Monitor Building

900–910 16th Street, NW

1971 I. M. Pei & Partners (principal designer: Araldo A. Cossuta)

TEL: (202) 833-3325

The Christian Science Church has a long track record as a patron of high-quality—and often quite progressive—architecture, including important early twentieth-century works in California by Bernard Maybeck and Irving Gill. The church's world headquarters complex in Boston includes a collection of striking concrete buildings by I. M. Pei & Partners, which were under construction while the firm was also working on Washington's modestly scaled Third Church of Christ, Scientist.

This church has an octagonal plan, which Pei adopted after abandoning his original, circular scheme for fear that it would be too expensive to build and would complicate the acoustics inside the sanctuary. The building's facets are clad in concrete panels, and are mostly windowless—light enters the interior primarily through a skylight tracing the perimeter of the roof. A cantilevered carillon, which required a zoning variance because it projects over the public sidewalk along 16th Street, is the most engaging element of the design; the low point is the decidedly inelegant emergency exit doorway on I Street, which passersby are presumably expected to ignore.

The main entrance to the church faces a small plaza, across which stands a small office building housing the Christian Science Reading Room. This sliver of a building, with its rectilinear plan and long ribbons of glass, is a geometrical and textural foil to the main structure.

J2   Barr Building

910 17th Street, NW

1926 B. Stanley Simmons

Rich ornament in the English Gothic Revival style lends a strongly ecclesiastical character to this office building—indeed, the vacant sculptural niches adorning its columns seem destined to accommodate saintly statuary. E. J. Applewhite declared the Barr Building to be "a rebuke to the boring borax banality of the computer-designed structures which adjoin it at either side." Though the adjacent structure to the north is new since Applewhite's time, his remark remains apt.

J3   Washington Square

1050 Connecticut Avenue, NW

1982   Chloethiel Woodard Smith & Associates

The intersection of Connecticut Avenue and L Street is sometimes called "Chloethiel's Corner" because the pioneering woman architect designed three of its four buildings (all but the one on the northeast corner). Of these, Washington Square is by far the most stylish, thanks to its serrated façades composed of shallow bay windows, its mezzanine-level outdoor terrace, and its pair of glassy, towering atria, all of which make it more like a glitzy convention hotel than a typical downtown office building.

J4   Mayflower Hotel

1127 Connecticut Avenue, NW

1925   Warren & Wetmore; Associated architect: Robert S. Beresford
1941   Partial interior renovation: Dorothy Draper Inc.
1958   Apartment wing converted to hotel rooms: Architect unknown
1984   Renovation: Vlastimil Koubek; Interiors: Louis Cataffo

While best known as the architects of New York's Grand Central Terminal, Warren & Wetmore also designed dozens of luxurious mansions, hotels, and office buildings that epitomized gentility and urbanity in early twentieth-century America. The Mayflower Hotel is emblematic of the era in its subdued elegance. The main body of the building is actually quite plain, with simple windows set into unadorned brick walls, but the hotel achieves quiet dignity thanks to its tastefully ornamented limestone base, the bold terra cotta quoins climbing the corners of each wing, the subtle curves of the two wings facing Connecticut Avenue, and the parade of loosely spaced urns running along the edge of the roof. Among the hotel's many famous guests was local resident J. Edgar Hoover, who dined here with his colleague and companion Clyde Tolson almost every evening for two decades.

In 1941, famed interior designer Dorothy Draper redid all of the guest rooms on the hotel's fifth floor. Draper was known for an over-the-top, florid decorative style, but ironically, this project in conservative Washington was one of her simplest and most modern. All of the hotel's rooms have since been redone a number of times.

J5 ABC News Washington Bureau

1717 DeSales Street, NW

1981 Kohn Pedersen Fox Associates

Now a global mega-firm, Kohn Pedersen Fox started out in 1976 as an office comprising only the three partners. ABC was the client that gave the young architects their big break, and the firm went on to design a number of facilities for the network, including the Washington News Bureau, one of their earliest completed projects. The major design gesture here is the taut, convex curve of the façade, which distinguishes the mid-block building from its neighbors without unduly disrupting the streetscape.

J6 National Geographic Society Headquarters

M Street between 16th and 17th streets, NW

1903 Hubbard Memorial Library: Hornblower & Marshall
1913–32 Administration Building: Arthur B. Heaton
1964 17th Street Building: Edward Durrell Stone

1984 M Street Building: Skidmore, Owings & Merrill
1984 Renovation of Hubbard Memorial Library: Keyes Condon
Florance Architects

TEL: (202) 857-7588   www.nationalgeographic.com

The National Geographic complex feels like a small, tightly packed academic campus, consisting of several quite disparate buildings that somehow cohere thanks to their complementary architectural qualities and unified landscaping. At the corner of 16th and M streets stands the original building, now known as the Hubbard Memorial Library, named after Gardiner Greene Hubbard, the first president of the society. It was Hubbard's son-in-law, inventor Alexander Graham Bell, who succeeded him and turned the organization into the famously popular enterprise that it is today. Adjacent to the library on 16th Street is an administrative building executed in a complementary Renaissance Revival style in 1932.

At the 17th Street corner is Edward Durrell Stone's 1960s tower, which is curiously reminiscent of an unbuilt Frank Lloyd Wright project from 1913 for the *San Francisco Call* newspaper, with slender, tightly spaced columns and a boldly horizontal, perforated "cornice." Unlike Stone's widely reviled Kennedy Center [see I14], which languishes by the Potomac like a beached whale, this building is welcoming and comfortable in its urban setting. It also houses the society's Explorers Hall, a small museum with rotating exhibitions.

At the center of the block lies the newest element of the complex, a modern rendition of a ziggurat, with an L-shaped plan creating a courtyard as a focal point for the motley campus. The new building's insistent horizontality offsets the equally emphatic verticality of Stone's structure, while mediating between the modern tower to its west and the older, classical buildings to its east.

J7 Sumner School and Sumner Square

17th and M streets, NW

1872 Sumner School: Adolf Cluss
1887 Magruder School: Architect unknown
1985 Restoration and additions to existing buildings:

Ehrenkrantz Group; New structures: Hartman-Cox Architects;

Associated architects: Navy, Marshall, Gordon, with RTKL Associates Inc.; Preservation architects: Oehrlein & Associates Architects

Largely thanks to Adolf Cluss, nineteenth-century Washington boasted a number of inventively designed public schools, and the city was even recognized with a "Medal for Progress" in school design at the Vienna World's Exposition of 1873. Named for abolitionist Charles Sumner, this particular school was a center of African American education during the era of segregation. Ironically, with integration came neglect, and the Sumner School sat, largely ignored and rapidly decaying, until the District's Board of Education finally decided to restore it and the Magruder School next door.

   The two historic schools became the centerpieces of a new commercial development, though the Sumner School was retained by the Board of Education for its own use. The underground component of the project required that the Magruder building be dismantled and reconstructed on a new foundation. The bulk of the new structure, by Hartman-Cox, is unobtrusively rendered in a gray curtain wall, making a true background building that avoids visual competition with the schools. One wing of the new building comes out to the street line, however, and for that part, the architects broke from the pure background approach. Instead, they covered it in a buff brick, which deftly relates the new wing to the existing buildings on either side—its primary material, brick, is the same as that of the Magruder School, while its beige color ties it to the Jefferson Hotel (1923—Jules Henri de Sibour) at the corner of M and 16th streets.

J8   St. Matthew's Cathedral

1725 Rhode Island Avenue, NW

1893 C. Grant La Farge (Heins and La Farge)
2003 Restoration: Oehrlein & Associates Architects

The 190-foot-tall copper dome of St. Matthew's, the seat of Washington's Catholic Archdiocese, was a prominent landmark for a half century before it was gradually surrounded by mid-rise office buildings. In its basic massing, proportions, and spartan decoration, the building recalls the architecture of early Christian churches (the one bit of *relative* exuberance, the mosaic over the main door, was added in 1970). The severe façade, however, belies the opulence of the interior, which teems with colorful mosaics and marble. Heins and LaFarge, both of whom apprenticed in the office of H. H. Richardson, were also the original architects of the gigantic and perpetually unfinished Cathedral of St. John the Divine in New York.

J9   1150 18th Street, NW

1991 Don M. Hisaka & Associates

In designing this small office building, Don Hisaka was eager to avoid not only the "granite or marble cliché" of traditional Washington architecture, but also the facile, banal curtain wall so common in the city's more recent commercial buildings. Nonetheless, the architect felt that his project must still fit comfortably into the cityscape. His solution was to create an elaborate, sunscreen-like façade of white-painted steel. In its color, depth, and interplay of light and shadow, the façade alludes abstractly to the city's classical landmarks, while its extruded steel components and industrial detailing firmly establish its modernity. By organizing the interior around a brilliantly bright atrium and cantilevering the upper floors over an adjacent alley, Hisaka was able to maximize both square footage and access to natural light on a very constricted site.

J10   National Permanent Building

1775 Pennsylvania Avenue, NW

1977 Hartman-Cox Architects

The National Permanent Building represents an unusual marriage of technological expressiveness and historical allusion. Its round concrete columns gradually decrease in size as the structure rises, reflecting the reduced load they carry at higher levels. Flanking the columns are what at first appear to be redundant columns painted black, but in fact, these are steel ducts that carry air from handlers on the roof, so quite logically, they *increase* in circumference as they rise. The skillful interweaving of these two complementary systems lends great compositional interest to the perfectly rational façade. Moreover, those myriad columns and ducts clearly evoke the ornate garb of Alfred B. Mullett's Eisenhower Executive Office Building just down the street. The visual connection is especially strong at the top of the Hartman-Cox building, where the large ducts are canted and the floors stepped back, yielding an inventive reinterpretation of Mullett's mansard roof.

J11 1915 I Street, NW

1917 Frank Russell White
1982 Addition: Kerns Group Architects

While the addition echoes the form of the original building's Dutch gable, its animated, multiple setbacks change what was previously an inconspicuous apartment building into a minor landmark. The stepped façades unabashedly reveal their false historicism at their edges, where they are offset from the side walls by glazed notches.

J12 **Millennium Building**

1909 K Street, NW

1999 Boggs & Partners Architects

In renovating and expanding a typical K Street office block, Joseph Boggs decided to preserve the faceted marble panels that lined the existing building's columns, and reuse them in essentially the same fashion on his new structure. Besides saving money and avoiding a waste of material, the decision resulted in a building that, while clearly new, has a welcome hint of historical continuity (even though the existing structure was just a few decades old). Boggs added three floors in order to fill out the allowable zoning envelope, and tied the new and old masses together with a curving element that lends sculptural relief to the understated façade.

J13   Brewood Office Building

1147 20th Street, NW

1974 Wilkes & Faulkner

A small surprise among the generic behemoths so common in this part of town, the Brewood Building is unusual in its use of board-formed concrete that reveals the pattern of the wood used as formwork. Cleverly, the façade details go a step further to suggest the patterns, scale, and connection methods of wood construction. As a result, the small building has an almost hand-crafted quality that is rare in modern commercial architecture.

J14   William P. Rogers Building

2001 K Street, NW

2000 Skidmore, Owings & Merrill

The Pepsi-Cola Headquarters (1959) in New York, by Skidmore, Owings & Merrill, presents a startlingly minimalist façade to Park Avenue, with broad windows, widely spaced mullions, and no structural columns along the exterior. The William P. Rogers Building, designed by the same firm four decades later, harks back to that earlier landmark, while making certain accommodations to its own context. The very thin curtain wall at PepsiCo, for instance, would have been hard to replicate in an era that demands greater thermal performance from building envelopes. Perhaps recognizing that greater depth was inevitable in the new structure, SOM used shadow-box spandrels—see-through glass panels with metal panels behind them—to modulate the visual depth of the façade. Also, while PepsiCo is raised off the ground on *pilotis,* such a move would be hard to justify in height-limited Washington, so here, the first floor is built out to the property line. The main entrance is marked with an extremely subtle setback running the full height of the building.

J15 2099 Pennsylvania Avenue, NW

2001 Pei Cobb Freed & Partners Architects; Associated architects: Weihe Design Group

Part of the new breed of modern Washington office buildings eschewing the historicist tricks that became so common in the 1980s and early 1990s, this structure is an exercise in pure solid geometry, its façades deliberately rendered as flat as possible so as to avoid compromising the perception of the basic forms. Unlike the Cato Institute Building [see G20], where two clearly differentiated cubes intersect, here the distinction between the two primary forms is subtle, marked by a minor change in the design of the ten-foot window modules—each of the windows in the "background" block has a wide mullion on one side, while in the "foreground" form the mullions are all hair-breadth thin.

J16 International Finance Corporation Headquarters

2121 Pennsylvania Avenue, NW

1996 Michael Graves & Associates; Associated architect: Vlastimil Koubek (Koubek Architects)

A division of the World Bank Group—which, if it were any bigger, would require its own world—the International Finance Corporation (IFC) occupies this mammoth building entailing more than one million square feet of office space. An example of the Aldo Rossi-esque style that Michael Graves has come to favor for commercial and civic structures, the IFC Building is daunting with its no-nonsense massing, its absurdly tall, four-story "base," and its dizzying array of perfectly cylindrical columns (especially on the K Street façade).

J17 2401 Pennsylvania Avenue, NW

1991 Keyes Condon Florance

This mixed-use building employs a whimsical assortment of materials and decorative motifs. The result is generally quite urbane—the base of the building holds the street line, while the upper stories are sculptural, yielding an unusually complex and visually rich work of architecture. Many of the details are subtly amusing, such as the donkey- and elephant-head-shaped brackets holding the cables that support the ground-floor canopies. Occasionally, the decorative devices dissolve into kitsch, as in the precast concrete flags at the southeast corner of the roof.

J18 Barclay House

2501 K Street, NW

1980 Martin and Jones

In Washington, the term *postmodern architecture* is popularly associated with rather straightforward historicism. Actually, the city has relatively few *truly* postmodern buildings—those that actively and deliberately seek to challenge modern orthodoxies. The Barclay House is an example of this more mischievous brand of postmodernism. Dozens of conventions are broken here—expected hierarchies are subverted, grids and planes dissolve and reappear seemingly at random, and projecting bays seem to hang illogically from columns.

J19 The Westin Grand Hotel

2350 M Street, NW

1984 Skidmore, Owings & Merrill

Although it is hard to imagine Greta Garbo or John Barrymore striding through this lobby, the building's name—originally just "The Grand Hotel"—is nonetheless important, for it indicates the developer's aspirations, namely, to revive some of the elegance and grandeur of luxury hotels from the early twentieth century. The resulting architectural expression is timidly historicist, with a few elements, such as the rusticated concrete base and the shallow dome over the corner entrance tower, conveying a modest monumentality.

J20 1250 24th Street, NW (B and W Garage)

1925 Designer-builder: Peter Reinsen
1988 New building incorporating existing façade: Hisaka & Associates Architects

This office building, like the garage that originally occupied the site, is simultaneously industrial and classical in spirit. The front façade of the two-story garage was preserved (though the deteriorating brick had to be painted), and now serves primarily as a screen defining small courts in front of the new building, which features a curving curtain wall bracketed by two painted brick towers that replicate the architectural vocabulary of the old garage. The bowed façade gives the building a formal presence, but does not overwhelm the low wall of the original structure.

The back of the building is less elegant, as one would expect, since that is not where architects generally want to spend their budgets. Recognizing, however, that there was a relatively prominent axial view of the building from 25th Street, Hisaka created a single projecting bay to serve as an appropriate terminus for the vista.

J21 2300/2400 N Street, NW

1983 Skidmore, Owings & Merrill

Taken as a pair, these fraternal twin buildings form an example of what the Germans would call *Stadtraum,* a term for "urban space" that implies not just the leftover area between buildings, but a deliberately sculpted outdoor "room." Here, at the end of a not-so-important street, these two buildings successfully create a strong sense of place. They do so not only through the geometry of their plans, but also through their distinctive red-brick-and-precast-concrete palette, which became a design signature of development in this part of the West End.

Georgetown

Forty years older than the city of which it is now a part, Georgetown was originally a small Maryland river town known simply as George—named not for America's first president, as many people suppose, but for King George II of England. The initial community covered about sixty acres between the Potomac and a line south of N Street (then known as Gay Street), bounded on the east by what is now 30th (then Washington) Street, and on the west by the land now occupied by Georgetown University. Even after it was absorbed into the newly established District of Columbia in 1791, Georgetown remained legally a separate jurisdiction until formal annexation by "Washington City" eighty years later.

While Georgetown is now virtually synonymous with gentility, much of its history is actually rather gritty. In its early days, Georgetown was a bustling port, thanks to its strategic location near the falls of the Potomac and its proximity to vast tobacco plantations that provided the primary commodity to be shipped. Like most ports of that era, it was a scrappy town, home to workaday wharves and rowdy taverns, populated by notoriously crude sailors and probably more than a few merchants with fungible business ethics. Abigail Adams dismissed the place as "a dirty little hole," and many other contemporary accounts were equally unfavorable.

The converse of the seedy side of ports, of course, is the wealth they generate for those positioned to reap the profits of commerce. Georgetown quickly grew a substantial class of prosperous entrepreneurs, many of whom were quite cultured, and who built houses that still reign as

This "View of Georgetown D.C.," published by E. Sachse & Co. in 1853, reveals that parts of the area retained a pastoral quality well into the nineteenth century.

some of the most elegant in the District. In fact, Georgetown's elite regarded the nascent—and, at the time, absolutely distinct—capital city to the east with some skepticism, suspicious as they were of the questionable enterprises (i.e., politics and government) practiced there. As late as 1826, one observer noticed that "the people of Georgetown . . . form a striking contrast to their neighbors in Washington, their minds being generally more cultivated. It is hardly possible to conceive how towns so near . . . should differ so widely."

As the nineteenth century progressed, however, Georgetown did not fare well. The river soon silted up, and the C & O Canal, dug to lure the rich Midwest trade to the Potomac, proved no match for the B & O Railroad. Trade bypassed Georgetown's once-flourishing port in favor of Baltimore. The Civil War brought significant social rifts, since Georgetown, though situated in the capital of the Union, still housed a number of prominent Confederate sympathizers (Georgetown University's official colors, blue and gray, reflect that school's divided loyalties). Following the war, the town absorbed an influx of freed slaves, most of whom were of course quite poor, and whose presence displeased some affluent Georgetowners, who moved elsewhere. The community grew increasingly shabby, and eventually even officially lost its name, when, upon annexation in 1871, it became legally known as "West Washington."

Georgetown then entered a period of quiescence that lasted until the New Deal, when the growth of the federal government—and the consequent rise in Washington's population—brought about the rediscovery of "West Washington" as a choice place to live, convenient to the office buildings of Foggy Bottom and downtown. The pace of this rediscovery quickened after World War II until it began to look as if Georgetown might be spoiled by its success. To ensure the preservation of the architectural character of their town, residents pushed the Old Georgetown Act through Congress in 1950. The act officially made Georgetown a historic district, and gave the U.S. Commission of Fine Arts the authority to appoint an advisory panel, the Old Georgetown Board, which to this day reviews proposals for additions and alterations to both public and private structures throughout the neighborhood.

Tourists are often surprised to learn that a substantial percentage of the "historic" houses in present-day Georgetown were actually built in the aftermath of the 1950 legislation. Many of these "Eisenhowerian" structures fit quite stealthily into the historic fabric, thanks to their modesty and reliance on red brick as the primary finish material. Even so, they are generally readily distinguishable by their less-grand proportions, smaller windows, shallower façades, and, in many cases, brick patterns that were uncommon in the nineteenth century.

Today, Georgetown may be appreciated as a microcosm of American urbanism, miraculously encapsulated within a small precinct of a large metropolis. Starting at the waterfront and walking northward, one passes the remnants of the town's industrial origins, moves through a thriving commercial and entertainment zone, and then traverses dense residential blocks. Continuing, one discovers streets lined with larger, detached houses, followed by an area of palatial "country" estates, and finally, the edge of Rock Creek Park—a swath of wilderness (well, almost) in the heart of the city.

K1 Georgetown University

The nation's oldest Catholic institution of higher learning, initially known as Georgetown Academy, was formally established in 1789 by Father John Carroll, the first American Catholic bishop. Carroll considered placing the new school on what is now Capitol Hill, but dismissed the site as being "too far in the country." Instead he opted for a high spot just upriver from the bustling port, enjoying a commanding view. The present campus is organized around two primary centers, with most of the historic academic buildings and residential clusters toward the southern end, and a sprawling medical school and hospital complex at the northern edge along Reservoir Road.

K1A Healy Hall

1877–1909 Smithmeyer & Pelz
1982 Restoration of Riggs Library: Environmental Planning and Research
1995 Renovation: Einhorn Yaffee Prescott

The architectural centerpiece of the campus is named for Father Patrick Healy, the university's dynamic president from 1874 to 1881. The son of an Irish father and a mother who was a slave, Healy was the first person of African American descent to earn a Ph.D. and the first to head a predominantly white university. Designed by the stylistically ambidextrous architects of the original Library of Congress building, Healy Hall has exterior walls of dark gray Potomac gneiss and is capped by a two hundred–foot clock tower, making it one of low-rise Washington's most widely visible landmarks. Glimpsed from the Potomac River or various spots along the Virginia banks, the imposing structure could almost be mistaken for a baronial fortress overlooking the Rhine. The building's most notable interior space is the Riggs Library, distinguished by four levels of delicate cast iron stacks.

K1B Old North Building

1797 Architect unknown
1983 Restoration: Mariani & Associates

The oldest extant academic building at Georgetown, Old North is typical of the simple but dignified Georgian and Federal structures, such as Princeton's Nassau Hall, found on a number of the country's most venerable campuses. It is also reminiscent of some of Washington's early residential blocks like Wheat Row [see C11].

K1C Joseph Mark Lauinger Memorial Library

1970 John Carl Warnecke & Associates
1991 Renovation: Einhorn Yaffee Prescott

The exposed-aggregate concrete surfaces and angular forms of the Lauinger Library are not widely favored today, but when it opened, the structure was praised—if rather faintly—for being deferential to its historic neighbors. *Washington Post* critic Wolf Von Eckardt declared that the architects of the library "managed to blend it into the cityscape, if not unobtrusively, successfully." Indeed, the new building's low physical profile preserves views to and from the older structures, while its incorporation of dark gray aggregate in the concrete and its abstract, asymmetrical towers are clearly deliberate allusions to Healy Hall.

K2 Georgetown Visitation Preparatory School/ Convent of the Visitation

1524 35th Street, NW

1821 Chapel: Joseph Picot de Clorivière
1832 Monastery: Architect unknown
1857 Additions/alterations to monastery and chapel: Richard Pettit
1874 Founders' Hall (Academy Building): Norris G. Starkweather
1995 Restoration of Founders' Hall: KressCox Associates
1996 Renovation of Chapel: KressCox Associates
1998 Athletic and Performing Arts centers: KressCox Associates

Founded in 1799 by three "Pious Ladies" under the auspices of Georgetown University's president, the Convent of the Visitation runs one of the oldest Catholic girls' schools in America. The campus is a catalogue of period architecture, from the austere Federal "monastery" building (at the corner of 35th and P), to the neo-Gothic, stuccoed chapel, to the ornate, Victorian Founders' Hall, with its mansard roof and elaborate brickwork. The last of these was the victim of a spectacular fire in 1993, after which the nuns not only oversaw a meticulous restoration of the damaged structure, but also embarked on a broader building and renovation campaign, adding new ancillary facilities designed in a low-key historicist mode. From around the corner, in the 3500 block of P Street, one can catch glimpses of the long wooden porches that line the rear of the monastery.

K3 Volta Bureau

1537 35th Street, NW (3417 Volta Place, NW)

1894 Peabody and Stearns
1949 Russell O. Kluge
2000 Renovation architects of record: Horsey & Thorpe; Interior: RTKL Associates

After the French government awarded Alexander Graham Bell the Volta Prize of 50,000 francs (about $10,000) in recognition of his invention of the telephone, Bell invested the money in further research that led to the graphophone, an improved version of the phonograph. The profits from this device helped him to establish the Volta Bureau, dedicated to the diffusion of knowledge about deafness, a subject near to Bell's heart because both his mother and his wife, Mabel Hubbard Bell, were deaf. The temple-like bureau seems to be from the same architectural vein as the small but impeccably detailed classical bank buildings that once stood on Main Streets in countless American towns. The entrance is marked by a pair of intricately decorated columns *in antis*, meaning that they are bracketed by the extensions of the side walls of the building. Note the contrasting east façade, which is composed of a series of slit windows suggestive of the rear of the former Central Library on Mount Vernon Square.

K4 Pomander Walk

Volta Place, between 33rd and 34th streets, NW

1885 Architects unknown
c. 1950 Renovations: Architects unknown

Formerly called Bell's Court, this row of ten tiny houses was once an alley inhabited by freed slaves living in desperate poverty. In 1950, the houses were condemned and the remaining residents forcibly evicted. Following renovation, the street was renamed after a small, private enclave in Manhattan's Upper West Side, which in turn had been modeled on the set of an early twentieth-century comedic stage play of the same name.

K5 St. John's Episcopal Church of Georgetown

3240 O Street, NW

1809 William Thornton
1870 Starkweather and Plowman
c. 1930 Parish Hall: Architect unknown
1995 Renovation and addition: Egbert & Houston

Thornton, the original architect of the Capitol, as well as of Tudor Place and the Octagon, provided the architectural inspiration for this church, if not the actual drawings. Early members of the congregation, which was founded in 1796, included Benjamin Stoddert and Francis Scott Key. President Thomas Jefferson contributed $50 to the building fund. The structure has been modified greatly over the years, but the foundations and most of the walls seem original. A new atrium connecting the church and the parish hall is crowned by a row of skylights between timber trusses.

K6   Smith Row

3255–3263 N Street, NW

c. 1815 Walter and Clement Smith, owner-builders
Numerous subsequent renovations and restorations: Various architects

Along with Cox's Row one block down N Street [see next entry], these five houses are classic examples of domestic architecture of the Federal period, with flat fronts, arched doorways, and generally restrained ornament. The houses in this series are more refined than the neighboring row in several subtle ways, most notably their raised parlor floors, elegant entrance steps, slightly more elaborate door treatments (note number 3259 in particular), and intimate relationship with the street.

K7   Cox's Row

3327–3339 N Street, NW

c. 1818 John Cox, owner-builder
Numerous subsequent renovations and restorations: Various architects

Built by Colonel John Cox, this row of Federal houses shows traces of Victorian remodeling and recent restoration projects, but enough remains of them to give a sense of how they must have looked when new. Cox engineered the gerrymandering of city boundaries so he could run for mayor of Georgetown; he won, entering office in 1823 and holding the post for a record twenty-two years. When the Marquis de Lafayette returned to town in 1824, he accepted Cox's offer to reside at 3337 N Street for his entire visit. In Lafayette's honor, it is said, local school girls sketched welcoming decorative flowers on the floor of the house with colored chalk. Cox and his wife lived next door at 3339.

K8 Holy Trinity Parish

3513 N Street, NW

1794 Original church (now Chapel of St. Ignatius Loyola): Architect unknown
1851 Present church: Architect unknown
1869 Rectory: Francis Staunton
1979 Renovation of main church: Giuliani Associates Architects
2000 Renovation of chapel and parish facilities: Kerns Group Architects

The three primary structures in this complex reflect three quite different eras in religious history. The original brick church on N Street was the first building in the District of Columbia erected for public Catholic services, and its small scale and modest character testify to the tenuous state of Catholicism in eighteenth-century America. (Before the First Amendment to the Constitution, which secured the right of "free exercise" of religion, the area's Catholic families had to conduct Mass in private.) That tiny church soon proved inadequate for the growing congregation, and it was superseded by the dignified Greco-Roman-revival structure on 36th Street, whose larger size and more refined architectural expression suggest American Catholicism's improved condition. Finally, the more elaborate, mansard-roofed rectory, around the corner on O Street, attests to the financial stability that was assured when millions of industrial-era immigrants arrived from Ireland, Italy, and elsewhere, swelling the ranks of the Roman Catholic Church in the United States. Less notable school and office structures complete the complex.

K9 Prospect House

3508 Prospect Street, NW

c. 1793 James Maccubbin Lingan,
owner-builder
1861–1951 Numerous alterations:
Architects unknown

The view down the Potomac provides
the name for this quintessential freestanding Federal town house. It is
believed that Lingan designed the residence himself, perhaps using one of
the architectural pattern books then popular among America's educated
builders. One of nineteen landowners who agreed to sell their holdings to
establish the District of Columbia, Lingan decided that the future lay in
the new, distinct capital city to the east, so he moved there and sold Prospect House in the 1790s. An outspoken opponent of the War of 1812, Lingan met his end in Baltimore when a hawkish mob stoned him to death.

A later resident was James Forrestal, the first person to hold the title
of secretary of defense, and namesake of the Department of Energy's
building at L'Enfant Plaza [see C1]. After Forrestal's death in 1949, the
federal government leased the residence as a guest house for foreign
dignitaries (while the Trumans were living at Blair House during the
renovation of the White House). The *Washington Times-Herald* soon
published an exposé about the "scores of Congressmen" who sullied the
grand dwelling with "stag entertainments . . . featuring liquor and femi-
nine companionship."

K10 3618 Prospect Street, NW

c. 1940s Architect unknown
2001 McInturff Architects

Although its front façade on Prospect
Street is unremarkable, the rear of this
house, visible from the stretch of M
Street just west of the Car Barn or from
the Key Bridge, is a local landmark.
Before the renovation, the entire rear
wall was becoming detached from the
main structure and was threatening to
tumble down the hill. This presented an

opportunity for McInturff to open up the façade dramatically in his redesign of the house. Now, in contrast to its tarted-up neighbors, with their profuse arches and other gimcrackery, 3618 Prospect presents a sleek and balanced composition of horizontal and vertical linear elements, which, from the inside, frame intriguing views while modulating sunlight.

K11 Capitol Traction Company Union Station (Georgetown Car Barn)

3600 M Street, NW
3520 Prospect Street, NW

1897 Waddy B. Wood
1911 Expansion: Architect unknown
1999 Renovation: Arthur Cotton Moore/Associates

Engaging the precipitous bluff at the western end of the Georgetown waterfront, this former streetcar storage facility towers over M Street, but appears from Prospect Street to be merely a series of modestly scaled pavilions and sunny terraces. In its original form, this was a highly complex building incorporating multiple levels of streetcar tracks, passenger stations, and offices. It is now leased by Georgetown University and accommodates part of the McDonough School of Business and other functions.

The vertiginous staircase immediately to the west of the Car Barn is the one made famous in the movie *The Exorcist*—happily, it is now more commonly populated by ambitious joggers than by plunging priests.

K12 Washington Canoe Club

K Street, NW, above Key Bridge

1904 Georges P. Hales

A classic example of early twentieth-century recreational architecture, this shingle-style boathouse conjures up images of the days of full-body bathing suits and Teddy Roosevelt's vigorous outdoorsy antics. Supposedly built by the club's members using wood salvaged from derelict barns, the structure contains a large ballroom with a massive brick fireplace, and a grill room on the first floor decorated by a cartoon frieze, executed by *Evening Star* cartoonist Felix Mahony, showing early members of the Washington Canoe Club. The organization was instrumental in the establishment of flatwater canoe racing as an Olympic sport.

K13 Halcyon House (Benjamin Stoddert House)

3400 Prospect Street, NW

c. 1787 Benjamin Stoddert, owner-builder
1900–38 Various alterations and additions: Albert Adsit Clemons
1994 Renovations and additions: Stavropoulos Associates; Landscape architect: James Urban

The bizarre history of this large urban estate, one of Washington's quirkiest buildings, could warrant a book in its own right. The short version begins with Benjamin Stoddert, merchant, landowner, and America's first secretary of the navy, who built Halcyon House "after the manner of some of the elegant homes I have seen in Philadelphia," which then reigned as the American model of urban sophistication. The south façade, which actually resembles those of several other local houses as much as it does anything along the Schuylkill, remains largely intact, but the north is another matter.

Albert Adsit Clemons acquired the mansion around 1900, and soon began to alter it. Supposedly convinced that he would die if he stopped working on the house, Clemons spent nearly four decades obscuring Stoddert's chaste structure in a labyrinth of rooms, hallways, and stairs, most of which no one ever used. The peculiar results of his obsession are still visible on the north façade—note, just for starters, the mix of irregularly shaped stone and brick, the Mannerist, broken bases under the engaged columns, the vertical recesses in the brickwork between windows on the second and third floors, and the chamfered windows in the pediment. According to the *Washington Times-Herald*, Clemons subsisted on money "provided by his wife on condition that he stay away from her." That condition didn't bother Clemons, who, legend has it, was particularly fond of one of his carpenters, with whom he lived in the basement while they both worked feverishly on the upper levels.

In 1978, sculptor John Dreyfuss moved into the mansion, and during the 1980s, he and his then-wife, photographer Mary Noble Ours, removed many of Clemons's greater excesses. They also commissioned a cavernous new studio space, under a revamped rear garden, which is illuminated by large skylights made of translucent, composite panels. Though still privately owned, the house may be rented for receptions and other events.

K14   Embassy of Ukraine (Forrest-Marbury House)

3350 M Street, NW

c. 1790   Uriah Forrest, owner-builder
Numerous alterations: Architects unknown
1988   Addition: Geier Brown Renfrow Architects; Restoration: MMP International

Here, in March 1791, Georgetown Mayor Uriah Forrest gave a quite consequential dinner party, the fruit of which was the District of Columbia. At the urging of George Washington, Forrest gathered together the area's leading landowners and convinced them to sell property to the new federal government. Shortly thereafter, Forrest sold the stolid brick house and moved away from Georgetown, to lead a quieter life at Rosedale [see O19], his farm in what is now Cleveland Park.

Baltimore attorney William Marbury bought the house in 1800. (Three years later he was a party in the landmark Supreme Court case of *Marbury v. Madison*, which established the principle of judicial review.) Forrest's old house proved too small for the Marbury clan, who built a two-story addition to the east around 1840 and added a third story to the main block about a decade later. After years of neglect, the house was adapted in the late twentieth century to new use as part of the Embassy of Ukraine.

K15 Cady's Alley, NW

2004 Master plan and bridge:
Shalom Baranes Associates;
Individual buildings and stores: Sorg
and Associates, Frank Schlesinger
Associates, McInturff Architects,
Martinez & Johnson Architecture,
and Shalom Baranes Associates with
Leopold Boeckl; Landscape architects:
The Fitch Studio

Cady's Alley runs between 33rd and 34th streets just north of the C & O Canal, but the name is also used loosely to refer to a broader area containing a burgeoning collection of stores selling high-style furniture and housewares. This publicly accessible design center was the brainchild of developer Anthony Lanier, who saw the long-neglected western end of M Street as ripe for rejuvenation as a retail destination. The complex is all the more interesting because a number of different architects had a hand in the various buildings, some of which are relatively edgy for Washington. Note in particular the corrugated metal façade of 3335 Cady's Alley, and the addition on top of 1028 33rd Street at the eastern end of the alley.

K16 The Flour Mill

1000 Potomac Street, NW

1845 George Bomford, owner-builder
Numerous alterations: Architects
unknown
1980 Peter Vercelli

Mills for cotton and flour were once
fairly common near the Georgetown
waterfront, yet of the many such buildings erected hereabouts, this is the
sole survivor. Colonel George Bomford
started a cotton mill on this site in the 1840s; later owners converted that structure into a flour mill in 1866; still later owners built some additions in 1883 and some more in 1932.

Peter Vercelli used the extant structure as the base for a vast condominium complex. The serrated balconies of the new buildings contrast dramatically with the planar façades of the original structure. This is one of a number of projects in Georgetown reflecting an almost fetishistic reliance on red brick as a medium for creating buildings that are clearly modern but still seem sympathetic to their historic contexts. While the results can be a little overwhelming, the technique was usually quite successful. The vaguely threatening bollards at the corner of the plaza to the northeast of the site are inexplicable, however.

K17 Dean & Deluca (Georgetown Market)

3276 M Street, NW

1865 Architect unknown
1992 Renovation: Jack Ceglic, designer; Associated architects: Core Group

Public markets have been held on this site since the mid-eighteenth century, and in 1795, the ground was formally deeded to the town "for the use of the market aforesaid, and for no other use, interest or purpose whatsoever." The current structure, reminiscent of a small Victorian train station, dates to the Civil War era. Generations of hucksters enjoyed a brisk business in the market until chain stores rendered the independent vendors obsolete. After a period of neglect, the old building, with its round-arched windows, bracketed cornices, and central parapet, has been carefully restored and now houses a highly fashionable food store. Excellent lighting and well-maintained displays conspire to make the fresh fruit, vegetables, and other foodstuffs on view almost irresistible.

K18 Chesapeake & Ohio Canal Warehouses (Canal House/Georgetown Park Apartments)

Along the C & O Canal

c. 1828 and after Architects unknown
1977–82 Chloethiel Woodard Smith/Lockman Associates et al.

Despite having George Washington and Thomas Jefferson among its backers, the C & O Canal, which ran roughly 185 miles from Cumberland, Maryland, to Alexandria, Virginia, never enjoyed the commercial success its illustrious sponsors had anticipated. The canal, obsolete even when new, could not compete with its archrival, the Baltimore & Ohio Railroad, which easily garnered most of the lucrative Ohio Valley trade. Closed to commerce since 1923, the canal is now simply a tourist attraction and a popular venue for evening constitutionals. A passenger barge operated by the National Park Service provides a sedate amusement ride for those so inclined.

Back in the early to mid-nineteenth century, the canal carried enough traffic to warrant several large warehouses, which, over a century later, caught the eye of developers eager to address the growing interest in loft spaces for both residential and commercial purposes. These dour, muscular buildings—rare in a city nearly bereft of industrial heritage—proved readily adaptable for modern living, retail, and office use. Old and new elements, while distinguishable by virtue of their differing materials and details, are nonetheless seamlessly integrated into a coherent and vibrant whole.

K19 City Tavern

3206 M Street, NW

1796 Architect unknown
1962 Reconstruction: Macomber & Peter

During the eighteenth century, Georgetown, located on a much-traveled post road, boasted several inns and taverns. Some voyagers used these more or less reputable establishments as places to refresh themselves with a glass of ale or a spot of dinner; others sought rest in the (literally) lousy upstairs sleeping quarters. While most of the inns went out of business and were demolished as the importance of the post road declined in the nineteenth century, this one managed to endure. Rather, parts of it have endured: the upper-floor rooms are original, but the lower floor and brick façade are new and date to the building's painstaking reconstruction. The tavern now functions as a private club.

K20 Grace Church

1041 Wisconsin Avenue, NW

1867 Architect unknown
1895 Rectory: Architect unknown
1898 Parish Hall: Architect unknown

Set back on a raised and tree-shaded courtyard, this humble granite Gothic revival church, built as a mission for boatmen on the nearby Chesapeake & Ohio Canal, seems oblivious to the passage of time and the substantial development that has occurred around it. Viewed from certain angles, the property evokes images of classic New England churchyards.

K21 Waterfront Center (Dodge Center)

1010 Wisconsin Avenue, NW

1813–24 Original warehouses: Architects unknown
1975 Hartman-Cox Architects

Its angled profile mimicking the natural bluff that rises steeply from K Street (formerly known as Water Street), this office building is one of several projects offering a modern take on the industrial character of the old Georgetown waterfront. The finish brick replicates the texture of that used in surrounding historic structures, including the onetime warehouse of Francis Dodge, at the corner of Wisconsin and K, which was incorporated into the new complex. The building's soaring, open-air atrium has a Piranesian quality—its overall shape not fully intelligible, its concrete frame soaring into the mysterious upper reaches of the space. This open-air lobby recalls the raw visual power of the area's old mills and warehouses, while affording intriguing views between the various offices and circulation spaces throughout the building.

K22 Canal Square

1054 31st Street, NW

c. 1850 Architect unknown
1970 Arthur Cotton Moore/
Associates

This seminal project was among the earliest successful examples of adaptive use of antique industrial facilities for contemporary commercial purposes. The new complex incorporates an existing warehouse that was the site of a historically significant event—here, in the 1880s, the computer age arguably began when Herman Hollerith perfected his pioneering punch-card tabulating machines. In 1890, Hollerith won the right to use his new gadget to tabulate that year's census figures, and he accomplished the job in a few weeks, compared to the many months it had taken clerks to do the work in 1880. Hollerith secured several other such commissions, but in 1911 he sold his Tabulating Machine Company to an upstart firm that came to be known solely by its initials: IBM.

The Canal Square project is also notable for another reason: it included what is believed to have been the first exposed-brick-hanging-fern restaurant in the country—a typology that soon became ubiquitous.

K23 The Foundry

1055 Thomas Jefferson Street, NW

1856 Architect unknown
1977 Renovation and new
construction: Arthur Cotton Moore/
Associates; Architect of record:
Vlastimil Koubek; Landscape
architects: Sasaki Associates

William Duvall's 1856 machine shop at 1050 30th Street, which was once used as a veterinary hospital for the mules that worked the canal, inspired the design and name of this complex. The terraced plaza, for instance, designed by Sasaki Associates, suggests the old building's raked profile. This development has struggled to retain retail and entertainment-oriented tenants—its movie theaters closed a few years ago, for instance—perhaps because the spaces devoted to these uses are relatively removed from the bustle of Georgetown's main commercial corridors.

K24 Washington Harbour

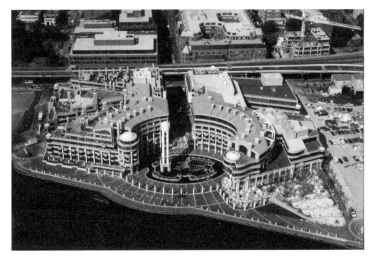

3000–3020 K Street, NW

1986 Arthur Cotton Moore/Associates

Dubbed "Xanadu on the Potomac" by the late J. Carter Brown, longtime chairman of the Commission of Fine Arts, Washington Harbour is a curious concoction of architectural motifs, which, according to the architect, refer to such diverse antecedents as the "exuberant three-dimensional vocabulary of Victorian Georgetown," the "classic, rhythmic, columnar quality" of Washington's monumental architecture, and even what he calls "Jeffersonian domes." Add to this the cartoonish metallic ornamentation that exemplifies Moore's "industrial baroque" style, and the result is visually staggering.

The mixed-use complex is, however, unquestionably successful in creating a *place*, predictably aswarm with diners, drinkers, boaters, and strollers on any remotely pleasant day. The slightly skewed, cross-shaped plan incorporates an implied continuation of Virginia Avenue (which actually dead-ends on the other side of Rock Creek), intersected by a pedestrianized extension of Thomas Jefferson Street, culminating in an oval plaza with a fountain and an idiosyncratic tower. The relative narrowness of the complex's "streets" provides a respite from the famous—and, sometimes, seemingly relentless—broad avenues of Washington. The freestanding columns that dot the perimeter of the development provide support for floodwalls that can be raised from below ground when the Potomac has one of its destructive mood swings.

K25 Four Seasons Hotel

2800 Pennsylvania Avenue, NW

1979 Skidmore, Owings & Merrill

The Four Seasons, often touted as among the best hotels in the country, stands at the primary gateway to Georgetown from central Washington, and is therefore one of the most prominent of the neoindustrial buildings hugging the steep slopes between M Street and the Potomac. This is architecture stripped bare, save for a few awnings and other limited decorative devices, that is rescued from abject banality by the texture of its brick façades and by its modestly inviting entry court. Miraculously, the minimalist brick clock tower, by virtue of its thoughtful placement and proportions, has achieved minor landmark status despite its spartan form.

K26 3001–3011 M Street, NW

c. 1789–1810 Thomas Sim Lee, Andrew Ross, and Robert Getty, owner-builders
c. 1955 Restoration: Howe, Foster and Snyder

Lee, a friend of George Washington and an ardent supporter of the patriot cause, served as a delegate to the Continental Congress and put in two terms as governor of Maryland. Like many prominent area politicians of the day, he dabbled in Washington real estate. One of his ventures involved building 3001–3003 M Street, originally a six-bay town house. Around 1805, however, Lee divided the building in two, selling one part and keeping the other. Lee's original lot extended far to the west and north. In 1810 he sold the unused land to Ross and Getty, who then built 3005–3011 M Street and 1206–1210 28th Street.

In the 1950s, after decades of neglect, developers, encouraged by Dorothea de Schweinitz and the nascent Historic Georgetown, Inc., restored the Lee-Ross-Getty houses. The developers' work—and financial success—spurred others to similar actions and may have been the single most important factor in bringing Georgetown's commercial district back to life.

K27 Old Stone House

3051 M Street, NW

1765 Christopher and Rachael Leyhman (or Layman), owner-builders
1767 Rear addition: Architect unknown
1959 Restoration: National Park Service

TEL: (202) 426-6851
www.nps.gov/olst

The aptly if unimaginatively named Old Stone House is the oldest extant structure *built in* the District (but arguably not the oldest *structure* [see P15]). Some District romantics claim that George Washington headquartered here in his surveying days; others steadfastly maintain that it was in this building that L'Enfant drew up plans for the new capital city. These and other traditional stories have been debunked, and most historians now believe that a Pennsylvania-born cabinetmaker built the simple structure to live in and to use as a shop. The narrow garden behind the house is the real star of the property.

K28 Washington Post Office, Georgetown Branch (Custom House)

1215 31st Street, NW

1858 Ammi B. Young
Numerous alterations:
Architects unknown
1997 Restoration: Sorg and
Associates

This former custom house serves as a reminder that Georgetown remained a prominent port well into the nineteenth century. The architect, a native of New Hampshire, had already designed the Vermont State Capitol (1832) and the Boston Custom House (1837) when the federal government called him to Washington in 1852 and made him supervising architect of the Treasury. In that capacity Young designed this impressively solid Italianate building with granite walls and trim.

K29 Wheatley Houses

3041–3043 N Street, NW

1859 Francis Wheatley, builder
Various alterations: Architects
unknown

This mirror-image pair combines the flat façades more typical of Federal row houses with details that reveal their true Victorian character—tall, narrow parlor windows, sinuous and organic cast iron window heads, and strongly rhythmic decoration on the cornices. By placing the first floor well above street level, Wheatley could drop the windows on that level to the floor and still preserve privacy for the rooms inside. Note the service entrance, suitable for hobbits, between the two houses.

K30 Laird-Dunlop House

3014 N Street, NW

1799 Original (central) section:
Attributed to William Lovering
Various additions and alterations:
Architects unknown

In the 1990s, German automaker BMW
used a block of N Street in Georgetown
as the backdrop for a series of ads for
one of its most luxurious models, el-
evating the street to iconic status as
a province of the wealthy. Exuding class and unimpeachable taste, the
street is lined with quietly elegant row houses such as this storied residence.

The inset, arched windows on the main floor of this house were unusual during the Federal period, though Lovering, a self-trained amateur
architect, used a similar motif on the Law House in Southwest. Thanks
to slight setbacks and changes in height, the additions mimic the scale
and rhythm of separate row houses, and thus disguise the true bulk of this
mansion. John Laird, a wealthy tobacco merchant, built the original house.
It later passed to his daughter, Barbara, and son-in-law, James Dunlop, a
judge whose Confederate sympathies led to his ouster by President Lincoln. Ironically, a subsequent owner was none other than Robert Todd Lincoln, Honest Abe's only surviving son. The most recent famous occupants
are former *Washington Post* editor Ben Bradlee and author Sally Quinn.

K31 Foxall House

2908 N Street, NW

c. 1820 Henry Foxall, owner-
builder
Various additions and
alterations: Architects
unknown

Dwarfed by its three-story
neighbors, this small three-bay
residence with a rare, wall-enclosed entry court has been much expanded. Foxall, who owned a thriving munitions foundry on the western outskirts of Georgetown and briefly served as the city's mayor, has

gained immortality (and an *h*) thanks to the twentieth-century suburban neighborhood that sprawls over the family farm just west of Georgetown University [see Tour Q: Foxhall].

K32 Susan Decatur House

2812 N Street, NW

c. 1779 Architect unknown
Various alterations: Architects unknown

The date of this house's original con-struction is unclear—various sources indicate that it was anywhere from 1779 to 1813. At any rate, it is a quintessen-tial Georgetown Federal house, with its well-articulated doorway, planar façade, and simple staircase that seems to leap toward the entry. Stephen Deca-tur's widow, Susan, moved here from Lafayette Square after he was killed on the dueling field in 1820.

K33 Trentman House

1350 27th Street, NW

1968 Hugh Newell Jacobsen

Jacobsen is best known for his abstract, freestanding houses—assemblages of white pavilions whose simple, iconic shapes remind some people of Monop-oly houses. In historic settings, how-ever, Jacobsen tended to pursue a more contextualist path. Acknowledging, but not quite replicating, the scale, color, and certain compositional elements of classic Federal row houses, the Trentman House is clearly modern, with sleek bay windows popping out from frames of highly unusual curved bricks.

K34 Mount Zion United Methodist Church

1334 29th Street, NW

1884 Architect unknown
1904 Alterations and addition:
Architect unknown

The area of Georgetown east of 29th Street and below P was once a predominantly African American neighborhood known as Herring Hill. Mount Zion, believed to have been the first organized African American congregation in the District of Columbia, was a major fixture of the community. The original church, built around 1816, actually stood on 27th Street above P, and served as a station on the Underground Railroad. This larger brick structure, built after the old church was destroyed by fire, bears a sober brick façade, but the sanctuary contains a rather elaborate stamped metal ceiling.

K35 Christ Church

31st and O streets, NW

1887 Cassell & Laws/Henry Laws
1923 Addition: Architect unknown
1968 Chapel of St. Jude: Philip Ives
2003 Interior restoration: STUDIOS

With its acutely angled gables and almost skeletal tower, this church suggests a Gothic cathedral rendered in miniature and in dark red, pressed brick rather than stone. Note the sharp right triangle implied by the overall composition of forms along the O Street side. Inside, the ceiling is supported by exposed scissor trusses.

K36 The National Society of the Colonial Dames of America (Dumbarton House)

2715 Q Street, NW

c. 1800 Samuel Jackson, owner-builder
1805 Alterations: Attributed to Benjamin Henry Latrobe
1915 Moved to present site
1931 Restoration: Horace W. Peaslee and Fiske Kimball
1991 Renovation: Martin Rosenblum

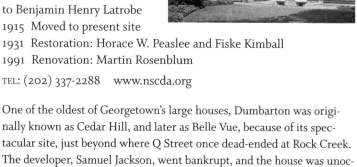

TEL: (202) 337-2288   www.nscda.org

One of the oldest of Georgetown's large houses, Dumbarton was originally known as Cedar Hill, and later as Belle Vue, because of its spectacular site, just beyond where Q Street once dead-ended at Rock Creek. The developer, Samuel Jackson, went bankrupt, and the house was unoccupied until Joseph Nourse, the first person to hold the position of register of the U.S. Treasury, bought it in 1804. It is believed that Latrobe had a hand in adding the portico and gently curving rear bays not long after Nourse moved in.

The origin of the Dumbarton name is convoluted. In 1703, Ninian Beall, a Scot who had been taken prisoner by Oliver Cromwell in the Battle of Dunbar in 1650, obtained a "patent" for a large tract of land in what is now Georgetown. He named the estate "Rock of Dunbarton" (sometimes rendered as "Dunbar-ton"), a wry reference to his defeat many years earlier, but also a bit of a pun, referring to the famous Dumbarton (with an *m*) Rock, a castle in Scotland.

Demolition of Dumbarton House seemed imminent in 1915, when the District government unveiled plans to extend Q Street into Georgetown across the new Buffalo Bridge. Preservationists managed to save the building and move it about a hundred feet to its present location. The National Society of the Colonial Dames of America, an organization dedicated to historic preservation and education, bought the house in 1928 to serve as its headquarters. The society soon undertook a restoration to remove Georgian appliqués, such as stone quoins at the corners of the house, which had been added in the early twentieth century. A more recent renovation added modern services and various facilities to meet the organization's needs.

K37 R. E. Lee House

2813 Q Street, NW

c. 1890 Architect unknown
1959 Addition: Hugh Newell Jacobsen

The original late nineteenth-century structure, the western half of this much-expanded house, proved too small for Lee, its mid-twentieth-century owner, and Jacobsen was brought in to oversee enlargements. Georgetown's large and vocal aesthetic rear guard was up in arms when the addition was announced, but Jacobsen's subdued modern solution won many converts after the fact. New window sashes and other contemporary exterior details clearly declare the finished house's modernity without unduly competing with the existing structure's Victorian character.

K38 Francis Dodge House

1517 30th Street, NW

1853 Andrew Jackson Downing and Calvert Vaux
Various alterations: Architects unknown

One of a pair of houses designed for the Dodge brothers, Francis and Robert, this grand residence, although significantly altered, remains a textbook example of Victorian Italianate design. (Robert's house stands at 1534 28th Street, at the corner of Q.) Vaux described both dwellings at length in his *Villas and Cottages* (1857). He lumped them together as "Design No. 17, 'Suburban Villa,'" but accurately noted that "although these two houses have their principal features in common, neither is a servile imitation of the other." Vaux also quoted an 1854 letter from Francis Dodge in which the client complained that the cost, $15,000, was "much beyond what Mr. Downing led us to expect." Dodge admitted, however, that the resulting products were "fine houses . . . very comfortable and satisfactory in every respect."

K39 Cooke's Row

3007–3029 Q Street, NW

1868 Starkweather and Plowman
Numerous alterations and additions:
Architects unknown

This parade of picturesque duplexes hints at the stylistic promiscuity of the Victorian era, while dramatically refuting the notion of Georgetown as solely an enclave of Federal architecture. The row's two end units are exuberantly Second Empire, while the middle two are equally elaborately Italianate. All four structures sport some of the most audacious brackets in the city, but the ones at 3007 and 3009 deserve particular note.

K40 Tudor Place

1644 31st Street, NW

1795 Architect unknown
1805–16 Addition and renovation: William Thornton
1914 Renovation: Walter Gibson Peter

TEL: (202) 965-0400   www.tudorplace.org

Tudor Place—William Thornton's masterpiece—marks a significant break with the Georgian architecture of the preceding generation as represented by the Bowie-Sevier House, directly across Q Street. Dressed in pale yellow stucco, with extensive wings and a domed, Tempietto-like porch, the finished house anticipated the stately demeanor of the Capitol itself, decades before the seat of government finally achieved its quintessential form.

Like the Capitol, Tudor Place began ingloriously as a pair of wings with no connecting body. Then, in 1805, these stubs and the eight-and-a-half-acre property on which they stood were bought by Thomas Peter

and Martha Custis Peter, granddaughter of Martha Washington, using $8,000 left to Mrs. Peter by her step-grandfather George. The Peters hired Thornton to remodel the wings and design the central connecting piece. The house is linear in plan, with the public rooms marching along the south side of the ground floor, and circulation and service spaces lining the north side. The engaged porch, which is a full circle in plan, leads to the saloon, a curious room given the convex arc that projects into the space. Huge windows in the arc can be lifted up into a hidden pocket above, creating a doorway through which guests once entered.

Incredibly, Tudor Place was continuously occupied by six generations of the Peter family over the course of more than 180 years. It is now a museum boasting extensive collections of art objects and household items, as well as meticulously maintained gardens. Martha Peter planted some of the Old Blush roses and the boxwood parterre, and her direct descendants added specimen trees and other features. Both house and gardens provide unparalleled insights into the evolution of domestic life in Washington in its first two centuries.

K41 Scott-Grant House

3240 R Street, NW

1857 A. V. Scott, owner-builder

1907, 1930 Alterations: Architects unknown

Representative of the gracious, freestanding estates that give the northern end of Georgetown its genteel suburban character, this highly formal house is loosened up by relatively florid decorative elements. Alabaman A. V. Scott, who built the place, had no use for it during the Civil War and leased it to a variety of tenants. General Ulysses S. Grant himself rented it during at least one summer, hence the second half of the house's name, but the most memorable lessee may have been General Henry Walker Halleck. He earned the enmity of his neighbors by quartering enlisted men in the house, turning R Street into a drill field, and having the company bugler sound taps and reveille at dusk and dawn each day.

K42 Dumbarton Oaks

3101 R Street, NW

1801 William Hammond Dorsey, owner-builder

c. 1865 Alterations: Edward Linthicum, owner

1922–59 Landscape architecture: Beatrix Farrand

1923 Alterations: Frederick H. Brooke

1929 Music room: Lawrence White/McKim, Mead & White

1938–46 Byzantine wing and other additions: Thomas T. Waterman

1963 Garden library: Frederick Rhinelander King

1989 Museum addition: Hartman-Cox Architects

1995 Pool renovation: Richard Williams Architect

2005 Library: Venturi Scott Brown Associates

TEL: (202) 339-6401   www.doaks.org

The house at Dumbarton Oaks has been so altered and extended that little of the original architecture is visible, but it remains a building of great character. Robert and Mildred Bliss (stepbrother and -sister, unrelated by blood, who were raised together and later married) acquired the house and fifty-three acres in 1920 and proceeded to change the already much-altered dwelling to accommodate their exceptional collections of Byzantine and pre-Columbian art. They also set to work on the gardens. The Blisses decided to keep as wilderness twenty-seven acres to the north of the house, the present Dumbarton Oaks Park, but wanted more formal gardens around the house. Beatrix Farrand's ten acres of terraced gardens with "garden rooms" are an undisputed masterpiece of American landscape architecture and the summation of her distinguished career. Her Dumbarton work captures her spirit of romance: she once wrote to the Blisses about a patch of woods near the music room, urging them "to keep it as poetic as possible . . . the sort of place in which thrushes sing and . . . dreams are dreamt."

The Blisses, whose wealth derived from their family's ownership of the patent for Fletcher's Castoria, a children's medicine, moved to California in 1940 and gave the bulk of Dumbarton Oaks to Harvard University (they sold the back part of the estate to the Danish government for a new embassy). Before heading west, Mrs. Bliss asked Farrand to draw up some maintenance guidelines for the grounds. Farrand complied and urged the university always to respect the dual nature of the property: on one hand it offers "a pleasant sense of withdrawal from the nearby streets"; on the other it allows "an intimate connection with all that a great city can offer."

Between August and October 1944, the estate was the site of a series of meetings collectively known as the Dumbarton Oaks Conference, in which senior representatives of the United States, Great Britain, Russia, and China lay the organizational groundwork for the United Nations.

K42A Pre-Columbian Museum

Dumbarton Oaks
Enter through 1703 32nd
Street, NW

1963 Philip Johnson

In a long but erratic career, which on the one hand produced the sublime Glass House in New Canaan, Connecticut, but also yielded a series of utterly fatuous postmodern skyscrapers, Philip Johnson has produced a few masterpieces. The Pre-Columbian Museum is among them.

It was the 1960s, and the idea of appending an abstract molecule of little pavilions made of marble, teak, bronze, and glass to a huge, historic brick mansion was less surprising than it would be now. For the visitor who can set aside any preconceptions about such a juxtaposition, this gem of a museum is a wondrous building to experience. In plan, it is rather like a tic-tac-toe board in which the perimeter spaces are filled with O's that have melted together and completely overtaken the grid. Eight domed exhibition pods surround a central, open court with a pool. Each pavilion is itself defined by a constellation of round columns, subtly recapitulating the larger organization of the structure. Despite its heavy classical and Byzantine undertones, this was the only Washington building to be included in the Museum of Modern Art's landmark 1977 survey exhibition of modern architecture.

K43 Montrose Park and Lovers Lane

3001 R Street, NW

This popular spot for dog-walkers occupies land that in the early nineteenth century was owned by rope-making magnate Richard Parrott, a neighborly gent who allowed Georgetown's citizens to use the tract for picnics and meetings. By the early twentieth century, Parrott's Woods, as it was then called, had grown rather scruffy; so a group of public-spirited women, headed by Sarah Louisa Rittenhouse, goaded Congress to buy the acreage and establish Montrose Park "for the recreation and pleasure of the people." Lovers Lane separates the park from the more formal gardens of Dumbarton Oaks.

K44 Oak Hill Cemetery

30th and R streets, NW

1833 Van Ness Mausoleum:
George Hadfield
1850 Chapel: James Renwick Jr.
c. 1853 Gatehouse: George de la
Roche
1872 Van Ness Mausoleum moved
from original site on H Street, NW

Laid out in a fashionably romantic
manner over four natural terraces, Oak
Hill Cemetery was chartered by Congress in 1849 on land donated by
banker and philanthropist William Corcoran. Local luminaries interred
here include architect Adolf Cluss, politico James G. Blaine, and Corcoran himself.

The Italianate gatehouse, by George de la Roche, who also designed
the overall cemetery plan, is of brick with red sandstone accents. Inside
the grounds, but visible from the street, is Renwick's impeccable little
Gothic revival chapel—a giant paperweight in local Potomac gneiss and
sandstone. Hadfield's design for the monument to the Van Ness family was
based on the ancient Temple of Vesta in Rome. Although it seems perfectly
at home perched on the cemetery's eastern hill, the mausoleum originally
stood on the family's private burial grounds at 10th and M, and it was later
moved to this site.

During much of its first century, Washington was generally a scruffy and inconsistently developed town with a few monumental buildings that stood out like ermine-clad royalty among the mud-soaked peasants. That began to change—slowly—in the 1870s with Boss Shepherd's highly successful but fiscally disastrous public works campaign. The city soon began to show a few more signs of architectural maturity and sophistication, and by the 1890s, to the astonishment of the upper classes everywhere, Washington was becoming a fashionable place for the wealthy—especially the newly wealthy—to hobnob, throw fabulous parties, and build immense mansions.

Around the turn of the twentieth century, more than a hundred grand residences sprang up along Massachusetts and Connecticut avenues and

Dupont Circle in the mid-1920s, after the original statue of Admiral Samuel Francis du Pont had been replaced with the more impressive fountain by sculptor Daniel Chester French and architect Henry Bacon (the same team responsible for the Lincoln Memorial). The Patterson House (now the Washington Club) is visible at the middle left. The large house at right was the mansion of dry-goods magnate Levi Leiter. It was demolished in 1947 to make way for what is now the Jurys Hotel.

on Dupont Circle itself, making this once-quiet section of the city suddenly the rival of New York's Fifth Avenue as *the* place in the nation to live. Perhaps Henry Adams was thinking of this trend when he wrote in 1904: "The American wasted money more recklessly than any one did before; he spent more to less purpose than any extravagant court aristocracy; he had no sense of relative values, and knew not what to do with his money when he got it, except to use it to make more, or throw it away." Later, the Dupont Circle phenomenon prompted Phillip Wylie to use his 1942 book, *Generation of Vipers*, to attack "every sullen, rococo, snarling, sick, noxious and absurd form of vainglorious house . . . [built here] to assuage the cheap pretensions of the middle class and the Middle West."

The evolution of the park in the circle itself reflects the broader trends in the neighborhood during that period. In 1882 Congress decided to commemorate Admiral Samuel Francis du Pont, a Civil War naval hero, by naming this new circle for him (the area had been known as "The Slashes") and by placing a small bronze statue of him in the center. That wasn't enough for the du Ponts, who, in good Gilded Age style, decided to circumvent the federal government by directly hiring the team that gave the city the Lincoln Memorial—architect Henry Bacon and sculptor Daniel Chester French—to build the present, far grander, Dupont memorial.

The Great Depression obliterated much of the wealth that had made all of this possible, and when World War II came, many of the grand mansions were lent, sold, or donated to governmental and other agencies to aid the war effort. By the 1950s, a number of the buildings here had been converted to boarding houses. The riots of the late 1960s along the nearby 14th Street corridor triggered a further decline in property values, but at the same time, the circle itself and some nearby buildings were becoming popular with hippies, artists, and other alternative types that the decade produced in abundance. Soon the area was recognized as a historic district, and, repeating a pattern common to analogous areas in so many American cities, gay men and lesbians began to move here in large numbers, leading a wave of renovation. Over the past generation, the Dupont Circle neighborhood has blossomed once again, becoming one of the most vibrant residential areas in the country, attracting new residents including young families, and boasting housing prices that suggest the arrival of a new Gilded Age.

L1 Dupont Circle Building

1350 Connecticut Avenue, NW

1931 Mihran Mesrobian
1942 Conversion from apartments to
offices: Architects unknown
1987 Renovation: Oldham and Seltz

The genius of this wedge-shaped structure lies in its masterful bas-relief ornament, which lends visual depth and
rhythm to the main façades, but keeps
the profile of the building taut and planar so as not to distract from its
apparent geometrical purity when viewed on end. In this regard, it out-
does New York's famous Flatiron Building, which has a heavily sculpted
skin that somewhat diminishes the drama of its acutely angled form.
Another notable element of the Dupont Circle Building is its stepped
mechanical penthouse—a technical necessity that Mesrobian turned
into an architectural asset.

L2 1818 N Street, NW

1984 David M. Schwarz/
Architectural Services;
Associated architect:
Vlastimil Koubek

Since John Carl Warnecke's
project for Lafayette Square set
a Washington precedent for pre-
serving low-rise structures and
adding taller buildings behind
them, local architects have experimented with numerous variations on
that theme. This complex on a narrow block of N Street represents a hybrid approach—in its materials, gabled forms, and stepped massing, the
newly constructed portion is deferential to the existing row houses, but
stops well short of replicating their decorative motifs or other historical
details. As a result, unlike numerous other examples of the genre, the
new high-rise structure successfully assumes a "background" quality.

L3 Sunderland Building

1320 19th Street, NW

1969 Keyes, Lethbridge & Condon,
Architects

This relatively small office building is
an intriguing geometrical exercise. The
façades of the rectilinear structure are
each animated by several asymmetrical
design gestures: first, the exterior columns (some of which house ventilation
ducts, rather than structural supports)
are flared on just one side of each vertical slit window; second, the regular grid of these slit windows on the second through seventh floors is interrupted by a large blank panel to the right; and third, on the top floor,
the pattern of solid and void is switched, with a large expanse of glass to
the right, and a smaller blank panel to the left. Taken together, the four
virtually identical façades thus create a dynamic composition suggesting
rotational movement.

L4 Christian Heurich House Museum (The Brewmaster's Castle)

1307 New Hampshire Avenue, NW

1894 John Granville Myers; Interiors:
Charles H. and Hugo F. Huber
1914 Addition: Appleton P. Clark

TEL: (202) 429-1894
www.heurichhouse.org

Knotty and lugubrious, the Heurich
House is an example of what histo-
rian Richard Howland dubbed "beer-barrel baronial" grandeur. Its New
Hampshire Avenue façade, made of dark, rough sandstone, is punctuated
by a chunky *porte cochere* bristling with gargoyles. Around the corner on
Sunderland Place, a somewhat less intimidating brick, terra cotta, and
sandstone façade ends with a copper-and-glass conservatory, the delicacy
and bright green patina of which contrast sharply with the main body of
the house. Supporting all of the robust masonry is a structure that was

innovative in its day—the first significant use of reinforced concrete in a residential building in the United States.

The shadowy interiors, intact and original, attest to the extravagant taste of the house's builder, Christian Heurich, a German immigrant who became a highly successful brewer and, at one time, the second largest landowner in the nation's capital, after the federal government. Heurich, whose company's slogan was "Beer recommended for family use by Physicians in General," made no bones about acknowledging the source of his wealth. The breakfast room in the basement is a case in point. Its walls are covered with murals depicting the virtues of beer-drinking interspersed with aphorisms such as "Raum ist in der kleinsten Kammer für den grossten Katzenjammer" ("There is room in the smallest chamber for the biggest hangover"). Clearly, Heurich, who actively managed the business until his death at the age of 102, loved his work.

Heurich's widow donated the house to the organization now known as the Historical Society of Washington, D.C. When the society moved to the new City Museum in Mount Vernon Square in 2003, two of Heurich's grandchildren bought the house back and formed a foundation to preserve it as a museum, to which they have now applied the regrettable, Disneyesque moniker "The Brewmaster's Castle."

L5 21 Dupont Circle, NW (Euram Building)

1971 Hartman-Cox Architects

All too often, a project that begins as an elegantly simple architectural diagram, when finally realized in three dimensions, lacks the purity and clarity of the initial concept. This modestly scaled building is a brilliant exception. Structurally, 21 Dupont Circle is composed of a series of post-tensioned concrete bridges, spanning between unadorned brick-clad piers at the corners of the site, and surrounding an open courtyard. The resulting office spaces are narrow and column-free, affording all tenants access to urban views and plenty of natural light. The principal façades neatly express the essential structural scheme, thanks in large part to the bands of floor-to-ceiling, mullion-less windows, which allow the bridge-like concrete beams to be read clearly.

L6 Blaine Mansion

2000 Massachusetts Avenue, NW

1882 John Fraser
1921 Renovation and additions:
George N. Ray
1949 Conversion to office use:
Maurice S. May

This brooding and grim mansion is the last of several dark brick Victorian structures that once loomed near Dupont Circle, and today it stands in apparent disapproval of the neighborhood's commercial bustle. The house was built for James G. Blaine, a man known to his friends as "the Plumed Knight of American Politics" and to his enemies as "Slippery Jim." One of the founders of the Republican Party, Blaine held a number of important posts, including Speaker of the House and secretary of state, and thrice ran unsuccessfully for the presidency. Soon after this house was finished, Blaine decided that it was too expensive to maintain, and leased it to some of his more cash-laden contemporaries, such as Levi Leiter, an early partner of Marshall Field, and George Westinghouse, whose surname speaks for itself. Westinghouse bought the place outright in 1901 and lived here until his death in 1914.

John Fraser, a former partner of the great Philadelphia architect Frank Furness, originally designed the house for a different site, which helps to explain its rather incidental relationship to adjacent streets. The one-story addition along P Street, dating from a 1921 renovation, is an unwelcome appendage, but the house has also suffered a few amputations. The west façade once bore a porch "commanding the gorgeous sunsets known to this latitude," according to one biography of Blaine. The mansion's roofscape was initially even craggier than it is now, but the bulbous caps that once crowned its chimneys were lopped off in 1944 following the discovery of alarming cracks.

L7 Embassy of Indonesia (Walsh-McLean House)

2020 Massachusetts Avenue, NW

1903 Henry Andersen
1952 Renovations: Architect unknown
1982 Addition: The Architects Collaborative

TEL: (202) 775-5306

In 1869, an Irish teenager named Thomas Walsh came to the United States to seek his fortune, and seven years later he found it during the Black Hills Gold Rush. He then struck it richer, as it were, when he bought the Camp Bird Mine, which was marked by one of the thickest veins of gold in the world (he later sold the mine for the then-impressive sum of $3 million plus a percentage of future yields). Obscenely rich, he moved his family to Washington in 1897 with the goal of joining "society."

Walsh quickly realized that one of the most important instruments of social status was an impressive mansion, so he commissioned this sixty-room extravaganza, and proudly embedded a slab of gold ore into the front porch to proclaim the source of his wealth. The house is organized around a three-story, galleried Art Nouveau stairwell that was copied from one of Walsh's favorite White Star ocean liners. The exterior, with its undulating walls, rounded corners, and even curving chimneys, defies stylistic nomenclature, but could be described generically and with some understatement as "neo-Baroque." "Baroque" also describes Walsh's lifestyle: at one New Year's Eve party, reported *The New York Times,* his 325 celebratory guests downed 288 fifths of scotch, 480 quarts of champagne, 40 gallons of beer, 35 bottles of miscellaneous liqueurs, and 48 "quarts of cocktails."

Walsh later grew reclusive, and in 1910 he died in virtual isolation. His daughter Evalyn inherited the house but refused to move into it, stating, "it was cold, but its deepest chill lodged in my breast." She married publishing heir Edward Beale McLean (his family owned the *Post*), and the pair lived lavishly at their estate on Wisconsin Avenue. According to James Goode's *Capital Losses,* the pair "managed to dissipate almost all of the vast McLean and Walsh fortunes, amounting to 100 million dollars." (She "dissipated" a portion of the money when she bought the Hope Diamond.) The Indonesian government purchased the Massachusetts Avenue mansion in 1951 for $335,000—a fraction of its original cost—and later added a new wing with a curving façade echoing the fluid form, but not the quirky character, of the exuberant main house.

L8 The Society of the Cincinnati Headquarters Library and Museum (Anderson House)

2118 Massachusetts Avenue, NW

1905 Little and Browne
1997 Exterior restoration and interior alterations: Archetype

TEL: (202) 785-2040
www.thesocietyofthecincinnati.addr.com

This is one of several grand residences in Washington—the Kreeger house in Foxhall being a more modern version—designed from the start for conversion to quasi-civic purposes following their owners' demise. Career diplomat Larz Anderson III and his heiress wife, Isabel Weld Perkins, commissioned the neo-English Baroque palace with the intention of giving it to the Society of the Cincinnati, a hereditary membership organization founded by a group of Revolutionary War officers. The society took its name from Lucius Quinctius Cincinnatus, a Roman "civilian general," who humbly returned to his farm after each of two victorious military campaigns. He was therefore seen as a parallel to America's own nonprofessional military hero, George Washington, who somewhat reluctantly agreed to become the society's first "president general," despite the objections of contemporary politicians who feared that it represented the beginnings of an American aristocracy.

The house's arched gateways and stately forecourt are highly unusual in Washington, and suggest the presumption that all visitors would arrive by carriage rather than on foot. Huge lanterns, suspended from curved iron armatures, hang just inside the archways. The mansion's cavernous interior, which is open to the public as a museum, is eclectically decorated, to say the least. Notable items on display include a set of Brussels tapestries originally woven as a gift of Louis XIII to Cardinal Barberini, papal representative at the French court. The premier space is the ballroom on the first floor, which boasts an astonishing cantilevered staircase leading to a musicians' balcony supported by spiral, red Verona marble columns. The building also houses a library notable for its eigh-teenth-century military history collections.

L9 Phillips Collection

1600 21st Street, NW

1897 Hornblower & Marshall
1907 Music Room:
Hornblower & Marshall
1920 Second-floor addition:
McKim, Mead & White
1923 Fourth floor: Frederick
H. Brooke
1960 Original annex: Wyeth
& King

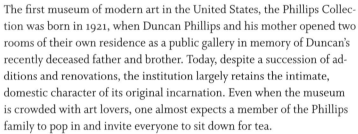

1989 Renovations and addition: Arthur Cotton Moore/Associates
2006 Addition and renovation: Cox Graae + Spack Architects

TEL: (202) 387-2151   www.phillipscollection.org

The first museum of modern art in the United States, the Phillips Collec-tion was born in 1921, when Duncan Phillips and his mother opened two rooms of their own residence as a public gallery in memory of Duncan's recently deceased father and brother. Today, despite a succession of ad-ditions and renovations, the institution largely retains the intimate, domestic character of its original incarnation. Even when the museum is crowded with art lovers, one almost expects a member of the Phillips family to pop in and invite everyone to sit down for tea.

The Phillips Collection, which is best known for its Impressionist and Post-Impressionist paintings, was actually conceived as a museum of "modern art and its sources," reflecting Duncan's interest in both contemporary art and past works that he considered to be important antecedents. An heir to the Jones and Laughlin steel fortune, Duncan developed his avocation early on—while still an undergraduate he wrote an article titled "The Need of Art at Yale," and he called his first book, published when he was twenty-eight, *The Enchantment of Art*. His wife, Marjorie, was a well-regarded painter in her own right.

The original mansion is a subdued, mildly eclectic affair, combining Georgian and Federal elements, and even a hint of Art Nouveau, in the decoration on the columns and frieze of the entrance bay. The house was modestly expanded several times in the early twentieth century, and the mansarded fourth floor was added to provide more living space after the initial rooms were opened to the public. By 1930, the collection had grown so large that the family had to move out entirely.

The original annex, as completed in 1960, was a necessary but uninspired addition, lending a more institutional tone to the complex. In 1989, the annex was thoroughly revamped to make it more compatible with the older structures and a more commodious setting for art in its own right. Yet another renovation of the complex, including the incorporation of an existing apartment building to the north, was recently completed.

L10 Cosmos Club (Townsend House)

2121 Massachusetts Avenue, NW

1901, 1904 Carrère & Hastings;
Landscape architect: Frederick Law
Olmsted Jr. (Olmsted Brothers)
1909 2164 Florida Avenue: Speiden
& Speiden Architects
1952 Alterations: Horace W. Peaslee
1962 Alterations and addition:
Frank W. Cole
1997 Renovation of 2164 Florida
Avenue (Hillyer House): O'Neil &
Manion Architects

Railroad money lay behind this entry to the unspoken contest to build the grandest house in turn-of-the-twentieth-century Washington. Richard Townsend's fortune came from the Erie Line and Mary Scott Townsend's from the Pennsylvania. The couple pooled their immense wealth and told Carrère and Hastings that they wanted a Washington chateau based on the Petit Trianon, an apt choice, given the New York architects' predilection for things French. The Townsends had the new house built around an older one, because a gypsy had once predicted that Mrs. Townsend was destined to die "under a new roof."

The couple's daughter, Mathilde, inherited the house in 1935; she had married Sumner Welles, a diplomat who played several crucial roles in FDR's administration. The prestigious and exclusive Cosmos Club acquired the property in 1950. In adapting the place for its new use, Peaslee had to take away much of the original landscaping—parking lots do take up room—but he was able to maintain surprisingly large sweeps of Carrère's interiors. Thus, the original structure, largely intact, forms a veritable museum of railroad-financed, Gilded Age grandeur.

L11 1718 Connecticut Avenue, NW

1982 David M. Schwarz/
Architectural Services

An architectural Jekyll and Hyde
(which is which depends on the viewer's own stylistic proclivities), this
retail and office building is fancifully
neo-Romanesque in front and no-nonsense International Style in back. A
bold diagonal line, best observed from
a vantage point a few blocks up Connecticut Avenue, strikingly cleaves the
two halves of the building. Although obviously more deliberate in this
case, the dichotomy evokes that of many historic Washington row houses
and commercial structures, which were often built with relatively ornate
fronts and quite plain rear façades.

L12 Woman's National Democratic Club (Whittemore House)

1526 New Hampshire Avenue,
NW

1894 Harvey L. Page
1967 Addition: Nicholas
Satterlee

A great cape of a roof—punc-
tuated by an occasional raised eyelid window—drapes languidly over
this spectacular mansion. Sarah Adams Wilcox Whittemore, a cousin of
Henry Adams, commissioned the house, whose modest entrance is partially sheltered by an overhanging, copper-and-leaded-glass bay window.
A parade of rather simple and serviceable brackets remarkably turns the
roof gutter into a substantive architectural element. Now the headquarters of the Woman's National Democratic Club, the building contains a
small museum of political memorabilia, including items pertaining to
Eleanor Roosevelt, a club member who, when she became First Lady,
used the organization as a vehicle to advance her social agenda. A starkly
contrasting, rough concrete addition houses event spaces and peripheral
functions.

L13 The Washington Club (Patterson House)

15 Dupont Circle, NW

1903 McKim, Mead and
White (Stanford White)
1951–56 Alterations and
addition: Architects unknown
1985 Restoration: Oehrlein &
Associates Architects

Designed by Stanford White for Robert Wilson Patterson, publisher of the *Chicago Tribune,* this palazzo appears extremely grand from Dupont Circle, but assumes a surprising intimacy up close thanks to its tiny forecourt defined by the two wings and angled entry connecting them. Lavishly iced with swags, fruit, and other sundries, the glazed terra cotta façades are further decorated with flat panels of variegated marble, which abstractly suggest framed paintings. This same variegated marble appears on the columns of the central porch, which became famous in 1927 when Charles Lindbergh, freshly returned from his daring flight across the Atlantic, was photographed there waving to crowds below. (Lindbergh was visiting President and Mrs. Calvin Coolidge, who were living at the Patterson mansion temporarily while their own White House was undergoing renovation.)

The most famous Patterson to live in the house was not Robert, but his redoubtable and scandal-prone daughter, "Cissy," who worked her way up through the family publishing business and ultimately purchased two newspapers that she combined to create *The Washington Times-Herald.* Briefly a countess by marriage, Cissy was a vociferous opponent of Franklin Roosevelt, and she used the medium at her disposal to disseminate a blizzard of highly sensational "news" that made her the bête noire of official Washington. "The trouble with me," she once said, "is that I am a vindictive old shanty-Irish bitch." Cissy's death in 1948 marked the end of a feverish era in the capital's social life. She left the building to the Red Cross, which sold it to the Washington Club in 1951.

L14 Embassy of Iraq (Boardman House)

1801 P Street, NW

1893 Hornblower & Marshall
Numerous alterations:
Architects unknown

Tricks with bricks—such as
the splayed jack arches over
the windows and the eccen-
tric, zigzag frieze between the first and second floors—help to animate
this otherwise stolid neo-Romanesque block. Also noteworthy are the
balustrades along the top of the bay window and on the small balcony
above, comprising rows of tiny Ionic columns. Curiously, the house's
most elaborate decorative element, a beautiful mosaic, is tucked under
the entry arch, where, on a sunny day, it is sometimes almost invisible in
the shadows. Mabel Boardman, the house's most notable occupant, was
well known for her work with the Red Cross. Boardman also cofounded
the Sulgrave Club, whose members met here until 1932, when they were
able to buy and remodel their present building across the street. Now,
after more than a decade of disuse between the two Persian Gulf wars,
this house serves once again as the Iraqi Embassy.

L15 Sulgrave Club (Wadsworth House)

1801 Massachusetts Avenue, NW

1901 George Cary
1932 Remodeling: Frederick H.
Brooke
1952 Alterations: Architect unknown

When built, this was a drive-through
house, incorporating an unusual *porte
cochere* running from what is currently
the main entrance on Massachusetts
Avenue all the way through to P Street. The residence was commissioned by Herbert Wadsworth, an engineer who also owned vast farms
in the Finger Lakes region of New York State, and his wife, Martha. During World War I, the Wadsworths turned the entire house over to the
Red Cross. In 1932, it was sold to a small group of women who formed a

private club named for George Washington's ancestral home in England, Sulgrave Manor. Architect Brooke, hired to convert the house to club use, also worked as the local consulting architect for Lutyens's British Embassy on Massachusetts Avenue.

L16 National Trust for Historic Preservation (McCormick Apartments)

1785 Massachusetts Avenue, NW

1917 Jules Henri de Sibour
1941–50 Interior alterations: Architect unknown
1979 Restoration/renovation: Yerkes, Pappas and Parker

TEL: (202) 588-6000
www.nationaltrust.org

The most assured and sophisticated of the numerous Beaux-Arts buildings in Dupont Circle, the current headquarters of the National Trust for Historic Preservation would be perfectly at home in the eighth *arrondissement* of Paris. Incredibly, the elegant structure was commissioned as a rental apartment building, albeit one with only six units. Full-floor apartments, each measuring a total of 11,000 square feet spread over twenty-five rooms, occupied the second through fifth floors. Residents included some of the wealthiest and most glamorous figures in the country.

The building was designed by the mellifluously named Jules Henri de Sibour. A descendant of French royalty, de Sibour arrived in Washington around 1900 following study at the famed École des Beaux-Arts. His client for this building was Katharine Dexter McCormick, whose husband was Stanley McCormick, son of Cyrus and heir to the International Harvester fortune. Stanley wanted to build "the most luxurious apartment house in Washington," but became incapacitated by mental illness before work on the project began. (Katharine became famous herself as a supporter of Margaret Sanger, and single-handedly funded the vast majority of research that led to the development of the birth control pill.)

The McCormick Apartments quickly became some of the most sought-after residences in the city, attracting such tenants as Pearl Mesta (later known as the "Hostess with the Mostest"), Lord Joseph Duveen, and Andrew Mellon. Duveen, an international art dealer, never actually lived in his apartment—he essentially rented it as a private gallery for the express purpose of selling to Mr. Mellon. The strategy worked, and Mellon eventually bought about $21 million worth of paintings and sculptures in one fell swoop, and soon donated the lot to the nation as the basis for the National Gallery of Art.

The armies of servants who looked after these nabobs lived in tiny rooms crowded onto eight mezzanine levels facing a narrow light well—you can catch a glimpse of this disparity from the alley at the northeast corner of the building, seen from P Street, where the larger number of shorter floors is apparent. Fortunately, the building offered several amenities to make work easier for the housekeeping staff, including a central vacuum system, centrally refrigerated tap water, and laundry chutes to individual washing machines in the basement.

L17 Institute for International Economics

1750 Massachusetts Avenue, NW

2001 Kohn Pedersen Fox Associates

A modern jewel set among the grand old buildings of Massachusetts Avenue, the Institute for International Economics demonstrates that even sensitive historic contexts can readily accommodate contrasting architecture when it is thoughtfully designed. The new building's form suggests a gable that has been split and reassembled in an unexpected way, creating a dynamic composition without relying on busy details or false decoration. Specialty glass lends an ethereal quality to the wall lining the assembly space to the left of the entrance. At night, when the interior lights are on, the curtain wall on the upper levels almost disappears, and the tidy individual offices read as rooms in a dollhouse. The only unfortunate note is the long, blank party wall along the east side of the property, next to the Embassy of Uzbekistan—if only it could have been executed in metal or stone rather than inexpensive, artificial stucco.

L18 Embassy of the Republic of Uzbekistan (Old Canadian Embassy)

1746 Massachusetts Avenue, NW

1909 Jules Henri de Sibour with Bruce Price
Various alterations: Architects unknown

Clarence Moore, a West Virginia tycoon, commissioned this Louis XV-style *palais,* but was able to enjoy it for only a few years before he had the misfortune to book passage on the maiden voyage of the *Titanic* in 1912. (Moore, a noted horseman and master of the hounds at the Chevy Chase Club, had been in England to buy dogs or ponies, depending upon which story you believe.) With its light-colored Roman brick, elaborate stone and iron ornament, and mansard roof, this house contrasts with the much more subdued Wilkins House (now the Peruvian Chancery), down the street at 1700 Massachusetts, which de Sibour designed a few years later. The Canadian government acquired the Moore property in 1927 and maintained it as a chancery until 1988, when embassy staff moved to their new quarters on Pennsylvania Avenue. It now serves as the Embassy of Uzbekistan.

L19 Benjamin T. Rome Building of the Johns Hopkins University (Forest Industries Building)

1619 Massachusetts Avenue, NW

1961 Keyes, Lethbridge & Condon, Architects
2000–2004 Interior renovations: Bowie Gridley Architects

Carefully considered proportions and deeply set windows distinguish this office building from more run-of-the-mill contemporaries. As a nod to the forestry-related association that commissioned the building, the window frames were originally made of wood—very unusual for a commercial structure—but later replaced with metal versions.

L20 Carnegie Institution of Washington

1530 P Street, NW

1909 Carrère & Hastings
1938 Delano & Aldrich
1998 Renovation: Florance
Eichbaum Esocoff King;
Preservation architects:
Oehrlein & Associates
Architects

In 1902 Andrew Carnegie gave funds to establish an institution to "encourage investigation, research, and discovery [and] show the application of knowledge to the improvement of mankind." This headquarters building by Carrère and Hastings soon followed. The architecture itself, though impressive, is a little odd in several respects. The huge portico, for instance, with its paired Ionic columns and heavy balustrade, seems as though it aspired to introduce a much larger structure—indeed, the architects diminished the building's scale several times during the design process in response to Carnegie's directive to avoid excessive grandeur. The scale of the portico is especially absurd now, since it no longer serves as the primary entrance. The main door is actually around the corner on the P Street side, under a relatively modest canopy, at the point where the original building meets the slightly watered-down addition.

L21 Church Place Condominium

1520 16th Street, NW

1964 Architect unknown
2000 Renovation: Eric Colbert &
Associates

The original, exceedingly banal apartment building had degenerated into a crowded tenement when an electrical fire and flood led to its condemnation. Colbert's colorful metal appliqués, which suggest the patterns of de Stijl architecture and painting, give life to the once drab façades. The architect worked to maximize window area in the new apartments to compensate for their low ceiling heights.

L22 The Cairo

1615 Q Street, NW

1894 Thomas Franklin Schneider
1904 Additions: Thomas Franklin
Schneider
1976 Renovation: Arthur Cotton Moore/
Associates
2000 Lobby renovation: James
Cummings AIA: A Collaborative Design
Group

"The Cairo is a very large curio. Some
might equate the building with one of
those rare objects occasionally encoun-
tered that appear so ugly or ungainly as to
attract rather than repel." —*Sixteenth Street
Architecture, Volume 2,* The Commission of Fine Arts, 1988.

Contrary to popular belief, the structure that engendered the District
of Columbia's first building height limitation was neither the Capitol nor
the Washington Monument but rather this bizarre, "Moorish" pile of
bricks and limestone. At a height of over 160 feet, the twelve-story tower
(whose height exceeded the reach of fire ladders available at the time) so
alarmed its neighbors that they successfully lobbied the District's Board
of Commissioners to enact restrictive zoning regulations in July 1894,
before the building was even finished. In truth, the Cairo's opponents
probably represented a strange alliance of architectural sophisticates
appalled by its ungainly design, and Luddites who ignorantly feared that
it was only a matter of time before sheer weight and hubris would cause
such a "skyscraper" to topple.

The architect was the enterprising T. F. Schneider, who had visited
the 1893 Columbian Exhibition in Chicago, marveled at the fair's literally
spectacular architecture, and, apparently, learned little. The Cairo is ill-
proportioned and capped by a ridiculously boxy cornice, but it does have
its charms—note the attenuated elephant heads that bracket the sills of
the two outermost windows on the first floor, and of course the great
entry arch, with its wispy lettering.

One of the first residential towers in America to employ steel-frame
construction, the Cairo was built in less than ten months. An effusive
promotional brochure touted it as "the most thoroughly equipped establishment of this nature south of New York," and even promised pleasant
summer living thanks to "cooling zephyrs" from Rock Creek Park, de-

spite the obvious fact that the park is not exactly nearby. The flyer also acclaimed the establishment's bakery, two billiard rooms, and rooftop garden complete with tropical plants and electrically powered fountains "bubbling here and bursting forth there." The building originally boasted a dining room on the top floor, marked by a change in window pattern that is still visible on the east façade.

The Cairo was converted into a hotel in the 1920s, beginning a slow but dramatic decline. By the 1960s, it was visited more frequently by police than by tourists, and rats outnumbered both. Finally, in 1976, a HUD-sponsored renovation, accomplished on the cheap, returned the building to apartment use. It became a condominium in 1979, and now, for all its quirks, the awkward tower reigns as one of Washington's guilty architectural pleasures.

L23 The Tapies Apartments

1612 16th Street, NW

2005 Bonstra Architects

Squeezed onto a twenty-one-foot-wide site previously occupied by a much-abused little wood-frame house, this svelte apartment building was conceived as a stretched, abstracted version of a typical row house with an asymmetrical bay. It accommodates just five apartments, four of them duplexes with living rooms almost as tall as the building is wide. A ladder-like trellis on the front façade, intended to serve as an armature for greenery, provides a series of small, horizontal counterpoints to the building's overall verticality. The landscaping of the front yard creates a surprisingly dense grove shading the sidewalk that zigzags toward the entrance.

L24 Church of the Holy City (Swedenborgian)

1611 16th Street, NW

1895 Herbert Langford Warren;
Associated architects: Pelz and
Carlisle
1912 Addition: Warren & Smith;
Associated architect: Paul Pelz

This rugged neo-Gothic structure was
designed by Herbert Langford Warren,
a Swedenborgian who later served as
the first dean of Harvard University's Faculty of Architecture. Construction was overseen by Paul Pelz, architect of the main Library of Congress
building. The south wing, added in 1912, contains a glorious, cantile-
vered spiral staircase that begins just inside the arched doorway.

L25 Toutorsky Mansion

1720 16th Street, NW

1894 William Henry Miller

This 12,000-square-foot mansion is in-
delibly associated with the beloved Russian music teacher Basil Toutorsky and
his Mexican wife María, even though
they did not move here until 1947 and
are now long gone. With its stepped
and scroll-edged gables, insistent rows
of windows, dark red brick, and strong
horizontal stone courses, it is a rare
iteration of Renaissance Flemish archi-
tecture in a city whose architectural ancestry is overwhelmingly English
and French.

L26 Scottish Rite Temple (House of the Temple)

1733 16th Street, NW

1915 John Russell Pope; Consulting architect: Elliott Woods

TEL: (202) 232-3579
www.srmason-sj.org/web/index.htm

"Supreme Council," answers the receptionist at the headquarters of the Ancient and Accepted Scottish Rite of Freemasonry, Southern Jurisdiction, USA. Subtlety is not a hallmark of the Masons, who are known for their pomp, circumstance, and elaborate rituals. Inspired by all that showmanship, John Russell Pope had a field day in designing the organization's seat. Basing his building on the Mausoleum at Halicarnassus, one of the Seven Wonders of the Ancient World, Pope erected an awe-inspiring temple in the midst of a quiet enclave of houses and apartment buildings.

As one would expect, the temple is replete with symbolism—some of it obvious, but some requiring a good deal of esoteric knowledge on the part of the viewer. The colonnade surrounding the building, for instance, consists of 33 columns, an allusion to the 33rd Degree (sometimes abbreviated as 33°), an honorary designation bestowed upon Masons for outstanding service to the fraternity. The front steps rise in flights of 3, 5, 7, and 9, alluding to Pythagoras's fascination with odd numbers. The steps are bracketed by a pair of monumental sphinxes, which guard the tremendous entry doors: *Wisdom,* to the south, has half-closed eyes and tranquil features, while the open-eyed *Power,* to the north, is fiercely determined. Inside the great bronze doors is the "Atrium," resplendent in Greek and Egyptian decorative motifs and rich in Masonic associations. The chairs, for example, are modeled after the throne at the Temple of Dionysus, and a pair of statues in ancient Egyptian style—three-dimensional representations of the hieroglyph that precedes the name of a god or of a sacred place—flanks the grand staircase.

Upstairs awaits the Temple Chamber, soaring roughly eighty-eight feet (the original height of Jenkins Hill, where the Capitol now stands—why does this seem significant?) to the inside of the stepped pyramidal roof. Visit the space on a bright day, if possible, to witness the spectacle of sunlight streaming in through the giant windows. The room is dripping with sumptuous materials, including marble, granite, bronze, and . . . and . . . are those *acoustical tiles lining the walls?* It seems that even the Masons occasionally must succumb to mundane practical considerations. Back downstairs are other intriguing spaces and displays, including a handsome library with stacks radiating along a gentle curve, and a room dedicated to none other than J. Edgar Hoover, 33°.

L27 Lauriol Plaza Restaurant

1835 18th Street, NW

1999 Singletary Rueda
Architects

The construction of a large, entirely new, freestanding restaurant in a dense, close-in residential area may have been the surest sign of Washington's urban renaissance at the close of the twentieth century. With its inviting sidewalk café, large expanses of glass, and a trellis-covered roof deck, this Tex-Mex restaurant is outrageously popular. Resisting all of the many clichés that such an establishment might normally invite—one could imagine cheesy "Mexican" decorative devices or cheap, pseudo-historical motifs intended to make the building "contextual"—the architects designed a resolutely modern building in brick, sheet metal, and wood. Although the exterior has a slightly industrial character, the structure sits comfortably in the historic residential neighborhood, thanks to its modest scale and carefully thought-out details. Inside, the soaring main space, with a mezzanine under a half-barrel vault, is one of the brightest and airiest dining rooms in the city.

The viewer should try to ignore the various temporary "additions"—such as plastic sheeting to enclose the roof deck—that currently diminish the appearance of the building from the street.

L28 American Geophysical Union

2000 South Florida Avenue

1994 Shalom Baranes
Associates

With a metal-and-glass prow seemingly breaking through a staid, more typically Washingtonian structure of masonry walls and punched windows, this building suggests the slow but inexorable tectonic processes by which the Earth forges new landscapes. The horizontal bands of the façades are meant to evoke the layers beneath the planet's surface, with thick, precast concrete bands at the base topped by lighter brick. The frieze that encircles the building represents the areas of scientific study in which the organization's members are engaged: the Earth, its atmosphere and hydrosphere, the other planets, and outer space. Note the decorative elements in the sidewalks adjacent to the building, in which the orbits of the planets in our solar system are indicated to scale.

L29 Thomas Nelson Page House

1759 R Street, NW

1896 McKim, Mead & White
(Stanford White)
1903 Alterations: Stanford White

Stanford White designed the Page House for the famous southern author and his wife in a Federal revival style, making a clean break from the faux chateaux then so popular with Washington's architects and their clients. The two main façades are quite different from each other—the R Street wall, which presaged McKim, Mead & White's later design for the Percy Rivington Pyne House on New York's Park Avenue, is formal and reserved, while that facing New Hampshire Avenue is more permeable and relaxed.

L30 International Temple, Order of the Eastern Star (Perry Belmont House)

1618 New Hampshire Avenue, NW

1909 Ernest Sanson; Horace Trumbauer

The Belmont House is symbolic of the era when many of the nation's wealthiest families routinely "wintered" in Washington to take advantage of the capital's then-fashionable social scene. In effect, this enormous slice of limestone pie with all the trimmings was built as a party house.

Diplomat Perry Belmont, a grandson of Commodore Matthew Perry, imported Ernest Sanson, a popular French architect, to design the house. Horace Trumbauer, who had a substantial portfolio of estates for American plutocrats, served as associate architect. The $1.5 million mansion was laid out in the preferred French manner of the time, with bedrooms on the first floor and the primary public rooms elevated to a *piano nobile*. Its highly ornate interior is replete with Italian marble, German woodwork, and metalwork from France.

Belmont sold the house during the Great Depression to the General Grand Chapter of the Order of the Eastern Star, an organization accepting both women and men as members, but widely known as the distaff counterpart to the Masons. The price tag of just $100,000 came with the stipulation that the order's Right Worthy Grand Secretary must live in the house. Thus, despite the building's institutional use, it is now actually a year-round residence—an awful lot of house for one family, no matter how right, worthy, or grand.

L31 Schneider Row Houses

1700 block of Q Street, NW

1889–92 Thomas Franklin Schneider

Built by Thomas Schneider of Cairo Hotel fame, these three-story brownand greenstone row houses form a parade of turrets, projecting bays, tiled mansard roofs, and Richardsonian Romanesque decorative detailing. Called a "young Napoleon" by one of his contemporaries, Schneider paid $175,000 for the long row of lots on the north side of Q Street and audaciously developed the whole tract in one fell swoop.

L32 Washington Chapter/AIA

1777 Church Street, NW

c. 1900 Architect unknown
1970 Renovation: Hartman-Cox
Architects
1995 Renovation: Fabry Associates
Architects

The local chapter of the American Institute of Architects bought this three-
story brick town house in 1968 and
then modified it to suit modern office
needs. The house was previously owned
for more than a half century by Mr. and
Mrs. L. Morris Leisenring, who bought
the building in 1917. Leisenring, chief architect for the Army Quartermaster Corps and the person responsible for the initial Washington
Architectural Registration Act, added a studio at the rear for his wife, a
distinguished sculptor, which now serves as the chapter's boardroom.
The house is unusual in that it breaks the regular rhythm of the row on
that side of the street—it is about five feet wider than its neighbors, and
the extra width allows for a delightful little oriel window and a bas-relief
decorative panel to enliven the façade.

No area in Washington experienced greater change in the 1990s and early 2000s than the interconnected neighborhoods of Logan Circle and Shaw, whose commercial spines are 14th Street and U Street, respectively. These long-decrepit business corridors—vexing symbols of urban decay—have rebounded dramatically to host some of the trendiest shopping and entertainment establishments anywhere in the region. The surrounding residential blocks, many of which were nearly abandoned just a couple of decades ago, now contain some of the city's priciest real estate.

The 14th Street corridor had its heyday in the 1920s, when it was Washington's "automobile row." Elegant but restrained car dealerships, typically sporting huge windows to show off their merchandise to good effect, lined the street. Peripheral businesses, such as auto repair shops, were also common along 14th and on adjacent blocks of several cross streets.

During the same period, U Street was a vibrant entertainment center for the city's African American community, rivaling and, in fact, exceeding the glamour of most "white" establishments in segregated Washington. Arguably the cultural capital of black America before the Harlem Renaissance, U Street was synonymous with jazz, attracting many of the world's great African American performers to its theaters and dance halls. Ironically, it was desegregation that ended all of this, as African American patrons quickly took advantage of their new freedom to visit previously segregated clubs and theaters.

The Logan Circle/Shaw area declined gradually until 1968, when a series of riots in the wake of the assassination of Martin Luther King Jr. dealt a devastating blow. Angry mobs set fire to businesses that refused to close in mourning of the slain civil rights leader, and the physical and psychological scars of that tragic period are still evident in various corners of the neighborhoods. The District government tried to spur redevelopment by building the Reeves Center (1986—VVKR, Devrouax & Purnell Architects-Planners, Robert Coles) at 14th and U to house various city services. It was the real estate boom of the 1990s, however, coinciding with a modest but sustained national trend toward renewed interest in urban living, that finally engendered a true resurrection of the area. In a city with little industrial heritage, the old car dealerships have proved to be popular for conversion to loft apartments, and U Street is once again one of the city's great spots for a meal or entertainment. Gentrification remains a delicate issue, as longtime residents are displaced by buyers of luxury condominiums, but for now at least, the 14th and U street corridors form the core of a diverse and vital community.

The duplex at 1–2 Logan Circle, built c. 1877 on what was then called Iowa Circle, exemplifies the elegant housing built for affluent Washingtonians in this neighborhood during the last quarter of the nineteenth century.

M1 Logan Circle

1875–Present Various architects

Proof that neglect is often the handmaiden of preservation, the houses surrounding Logan Circle, along with those lining adjacent streets (note, for example, the beautiful rows along the

1300 block of Rhode Island Avenue), form Washington's finest enclave of intact and carefully restored Victorian town houses. Most were built during a twenty-five-year period from about 1875 to 1900 to house the District's powerful and wealthy, such as John A. Logan, prominent Civil War general and, later, senator from Illinois, who lived at 812 12th Street. Logan originated the idea of Memorial Day. The government named the former Iowa Circle for him in 1930 notwithstanding his efforts to have the national capital moved to St. Louis. (Perhaps as vengeance, city officials allowed his house to be destroyed to make way for a parking lot.) In the early twentieth century, Washington's fickle society folk abandoned the neighborhood for Dupont Circle, and Logan Circle entered a deep sleep. Having miraculously survived an excruciating period as one of the city's most prominent drug and prostitution centers, the neighborhood has recently been attracting a great deal of local and national press attention as a highly desirable place to live.

M2 Luther Place Memorial Church

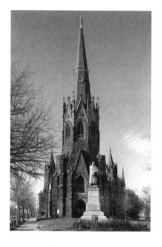

1226 Vermont Avenue, NW (at Thomas Circle)

1874 John C. Harkness and Henry S. Davis, based on original design by Judson York
c. 1884 Towers: Architect unknown
1905 Restoration: Frank H. Jackson
1951 Parish House: L. M. Leisenring
1969 Renovations: Neer and Graef
1990 Parish House addition and renovation: Weihe Partnership

Built as a gesture of thanksgiving for the end of the Civil War, this red sandstone, neo-Gothic church contrasts sharply with the classical National City Christian Church across the street. The structure's unusual plan derives from the acute angle of its site. The church operates N Street Village, a social service organization for homeless women and low-income families, which occupies a complex of historic and new structures designed by Shalom Baranes Architects, just north of the church building. A renovation of the nave by Kerns Group Architects is currently in the works.

M3 National City Christian Church

14th Street and Massachusetts Avenue, NW (Thomas Circle)

1930 John Russell Pope
1952 Addition: Leon Chatelain Jr.
1986 Addition: Architect unknown

This huge structure—its immense size becomes apparent only as the viewer approaches—was partly inspired by the early eighteenth-century church of St. Martin-in-the-Fields, on Trafalgar Square in London, designed by James Gibbs. National City is thus in good company, as Gibbs's iconic composition of pedimented front and stepped tower has served as the inspiration for countless Protestant churches throughout the United States. John Russell Pope took some liberties, of course, most notably by placing the structure atop a substantial mound, thereby necessitating the intimidating staircase leading to the portico, and by terminating the tower in a small dome rather than a pointy, conical spire.

M4 Post Massachusetts Apartments

1499 Massachusetts Avenue, NW

2002 Esocoff & Associates Architects

The exterior design of this large apartment building is clever in several respects. Its scalloped façades and vibrant blue projecting bays establish a strong rhythm of vertical elements that diminish the building's apparent bulk, while also yielding a sculptural quality that is rare in the bottom-line world of developer-driven construction. This design strategy was no mere caprice, however. It emerged logically from two factors: first, the prevalence of flat-plate concrete construction in Washington—commonly used because it often allows architects to squeeze an extra floor in commercial buildings governed by the city's height restrictions—and second, the District's public space regulations, which allow parts of residential buildings to project beyond the property line within certain guidelines. In flat-plate construction, it is relatively easy to create unusual shapes at the edges of the concrete floor slabs, so the scalloped façade design took advantage of local building traditions to make curved forms efficiently and economically. Meanwhile, under District law, the projections into public space—in this case, over the sidewalks—do not count against the maximum floor area permitted by zoning regulations, so the developer can build a larger building, gaining extra rentable space on a given piece of land.

The architect cites the work of Gaudí as one source of inspiration, and indeed, this building would fit well in Barcelona or many other European cities. It is one of a series of structures by Esocoff employing similar façade design strategies, including 400 Massachusetts Avenue, NW, and Quincy Park at 1001 L Street, NW.

M5   Whole Foods Market

1440 P Street, NW

2000 Mushinsky Voelzke and Associates

When the parent company of what was then called Fresh Fields announced an interest in opening one of its markets on an urban site in Washington, a group of Logan Circle residents launched a concerted effort to bring the natural food store to their neighborhood. The campaign was successful, and all parties are thrilled with the results. Not only is the store, now officially a Whole Foods Market, an excellent performer for the chain, it also served as a major catalyst for additional commercial and residential development in the area. Built on the site of a former service garage, the new building includes both underground and rooftop parking. Conceptually, the main façade is a stretched and folded storefront inspired loosely by the industrial architecture of the neighborhood, though it also bears hints of Art Deco, Amsterdam School modernism, and 1950s commercial architecture. Note the subtle green and blue colors in the small panes of glass at the top of the serrated windows.

M6 Rainbow Lofts

1445 Church Street, NW

1929 Architect unknown
2004 Renovation and
addition: Eric Colbert &
Associates

A façade-wide sign of individual
letters declares the original purpose of this former auto body
repair garage, and explains the derivation of the condominium project's otherwise corny-sounding name. The apartments in the existing,
three-story brick-faced structure are quite raw, with exposed concrete
block walls and industrial, pivoting steel-frame windows. The addition,
running up the west wide and across the top, is a dramatic contrast,
sheathed in white Alucobond panels (each composed of a polyethylene
core sandwiched between two aluminum sheets) and large expanses of
glass. Sunscreens partially shield the windows of the addition, while
ultra-minimalist glass railings line the edges of the roof deck and upper-
level terraces.

M7 The Studio Theatre

14th and P streets, NW

1919 1501 14th Street: Murphy & Olmstead
1920 1507 14th Street: Architect unknown
1922 1509 14th Street: John Mahon Donn
1987 Renovation: Devrouax & Purnell
Architects-Planners; Theater designer: Russell
Metheny
1997 Renovation: Russell Metheny; O'Marah
& Benulis
2004 Renovation and addition: Bonstra
Architects; Theater designer: Russell Metheny

One of the harbingers of the urban revitalization
to come, the Studio Theatre, founded in 1978,
moved to a former automobile showroom at 14th and P streets in 1987.
The original renovation preserved the essential character of the existing
building, while adding striking graphic elements—a giant sign, rendered
in dressing room–style lights, cleverly set within the windows along P

Street, and large, high-contrast black-and-white photographic images of faces, filling in the window areas to create the enclosure necessary for the theater spaces.

The well-regarded and successful theater company embarked on a major expansion in 2002, buying the two buildings along 14th Street immediately to the north of the original facility. The separate structures were combined, and visually unified by a glassy atrium atop the middle building, where the entrance to the complex is now located. Inserting a new theater in the northernmost building, long occupied by the Ace Electric Company, required the removal of the second-floor slab, and the transfer of structural forces to a series of three-foot-deep steel beams spanning the width of the building. The latest renovation also updated the large photographic faces, adding backlighting to create a glowing band of images.

M8   Whitelaw Hotel

1839 13th Street, NW

1919   Isaiah T. Hatton
1992   Restoration: Manna

The Whitelaw Hotel is most notable for its history, but the physical manifestation of that history is noteworthy by extension. It was developed by John Whitelaw Lewis, who made his money in banking and other business enterprises, as the city's premier accommodation for African Americans. During the glory days of U Street, the Whitelaw hosted nearly every famous black entertainer, as well as civic and political leaders, such as future Supreme Court Justice Thurgood Marshall. As a building, it reflects a dignified modesty, deriving its character not from expensive ornament, but from thoughtful proportions, a logical plan, and a considered formality. Hatton, the architect, also designed the headquarters of the Industrial Savings Bank at 11th and U, which Lewis owned. The Whitelaw was restored, albeit on a very modest budget, by Manna, a low-income housing developer, in 1990.

M9 National Minority AIDS Council

1931 13th Street, NW

1995 CORE

The architects and clients shared a vision for this project: that it somehow represent both the ongoing struggle against AIDS and a profound hope for a future free of the disease. This vision led to a design marked by the seamless blending of historic and new architectural elements. Galvanized steel sheets and brightly painted metal rails meld with the brick and wood that one would normally expect in buildings of this kind. The goal was to create architecture that, at first glance, seems perfectly a part of its community, but upon a second look, is revealed to be something special in its own right—a metaphor, it was felt, for the experience of many members of minority groups whose HIV status sets them apart in ways that may not be readily apparent. Inside, the two existing row houses were combined and heavily remodeled to introduce open, flexible spaces. A "wonder wall" serves as a primary element, incorporating storage and workstations while defining spaces without traditional enclosure.

M10 Lincoln Theatre

1215 U Street, NW

1922 Reginald Geare
1994 Restoration: Sorg and Associates; Preservation architects: Oehrlein & Associates Architects; Architects of record: Leo A Daly

At the height of the jazz era, U Street reigned, in the words of native Washingtonian Pearl Bailey, as the "Black Broadway." Its grand theaters and lively nightclubs, which regularly featured the most inventive and talented musicians in the world, provided elegant entertainment venues for African Americans living in segregated Washington. The Lincoln Theatre was instantly popular as a first-run movie and Vaudeville house, which the *Washington Afro-American* declared to be "perhaps the largest and finest for colored people exclusively anywhere in the United States." Immediately behind the theater once stood the Lincoln Colonnade, a dance hall that was a prestigious site for proms and other celebratory events, and which was among the establishments frequented by jazz greats like Duke Ellington, who grew up in the neighborhood. The Colonnade was demolished in the 1960s, and the Lincoln Theatre itself closed its doors in 1979.

As the U Street corridor began its slow resurgence in the early 1990s, the District of Columbia government assumed ownership of the theater and sponsored its restoration. Behind the unprepossessing façade is a somewhat more ornate interior, with a lobby that instantly evokes the heyday of silent films, and an auditorium surrounded by curved balconies and an elaborate proscenium stage bracketed by large Palladian arches. The restored theater hosts live performances, film festivals, and a variety of special events.

M11 Logan Heights Row Houses
2114–2122 10th Street, NW
2002 diVISION ONE

Eager to bring innovative design to one of Washington's rapidly gentrifying urban areas, the architects of this series of five row houses ended up developing the project themselves after they were unable to find an established company willing to do so (they also served as general contractors). The freely composed façades differ from neighboring houses in their abstract forms, lack of traditional compositional hierarchy, and alternative colors and materials, but are nonetheless sympathetic in terms of essential scale, visual depth, and rhythm along the streetscape. The interior spaces are relatively open for row houses, and more classically modern than the slightly funky exteriors.

CALVERT ST

⑪

COLUMBIA RD

18th ST

⑩

800 ft

Meridian Hill/Adams Morgan

In the late 1880s, former Missouri Senator John Brooks Henderson, who had drafted the constitutional amendment abolishing slavery, built a gruff stone "castle" at the corner of 16th Street and what is now Florida Avenue, just beyond the "boundary" of L'Enfant's plan. His wife, Mary Foote Henderson, alarmed to find herself living in semi-rural suburbia, soon began an audacious—and ultimately quite successful—campaign to turn the pastures around her house into a fashionable residential enclave. Mrs. Henderson thus became, in effect, one of the country's earliest female real estate developers, and however selfish her motivations, and despite numerous setbacks, her efforts yielded an extraordinary park and a collection of grand buildings that brought new glamour to the capital city.

One of Mrs. Henderson's ideas for improving the neighborhood was to try to convince Congress to declare the area Washington's official Embassy Row. She failed, but a few brave—or possibly intimidated—governments did establish outposts here. She later sought to have 16th Street permanently rechristened the "Avenue of the Presidents." Other ambitious schemes included commissioning Paul Pelz to design an imperially scaled new Executive Mansion for "her" hill, and lobbying Congress to place the proposed new Lincoln Memorial there. Even though all of

The "castle" of Senator and Mrs. John Henderson once loomed over 16th Street at the base of Meridian Hill, just beyond the boundary of L'Enfant's original plan. All that remains of the estate today are the craggy walls along the public sidewalk.

these initiatives came to naught, Mrs. Henderson nonetheless achieved great success in her broader goal of acquiring socially desirable neighbors. Meridian House, perhaps the most elegant private house in town, bears witness to her labors. Mrs. Henderson died in 1931, possibly after learning that Sinclair Lewis wrote most of *Main Street* while living near her at 1814 16th Street.

As for "Henderson Castle" itself, the main structure was demolished in 1949, leaving only the dark red stone retaining walls running along 16th Street and Florida Avenue. The actual site of the house is now occupied by the distressingly mundane Beekman Place condominiums.

N1 Meridian Hill Park (Malcolm X Park)

16th Street between Florida Avenue and Euclid Street

1914–36 Horace W. Peaslee, based on designs by George Burnap and Vitale, Brinckerhoff & Geiffert; with John Joseph Earley
2006 Restoration: architrave, p.c., architects

Meridian Hill gets its name from the official meridian of the United States, which runs through the center of the White House. The "hill" is actually the edge of the fall line, a steep bluff that served as a natural boundary to L'Enfant's original plan for the city. The top of this bluff affords outstanding views of the capital's monumental core. Placing a park here was, not surprisingly, the brainchild of Mary Foote Henderson, who proposed the idea in 1906 and secured the approval of the Commission of Fine Arts in 1914. Construction of the park spanned two decades. Horace Peaslee wrote that he based the park's lower level, with its axial plan, thirteen graduated pools, and cascading falls, on "the Pincian Hill in Rome," but at various other times he said he relied on the Villa d'Este and on Rome's Villa Medici for inspiration. At any rate, the upper terrace is clearly of French origin: dead flat for some nine hundred feet from the edge of the hill, it is centered on a broad grass mall with promenades and hemlock hedges all culminating in a bronze statue of Joan of Arc.

Peaslee's luxuriant plantings contrast with the rough, exposed-aggregate concrete, a surprising choice of material, used throughout in the massive retaining walls, walks, and basins. As the city's chief engineer observed in 1926, "Meridian Hill Park is neither wholly architecture nor yet is it landscape design. There is nothing like it in this country." Miraculously, the park has survived more or less as Mrs. Henderson and Peaslee envisioned it, despite a period in the 1970s and 1980s when it was a notorious haven for drug dealers. Unofficially but commonly called Malcolm X Park, the site was, to many, a symbol of racial and economic strife. The real estate boom of the 1990s, abetted by a nationwide drop in drug-related crime, led to rapid gentrification of the surrounding neighborhood and, in turn, to the park's rejuvenation.

N2 Josephine Butler Parks Center

2437 15th Street, NW

1927 George Oakley Totten Jr.

Architect Totten, working on Mary Foote Henderson's dime, designed nearly a dozen residences in the Meridian Hill area as part of his sponsor's grand plan to make the neighborhood a center of international society. Formerly the Embassy of Hungary and of Brazil, this building now serves as the headquarters of Washington Parks & People, along with a number of other small cultural and service organizations. It is named in honor of Josephine Butler, a longtime community activist who was a founder of the District of Columbia statehood movement and an influential advocate of urban park revitalization, including Meridian Hill Park. The *porte cochere,* yellow stucco, generous windows, and metal balcony railings lend the building a decidedly Mediterranean air.

N3 Ecuadorian Embassy

2535 15th Street, NW

1927 George Oakley Totten Jr.

Another of the speculative mansions developed by Mary Foote Henderson, the Embassy of Ecuador suggests that Totten was looking toward Mansart for inspiration here. Other mansions by Totten, in an array of architectural styles, include the Pink Palace at 2600 16th Street, the former French Embassy at 2460 16th, and the old Spanish Embassy at the corner of 16th and Fuller streets.

N4 Meridian House (Meridian International Center)

1630 Crescent Place, NW

1922 John Russell Pope
1960 Alterations: Faulkner, Kingsbury & Stenhouse
1994 Renovation: Archetype

Pope designed Meridian House for Ir-win Boyle Laughlin, heir to one of the country's more sizeable steel fortunes. Laughlin, a career diplomat, purchased the hilltop site for his chateau in 1912, but postings abroad kept him from building anything until 1920. A recognized scholar of eighteenth-century French art, Laughlin worked closely with Pope on the project. A 1929 article on the building in *Architectural Record* commented, "Because of [Laughlin's] detailed knowledge of the art and architecture of that period and because of his indefatigable interest in every detail, Meridian was immediately recognized as one of the finest examples of architecture in the French style in America." Laughlin continued the French themes out into the terraced garden, whose pollarded trees and raked gravel strongly evoke the quietly elegant landscapes of Parisian palaces.

Laughlin maintained his interest in art and architecture throughout his life. He helped his friend Andrew Mellon organize and plan the new National Gallery and, according to David Finley, the gallery's first director, the steel heir influenced everything about the new building, down to details such as choosing the fountains for the garden courtyards and the paint colors for the galleries. Laughlin died in 1941, just missing the National Gallery's opening.

Next door is the White-Meyer House (1912), which was also designed by John Russell Pope. It was for many years the home of Eugene Meyer, owner of *The Washington Post,* and his wife Agnes (their daughter Katharine Graham later became the newspaper's publisher). Both the Meridian House and the White-Meyer House are now parts of the Meridian International Center, an organization that promotes international understanding through cultural exchange and other programs.

N5 Pink Palace

2600 16th Street, NW

1906 George Oakley Totten Jr.
1912, 1920 Addition and alterations:
George Oakley Totten Jr.
1923–86 Numerous alterations and
additions: Various architects

This neo-Venetian Gothic mansion,
known as the Pink Palace because of
the original color of its stucco walls,
was the first building completed as
part of Mary Foote Henderson's efforts to make Meridian Hill the center
of Washington's social life. Notable residents included Secretary of the
Treasury Franklin MacVeagh (before he moved across the street to 2829
16th) and Delia Spencer Caton Field, the extremely wealthy widow of
Marshall Field. The building has been altered significantly, including the
removal of several balconies on the main façade and the enclosure of the
formerly open-air galleries along the south face.

N6 Warder-Totten Mansion

2633 16th Street, NW

1888 H. H. Richardson
1925 Reconstruction: George
Oakley Totten Jr.
2002 Renovation/restoration:
Sadler & Whitehead
Architects/Commonwealth
Architects

Benjamin Warder, a Midwestern industrialist who moved to Washington in 1885, commissioned Henry Hobson Richardson's firm to design a
house for him, but Richardson himself seems to have had a rather limited role in the project, which began construction just two months before the architect's death. It is likely that George Shepley, Charles Rutan,
and Charles Coolidge, who were the senior designers under Richardson,
shared responsibility for the neo-French chateau. The house originally
stood on K Street, between 15th and 16th streets, NW. When Totten,
himself a pupil of Richardson's, learned that the house was being demolished, he bought most of the original structure's elements from the

wrecker, hauled them across town, and reassembled them in a slightly different configuration on this site. After years of neglect and abandonment, the building was renovated in 2002 and converted into a thirty-eight-unit apartment complex.

N7 Mexican Cultural Institute (Mexican Embassy)

2829 16th Street, NW

1911 Nathan C. Wyeth
1922 Additions: Clarence L. Harding
1942 Addition: Marcus Hallett

TEL: (202) 728-1628
www.embassy.org/gallery/historical/
history001.html

Commissioned by Emily MacVeagh as a surprise gift for her husband, Franklin, who was secretary of the treasury under William Howard Taft, this mansion is marked by a high ratio of wall to window area and rather oddly stretched proportions. After his wife died, MacVeagh made the building available to the federal government as a guesthouse for visiting dignitaries. In 1921, the Mexican government purchased it for use as its embassy, and shortly thereafter added the boxy Italianate portico and a new office wing.

Mexico produced a number of great muralists, and the three-story stairwell of this building features a colorful and richly layered mural by Roberto Cueva del Rio, depicting the history of the country. The building now houses the embassy's cultural arm, which sponsors a variety of programs and events.

N8 All Souls Church, Unitarian

16th and Harvard streets, NW

1924 Coolidge & Shattuck / Coolidge, Shepley, Bulfinch and Abbott
1936 Expansion: Ernest D. Stevens
1968 Alterations: Grigg, Wood, and Browne

The design of this Unitarian church, the result of a limited architectural competition, is very directly derived from the Baroque Church of St. Martin-in-the-Fields on London's Trafalgar Square. The tall spires of All Souls, the Unification Church [see N9] across the street, and the National Baptist Memorial Church a block to the north make this stretch of 16th Street one of the most architecturally dramatic nongovernmental enclaves in the city. All Souls has a long history of social activism, particularly in its early advocacy of abolition of slavery and, in the twentieth century, support for civil rights. The church's bell, which was moved from an earlier structure, was cast by Paul Revere's son, Joseph, in 1822.

N9 Unification Church (Church of Jesus Christ of Latter-day Saints)

2810 16th Street, NW

1933 Don Carlos Young Jr. and Ramm Hansen

Severe and insistently vertical, this former Mormon church is certainly reminiscent of the multispired Mormon Temple (not the Tabernacle) in Salt Lake City, but also reflects the influence of Art Deco and the stripped classicism so prevalent in the 1930s. One of the architects, Don Young, was a grandson of Brigham Young, the influential successor to Mormon Church founder Joseph Smith, and the bird's-eye marble that covers this church was quarried in Utah. Rather surprisingly, the underlying structure is steel frame. The building is now owned by the controversial Unification Church of Sun Myung Moon.

N10 The Lofts at Adams Morgan

2328 Champlain Street, NW

2001 Project designers for base building: Devrouax & Purnell Architects-Planners; Interior architects and architects of record: Eric Colbert & Associates
2003 Addition on 18th Street: Eric Colbert & Associates

Decades ago in New York and other industrial cities, loft apartments developed logically as architects and property owners sought new uses for deserted warehouses and similar structures that no longer served their original purposes. The result was a new type of urban dwelling with unusually generous interior space and a chicly gritty character that many buyers and tenants found refreshing. In white-collar Washington, however, there were few industrial buildings available for conversion, so when local developers sensed a market for loft-style living, they decided to create facsimiles from scratch.

Thus derives the faux-warehouse aesthetic of the Lofts at Adams Morgan, one of the earliest loft apartment projects built from the ground up as such. It is composed of two main wings on either side of a pedestrian passage, which also accommodates cars entering a large parking garage beneath the apartments. Contrary to appearances, this passage is not a public right of way—it is actually on private land, and was incorporated as a civic amenity in response to community concerns raised during an arduous and lengthy public review process. Spanning the passage is a glassy, two-level bridge that contains lobby-like lounge spaces for residents. A third wing, completed a couple of years later, reaches out to 18th Street and contains apartments above retail space.

N11 Fitch/O'Rourke Residence

1918 Calvert Street, NW

1999 Robert M. Gurney

The front of this row house offers few hints that it is anything out of the ordinary, but the rear elevation is an architectural gem that warrants a walk down the alley. A skillful, balanced composition of horizontal and vertical lines and planes, the façade combines transparent, translucent, and solid surfaces to suggest a beautifully intricate three-dimensional puzzle. Inside, curved walls and other elements generate geometrically complex spaces. Perhaps most remarkable is the architect's success in controlling a diverse mix of materials—including Kalwall, sandblasted glass, various metals, concrete, and wood—which could have easily devolved into visual cacophony, but instead yields a seamless and congenial array of colors and textures.

Cleveland Park / Woodley Park

In the nineteenth century, many people believed that low-lying urban areas harbored "miasmic vapors"—mysterious gases that somehow caused illness, especially during hot, humid weather. An easy solution for Washingtonians who had the wherewithal was to seek weekend or summer refuge in the nearby sylvan highlands. Though now considered quite close to downtown, Cleveland Park and Woodley Park were, in those days, unquestionably "in the country," and were popular sites for second houses of wealthy city dwellers. Named after a prominent summer visitor (Grover Cleveland, who stayed at Red Top, now demolished) and a specific estate (Woodley, built by Philip Barton Key), these areas gradually developed into bucolic, close-in suburbs known for large detached houses with commodious porches. Today they are among the most storied neighborhoods in the city, popularly—and not inaccurately—associated with well-to-do professionals with a penchant for driving Volvos and listening to (and in some cases, working for) National Public Radio. Meanwhile, the Woodley Park and Cleveland Park commercial strips along Connecticut Avenue attract patrons from near and far, while the National Zoo and Rock Creek Park, which flows nearby, are major recreational attractions for the entire region.

In 1905, Easter Monday was a popular day for a stroll at the National Zoo.

O1 Rock Creek Park

Established 1890

One of the city's greatest natural features, Rock Creek cuts a deep, green
swath through Washington, helping to
define a number of distinct neighborhoods as it flows southward toward the
Potomac. The once powerful creek,
which in colonial days was navigable
well into the District, made a strong
impression on many early visitors—in the 1830s, for example, Frances
Trollope marveled at the "dark, cold little river . . . so closely shut in by
rocks and ever-greens, that it might serve as a noon-day bath for Diana
and her nymphs."

In 1890, in response to lobbying by banker Charles C. Glover and others, Congress approved funding to acquire and safeguard Rock Creek's
streambed, and to create a "pleasuring ground for the benefit and en-
joyment of the people of the United States," while providing for "the
preservation . . . of all timber, animals, or curiosities . . . in their natural
condition." In the early twentieth century, Frederick Law Olmsted Jr.
convinced Congress to enlarge the park to include portions of the creek's
tributaries.

Now sprawling over some 1,800 acres, Rock Creek Park forms the
largest single element in the National Capital Parks system. Both the
park and creek begin miles beyond the Beltway, near the (relative) wilds
of outer Rockville, and then gradually meander their way into the city,
passing the high ground of the National Zoo, running alongside Dumbarton Oaks Park, Montrose Park, and Oak Hill Cemetery, and ultimately
tumbling down to meet the river near the Kennedy Center.

O2 Duke Ellington Bridge (Calvert Street Bridge)

Calvert Street over Rock Creek, NW

1935 Paul Philippe Cret

One of several notable bridges in the
area, this handsome structure, with its
wide sidewalks and graceful stone-cov-
ered concrete arches, carries motorists

and pedestrians over Rock Creek, which gurgles along more than a hundred feet below. The triangular pylons that buttress the bridge are embellished with stylized sculptures symbolizing travel by air, rail, water, and highway. Unfortunately, the bridge, which was named in Ellington's honor in the 1970s, became a popular platform for suicidal jumpers, leading to the addition of spiky metal railings, which, though reasonably well integrated, greatly diminish the pleasure of crossing.

O3   Omni Shoreham Hotel

2500 Calvert Street, NW

1931 Joseph Abel
1935 Addition: Dillon and Abel
1946, 1950s Renovations: Architects unknown
1949 Addition: Architect unknown
1998 Renovation: Brennan Beer Gorman; Interiors: Hughes Design Associates

The exterior of the Shoreham is a somewhat timid rendition of jazz-age architecture, bearing hints of Art Deco, Renaissance Revival, and even Frank Lloyd Wright. The best aspect of the complex lies at the rear, where elegant dining and recreational terraces overlook the lush greenery of Rock Creek Park. Partially embraced by the building's sprawling wings, the pool deck in particular is remarkably secluded from the bustle of the city that surrounds it.

O4   Wardman Tower (Wardman Park Marriott Hotel)

2600 Woodley Road, NW

1928 Mihran Mesrobian
Numerous alterations: Various architects

The Wardman Tower was built as an apartment annex to the adjacent Wardman Park Hotel, completed about ten years earlier. Developer Harry Wardman tore down his own house to make way for the tower, which enjoyed a pastoral but still convenient setting that quickly made it one of the most prestigious addresses in Washington. The roster of famous residents remains unmatched by any other single structure in the capital save the White House, and includes former President Herbert Hoover, future President Lyndon Johnson, a bevy of vice presidents and cabinet officials, and more senators than you could shake a gavel at. Beginning in 1973, the apartments were gradually converted to hotel use, relegating the tower to secondary status as part of the larger complex. A few years later, the original Wardman Park Hotel next door was demolished and replaced by the current red brick behemoth.

Mesrobian's design skillfully diminishes the apparent bulk of the cross-shaped building while establishing a tone of posh domesticity. Subtle brick quoins modulate the scale of the tower at the corners, while stacks of balconies lend vertical emphases to counter the building's great breadth. His cleverest design move, though, was the incorporation of diagonal bays at the intersection of the two cross axes, thereby reducing the apparent length of each wing while providing prime spots for what were originally grand parlors with spectacular views from the upper floors.

O5   **Embassy of Switzerland**

2900 Cathedral Avenue, NW

1959 William Lescaze
2004 Renovation and
restoration: Leo Boeckl and
Herbert Furrer

Characteristically Swiss in its
no-nonsense modesty, this embassy could almost be confused
with a relatively refined suburban elementary school. Designed late in Lescaze's career, the structure suggests the influence of Mies van der Rohe, with a simple office block of buff-colored brick and steel-and-glass pavilions housing more ceremonial spaces. Lescaze, who was born in Switzerland and immigrated to America in 1920, is best known for the Philadelphia Saving Fund Society (PSFS) Building (1932), which was designed in partnership with George Howe and widely acknowledged as the first International Style skyscraper in the United States.

In 2004, the embassy announced plans to build a new ambassador's residence designed by Steven Holl in association with Swiss architect Justin Rüssli, which will be located on the grounds near the Lescaze building.

O6 Woodley (Maret School Main Building)

3000 Cathedral Avenue, NW

c. 1801 Philip Barton Key, owner-builder
1867, 1900, 1929 Additions: Architects unknown
1952 Renovation: Architect unknown

Philip Barton Key, an uncle of Francis Scott Key, was a loyalist who joined the British army soon after the colonies declared independence. He was captured and imprisoned by Revolutionary forces, and then fled to England upon being paroled. Key later returned to the United States, renounced his allegiance to the crown, and eventually managed to redeem himself sufficiently in the eyes of his countrymen to get elected to Congress representing Maryland. He reportedly modeled this mansion on Woodley Lodge, an eighteenth-century manor house that he had visited in Reading, England (and which was demolished in 1962). Key's estate went on to serve as the summer White House for several presidents, including Martin Van Buren and Grover Cleveland, and housed a number of prominent cabinet members. In 1946, then-owner Henry Stimson, former secretary of war, gave Woodley to the Phillips Academy Andover. The Maret School acquired the property in 1950.

O7 Smithsonian National Zoological Park

3001 Connecticut Avenue, NW

1890 Initial layout based on plan by Olmsted Brothers
1907–present William Ralph Emerson, Hornblower & Marshall, Glenn Brown, and many others

http://nationalzoo.si.edu

The basic plan of the 176-acre National Zoo, which was established in 1889 and became part of the Smithsonian Institution the following year, reflects the ideas of landscape architect Frederick Law Olmsted and his son and stepson, who advised Smithsonian Secretary Samuel P. Langley and animal curator William T. Hornaday on the project. Their goal was to create a "city of refuge" for bison and other endangered American species.

Several of the earliest structures at the zoo were designed by Boston architect William Ralph Emerson. The prominent firm of Hornblower and Marshall was commissioned to renovate an existing building into an aquarium, possibly on the basis of their experience incorporating fish tanks into the Children's Room at the Smithsonian Castle (though the tanks were actually designed by the institution's secretary himself). The firm's Small Mammal House, the oldest extant building at the zoo, was completed in 1906. It later served as the Monkey House, and now houses Think Tank, an exhibition exploring cognitive thinking in primates.

O8 Kennedy-Warren Apartments

3133 Connecticut Avenue, NW

1931 Joseph Younger
1935 Addition: Alexander Sonnemann, based on plans by Younger
2004 Restoration and addition: Hartman-Cox Architects; Interior design: Johnson-Berman, Hartman Design Group

The Kennedy-Warren represents the zenith of Art Deco architecture in the nation's capital. Named after its developers, who, like so many of their cohort, went bankrupt in 1931, the building is richly ornamented without seeming as frenetic as many other works of the same era and style. The welcoming forecourt, jazzy aluminum marquee, exuberant lobby, and ornate ballroom give the apartment house a decidedly theatrical air.

The building is even larger than it first appears. Thanks to the dramatic slope of the land at the northern and eastern sides of the site, there are actually six floors below the entrance level, including two floors of apartments, the ballroom, and several levels of parking and service spaces. An innovative forced-air ventilation system uses giant fans at the rear of the building to suck in cool air from the park floor and then distribute it through the corridors.

More than seventy years after the building's opening, the owner obtained necessary approvals to build the unrealized south wing that had been part of the initial plan. The addition is remarkable in its impeccable replication of the original's buff brick, aluminum spandrel panels, and other details. The layout of the apartments in the addition is quite different from Younger's arrangement, however, and while they are relatively spacious, the new units have a generic character that picks up on few of the motifs that made the main building one of the most glamorous places to live in the city.

O9 Klingle Mansion (Linnean Hill)

3545 Williamsburg Lane, NW

1823 Joshua Peirce, owner-builder
1840s–1850s Additions: Architects unknown
1936 Renovation: National Park Service staff architects
1994 Rehabilitation: National Park Service staff architects

Established by a son of mill owner Isaac Peirce (whose relatives sometimes spelled the name as "Pierce" or even "Pearce"), this estate contains many elements that reflect the family's Pennsylvania origins, including the beehive oven and the bank barn. Young Peirce, a noted horticulturist, created extensive gardens around the granite-walled, center hall–plan dwelling; a few of his plantings have survived, as has his two-story utility house with its built-in potting shed. The National Park Service restored the house and grounds in 1935, and now uses it as the park's administrative headquarters.

O10 Peirce Mill

2311 Tilden Street (at Beach Drive), NW

c. 1820 Isaac and Abner Peirce, builders
1936 Restoration: Thomas T. Waterman; Landscape architect: Malcolm Kirkpatrick

Rock Creek's formerly strong current once powered eight separate mills, grinding corn, rye, oats, and wheat grown by local farmers. The 1932 *Washington Sketch Book,* in fact, observed that the creek "was originally a racing stream, deep enough where it flowed into the Potomac to anchor seagoing ships," but "gradually the little harbor filled up." Simultaneously, changes in land use spelled extinction for major local agricultural enterprises. Of those original eight mills, only this one remains.

Peirce Mill and surrounding acreage were absorbed into the park in 1892 and Works Progress Administration staff restored the industrial building to working order in 1936. Flour produced here helped to stock government cafeterias of the 1930s and 1940s. The mill stopped working again in 1993, and another preservation effort is under way as of this writing. Other survivors of the once-flourishing Peirce family compound include a distillery (c. 1811), which is now private property, a stone springhouse (c. 1801), and the adjacent Linnean Hill/Klingle Mansion property. Though the mill is currently closed to the public, the nearby barn is open for exhibits and education programs.

O11 Hillwood

4155 Linnean Avenue, NW

1926 John Deibert; Landscape architect: Willard Gebhart
1957 Renovation: Alexander McIlvaine
1955–65 Landscape architect: Perry Wheeler
1957 French garden: Innocenti and Webel
1985 Indian Artifacts Collection: O'Neil & Manion Architects
1986 Café: O'Neil & Manion Architects
1988 Conversion of chauffer's house to library: Fisher Gordon Architects
1998 Visitor Center and renovation of Greenhouse: Bowie Gridley Architects; Visitor Center schematic design: Quinn Evans
1999 French garden renovation: Richard Williams Architect
2000 Restoration of main house: Bowie Gridley Architects; Preservation architects: Oehrlein & Associates

TEL: (202) 686-5807   www.hillwoodmuseum.org

This multifaceted museum complex is the legacy of cereal heiress Marjorie Merriweather Post, who in 1955 bought what was then known as Arbremont, a red brick neo-Georgian mansion standing amid twenty-five acres of gardens and woods, and promptly changed the estate's name to Hillwood. She then embarked on what might be called, in contemporary parlance, an "extreme makeover" to create a showcase for her unparalleled collections of French and Russian art.

Post, who was born in 1887, had begun collecting French decorative arts while she was in her thirties and married to her second husband, financier E. F. Hutton, who took over her family's company and turned it into General Foods Corporation. She divorced Hutton in 1935, and soon married Joseph E. Davies, who became the American ambassador to the Soviet Union. While living in Moscow, she developed a profound love of Russian imperial art, which she was able to amass easily in exchange for the hard currency the Soviets then desperately needed. After divorcing Davies, Post (who eventually returned to using her maiden name after her fourth and final marriage to Herbert May) bought the glorious estate that was to become her favorite project.

Mrs. Post, as she is still reverentially called by many Hillwood staff members decades after her death, terrorized workmen for years, micromanaging the building and remodeling until the mansion achieved its present thirty-six-room bulk. On the interior, the result is sort of a Beverly Hills take on the eighteenth-century French mode—the master dressing room, in particular, looks a bit like a set from *Mommie Dearest*. At the same time, Post was commanding Perry Wheeler, who had proved himself by designing the White House Rose Garden, to add a French garden, a Japanese garden, a Scots garden, and so on, to the rolling grounds. Once Hillwood finally met her standards, she began to fill it with her treasures, including an array of Russian Orthodox icons and an impressive clutch of Fabergé eggs.

In her will (Post died in 1973), she bequeathed Hillwood to the Smithsonian, which in turn gave the property to the Post Foundation in 1976. Additions to the estate since then include a building modeled after Post's camp in the Adirondacks, where she kept a significant collection of Native American artifacts, and a Russian dacha.

O12 University of the District of Columbia

Connecticut Avenue and Van Ness Street, NW

1976 and later Bryant and Bryant, Ellerbe Becket, Charles Cassell, et al.

A typical example of the Brutalist architecture that was the default style at American colleges in the 1970s, the District of Columbia's public university occupies an abstractly arranged campus of about a dozen raw-concrete-and-dark-glass buildings. Adjacent to the campus is the mixed-use Van Ness Station building, at 4250 Connecticut, by Hartman-Cox Architects (1984), which picks up on the buff brick and streamlined aesthetic common to many of the 1930s apartment buildings along the avenue.

O13 Intelsat Headquarters

3400 International Drive, NW

1988 John Andrews International; Associated architects: Notter Finegold + Alexander

A rare example of high-tech architecture in Washington, this assemblage of steel-and-glass pods and cylindrical, glass-block stair towers serves as the headquarters of a telecommunications satellite consortium. The building incorporates a number of environment-conscious features, including a network of atriums that bring natural light to interior spaces, roof gardens that enhance insulation and minimize unnecessary water run-off, and shimmering sunscreens that reduce thermal gain. Without being overly literal about it, the precisely honed structure suggests a flotilla of spacecraft.

O14 International Chancery Center

Both Sides of Van Ness Street between Connecticut Avenue and Reno Road, NW

1970–Present Initial plan: Edward D. Stone Jr. and Associates; Landscape architects: Oehme, van Sweden & Associates

In the 1960s, as foreign governments were clamoring for more space for their Washington outposts and real estate pressures were making inner-city neighborhoods less viable for such facilities, the State Department began seeking a large tract of land to accommodate a number of completely new embassy buildings. The chosen site, formerly occupied by the National Bureau of Standards, was divided into twenty-three one-acre plots plus one larger parcel that was set aside for Intelsat. The State

Department decreed that each embassy must be of essentially domestic scale and somehow reflect the architectural character of the home country. The result is the International Chancery Center, though a better name for this suburban assembly of disparate, detached buildings might be "Embassy Acres." Although a few buildings in the complex stand out, most are dreadful pastiches of pseudo-vernacular forms.

O14A Embassy of Singapore Chancery

3501 International Place, NW

1993 RTKL Associates

With its cruciform plan, low-pitched roof, broad eaves, and horizontally striated façades, this chancery inevitably suggests a debt to Frank Lloyd Wright's Prairie-style houses, but the resemblance is accidental. Such forms are also characteristic of the vernacular buildings of Singapore. Of course, Wright's work was strongly influenced by Asian architecture, so the evocation is understandable. The result, however, is a structure that reflects certain building traditions of both the home and the host countries without resorting to hokey, superficial imitation.

O14B Embassy of Kuwait Chancery

3500 International Drive, NW

1982 Skidmore, Owings & Merrill

One of the first buildings in the new International Center enclave was the sleekly geometrical Kuwaiti Chancery. Although relatively small, the structure has great presence thanks to the dramatic cantilever shielding its glassy corner entrance. Canted at forty-five degrees from the primary grid, the entrance is part of a system of diagonal elements in both plan and elevation, including the filigree screen in the lobby that, in certain light, is visible from the outside.

O14c Embassy of Bangladesh Chancery

3510 International Drive, NW

2000 SmithGroup

Water is an ever-present feature in swampy Bangladesh, and the architects of the country's new chancery incorporated a number of design elements alluding to this essential aspect of the nation's culture. The inverted gable hovering over the building, for example, is intended to suggest a water lily, while on the interior, various colors and textures of slate flooring are used to suggest a riverbed running through the main space. Kasota limestone on the front and rear façades adds warmth, and hints at the sandstone common in Bangladesh; for budgetary reasons, ground-face concrete-block was used instead on the side elevations.

O14d Embassy of Nigeria Chancery

3519 International Court, NW

2001 Shalom Baranes Associates

In approaching the Nigerian Chancery, the visitor first passes alongside a sweeping, limestone-clad wall that closely adheres to the curve of the street. Although this is the rear façade of the chancery, and it reflects the setback requirements common to all of the embassies in the International Center, its detailing, its fenestration pattern, and especially its respect for the street line make this one of the most urbane buildings in the complex. Around front, the primary façade, which is rectilinear and unpretentious, culminates in a modest, angular tower that houses a ceremonial "grand hall." In the middle of the building is a glass atrium that unites the curving wing and the rectilinear wing. The basic plan abstractly refers to a common West African building typology, in which separate structures surround a courtyard covered with a communal roof.

O14ᴇ Embassy of Brunei Darussalam

3520 International Court, NW

1999 RTKL Associates

Brunei Darussalam is a tiny sultanate on the island of Borneo in the South China Sea, and both the country and its monarch virtually ooze wealth thanks to huge deposits of oil and gas. The design of this chancery draws not only on building strategies that are common in Southeast Asia, such as post-and-beam construction and steeply pitched roofs, but also on forms that are more particularly associated with Brunei. The chancery's most direct antecedent is the "Kampung Ayer," or "Water Village," in Brunei's capital city, which is filled with simple gable-roofed houses on stilts.

O15 Sidwell Friends' School Administration Building (The Highlands)

3825 Wisconsin Avenue, NW

c. 1827 Charles Joseph Nourse, owner-builder Numerous alterations and additions: Various architects 2004 Interior renovation: Outerbridge Horsey Associates

One of the few remaining nineteenth-century houses in the area, the Highlands once presided over hundreds of acres of farmland. Joseph Nourse, who more or less ran the Treasury Department around 1800, gave the land to his son Charles, chief clerk at the War Department, and daughter-in-law, Rebecca. The couple then built this house using stone quarried on the property. As Anne Hollingsworth Wharton observed in *Social Life in the Early Republic* (1904), "no house in the vicinity of Washington is more replete with associations of the past than The Highlands, where the Madisons, Thomas Jefferson, . . . and other distinguished people of the day were wont to congregate." The square pillars on the west front are comparatively recent additions. The building is now the administration building of a prestigious private school whose alumni include several children of sitting U.S. presidents.

O16 Slayton House

3411 Ordway Street, NW

1960 I. M. Pei & Associates;
Associated architect: Thomas
W. D. Wright
2003 Renovation: Hugh
Newell Jacobsen; Landscape
architect: Jay Graham

A trio of barrel vaults peeks out
impishly from behind a plain brick wall, inviting observant passersby to
stop and investigate the unexpected form on an otherwise typical Cleveland Park street. Standing amid a well-landscaped garden is a modern
pavilion rendered in concrete, brick, and glass. The house was one of a
very small number of private residences designed by I. M. Pei, architect
of the National Gallery of Art's East Building. The client, William Slayton, managed this coup because he was a former associate of Pei's, who
came to Washington to serve as commissioner of the U.S. Urban Renewal Administration and later became executive vice president of the
AIA. He was locally renowned as the centerpiece of the "Slayton Irregu-
lars," an amorphous group of architects and related professionals who
often got together for conversation and lengthy meals.

The house is a zigzag in section—a sort of trilevel plus basement—
with the main living space in front facing the street, two bedrooms on
the upper level toward the rear, and a dining room, kitchen, and guest
room below. As renovated by Hugh Newell Jacobsen, the house is remarkably improved while remaining true to Pei's fundamental intent.
The top level of the central bay, for instance, which was originally enclosed, is now an open library and sitting area, allowing views from the
front yard all the way through the house.

O17 Winthrop Faulkner Houses at Rosedale

Ordway and 36th streets, NW

1964–78 Winthrop Faulkner

Son of architect Waldron
Faulkner and grandson of famed
architectural patron Avery
Coonley [see O19], Winthrop

Faulkner designed this group of houses—including 3530 Ordway, 3540 Ordway, 3407 36th Street, and 3411 36th Street—to surround his own residence at 3403 36th Street. Simultaneously modest and striking in their simplicity, the cleanly modern houses fit comfortably among more traditional neighbors.

O18 Waldron Faulkner House

3415 36th Street, NW

1937 Waldron Faulkner
1964 Landscape architect:
Lester Collins

The house Waldron Faulkner designed for his own family is a domestic version of the stripped classicism that swept 1930s Washington. Vaguely classical, not quite Art Deco, and almost modern, it exemplifies the struggle of Depression-era architects to reconcile broader architectural trends with the aesthetic conservatism that defined the nation's capital.

Though the house is now largely obscured by foliage, one can still see portions of its limited ornament, including a colorful frieze running a couple of feet below the roofline, and one little moment of exuberance— a somewhat modernized version of an anthemion (a classical floral motif) directly above the front door. Faulkner also designed the guesthouse at 3419 36th Street, completed in 1940, for which his son Winthrop designed an addition completed in 1992. The late Winthrop's brother Avery Faulkner is also an architect.

O19 Rosedale

3501 Newark Street, NW

c. 1793 Uriah Forrest,
owner-builder
2003 Addition and
renovation: Muse Architects

Rosedale was the summer retreat of General Uriah Forrest, whose house in Georgetown was the site of the influential dinner party where George Washington convinced prominent area landowners to sell property to the government for the new District of Columbia. Within a few years Forrest succumbed to the farm's charms and decided to abandon his M Street residence and live at Rosedale year-round. The small cottage that constitutes the oldest part of the house is believed by some historians to date to 1740, which would make it the oldest extant structure in the District, but this has not been proved.

The house was later owned by Avery Coonley, who had previously commissioned Frank Lloyd Wright to design a house in Riverside, Illinois, which became one of the architect's most admired works. Coonley left the estate to his daughter, Elizabeth, whose husband was Waldron Faulkner [see O18].

O20 Highland Place

Between 34th and Newark streets, NW

Mid- to late nineteenth century Various architects and builders

Romantic architecture, copious porches, and yards full of majestic, gnarled oaks make Highland Place one of the most picturesque streets in the city. Sequestered in the middle of a city block and easily overlooked, it is unknown even to many longtime Washingtonians.

MASSACHUSETTS AVE

WISCONSIN AVE

34th ST

25

24

23

22

21

20

2000 ft

Massachusetts Avenue / Kalorama

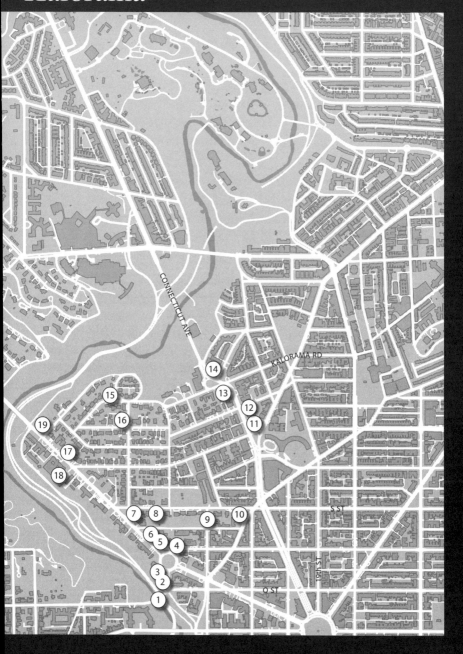

K*alorama* is an artificial word derived from the Greek for "good view" and is the fitting name that poet, liberal activist, and diplomat Joel Barlow gave to the estate he created on "the heights" above the new federal city and the older Georgetown. Barlow, one of Thomas Jefferson's most trusted friends, embraced whatever was new and advanced in any field—politics, literature, science—as long as he thought it would improve the condition of humankind. For him, that urgently included improving the condition of the new United States: "My object is altogether of a moral and political nature," he wrote. "I wish to encourage and strengthen in the rising generation, the sense of the importance of republican institutions."

If Barlow's house still stood, it would be on the corner of 23rd and Bancroft, but it was demolished around 1890, after which Kalorama Woods, as realtors originally called the neighborhood, quickly took on its present appearance, and the rich, famous, and powerful raced in to build their mansions and gardens. The area's architectural purity and unimpeachably tasteful landscaping prompted Russell Baker to quip, "Kalorama has the quiet, slightly sinister atmosphere of the aristocratic quarter of a Ruritanian capital."

Baker might have extended his criticism to cover most of Massachusetts Avenue, the city's longest and one of its grandest boulevards, a stretch of which skirts the western edge of Kalorama. "Mass Ave," as it is colloquially known, was perhaps the most sought-after address for the many robber

Cyril Farey's preconstruction (c. 1925) impression of the British ambassador's residence. Architect Edwin Lutyens signed the watercolor, apparently to signify his approval.

barons and aristocrats who moved to Washington in droves during the late nineteenth and early twentieth centuries. Life along the avenue changed perforce, however, during the Great Depression, as suddenly impoverished dowagers and debutantes slipped out the back door and diplomats from around the world strode in the front, and "Embassy Row" was born.

P1 Buffalo Bridge (Dumbarton Bridge)

23rd and Q streets, NW

1914 Glenn and Bedford Brown; Sculptor: A. Phimister Proctor

Brown *père* and *fils* designed this amazing bridge to join George-town with the then-developing Dupont/Kalorama area. Curving in plan, supported on large semicircular arches, and crowned by a cantilevered row of smaller, bracketed arches supporting the walkways, it is a visually powerful structure evoking Roman aqueducts and medieval fortifications. In contrast to such ancient European imagery, the decorative scheme is pure Americana, from the giant buffalo that give the bridge its unofficial but widely used name, to the series of heads sculpted from a life mask of the Sioux chief Kicking Bear.

The lower part of Rock Creek is traversed by a number of other noteworthy bridges, including the majestic William Howard Taft Bridge of 1906, which carries Connecticut Avenue over the creek (George Morison, architect; Roland Hinton Perry, sculptor), Paul Cret's 1931 bridge over Klingle Valley (Connecticut Avenue just north of the Kennedy-Warren Apartments), and the Duke Ellington Bridge at Calvert Street [see O2].

P2 Turkish Ambassador's Residence (Everett House)

1606 23rd Street, NW

1915 George Oakley Totten Jr.
2006 Renovation and restoration: Archetype

The prolific Totten, like many architects of his day, was stylistically promiscuous—compare his Venetian Gothic

"Pink Palace" on Meridian Hill [see N5] or his Beaux-Arts Moran House [see P6] to this restless classical mansion. The gently bowed front portico brings to mind the south façade of the White House, but the two buildings differ greatly in their proportions, window patterns, ornamentation, and almost every other aspect. Inside, eclecticism reigns, with an Italianate ballroom, an English dining room, and a French drawing room. The basement swimming pool and similar excesses earned this place the sobriquet "San Simeon on the Potomac."

Edward Hamlin Everett, who commissioned the mansion and moved here from his native Cleveland, was one of scores of industrialists who flocked to Washington in the Gilded Age. Everett derived some of his evident wealth from the usual sources, such as mining, oil and gas, and beer, but a sizeable chunk had more idiosyncratic origins—royalties from his invention of the fluted bottle cap.

Though built for Everett, the house may have been destined to serve as the Turkish Embassy. Totten had visited Turkey in the early 1900s, and designed the American Chancery there, as well as a residence for the prime minister. Sultan Abdul-Hamid was so impressed with these buildings that he offered Totten the position of "personal and private architect to the sultan." The architect accepted, but the sultan was deposed the next year and Totten returned to the United States to resume his career.

P3 Embassy of Latvia (Alice Pike Barney Studio House)

2306 Massachusetts Avenue, NW (on Sheridan Circle)

1902 Waddy B. Wood
2005 Renovation: Armands Bisenieks Architects

In the early 1900s, this eccentric and eclectic house was a nexus of cultural life in Washington, under the auspices of artist, patron, and social activist Alice Pike Barney. Designed by Waddy Wood with substantial input from Barney herself, it was the site of concerts, theatrical performances, exhibitions, and parties where artists and socialites mixed liberally. Barney once complained, "What is capital life after all? Small talk and lots to eat, an infinite series of teas and dinners. Art? There is none." Doing her part to change this situation, she painted and wrote plays, one of which was attended by Sarah Bernhardt, who arrived in a litter carried by four liveried footmen. Also a well-regarded musician, Barney received a commission from no less than Anna Pavlova to score a ballet for the great Russian dancer to use on her triumphant 1915 tour of America.

Barney died in 1931, and several decades later her daughters donated the house to the Smithsonian Institution, which never quite figured out what to do with it. The Smithsonian finally unloaded the charming but fallow building in 1999, and it now serves as the Latvian Embassy.

The Barney Studio House faces Sheridan Circle, named after General Philip H. Sheridan, who built his reputation on the scorched-earth Valley Campaign in Virginia during the Civil War and subsequently on the slaughter of countless Native Americans out west. The equestrian statue of the general is the work of Gutzon Borglum, who later showed what he could do at a larger scale when he created Mount Rushmore.

P4   Egyptian Ambassador's Residence (Joseph Beale House)

2301 Massachusetts Avenue, NW

1909 Glenn Brown
2000 Renovation and restoration: Archetype

Commissioned by Joseph Beale and now the Egyptian ambassador's residence, this Italianate palazzo is an exceptionally skillful composition. The central Palladian arch, marking a recessed loggia, creates a void that plays off against the subtle convex curvature of the façade. Note also how the bulging belt course low on the façade meets the projecting benches.

P5 Embassy of Haiti (Fahnestock House)

2311 Massachusetts Avenue, NW

1910 Nathan C. Wyeth

Haiti is one of several underdeveloped countries whose Washington embassies incongruously occupy opulent mansions. This grand Beaux-Arts town house, commissioned by financier Gibson Fahnestock, harmoniously blends with the rows of similar *hôtels* that line the blocks around Sheridan Circle. In contrast with the Moran House next door, however, this is a rather restrained and tightly controlled composition. Because of the tautness of the façade and shallowness of the pilasters, the Corinthian capitals seem to explode like fireworks from the wall plane.

P6 Moran House

2315 Massachusetts Avenue, NW

1909 George Oakley Totten Jr.

This building and its counterpart next door were commissioned by different plutocrats and designed by different architects, but appear as harmonious neighbors, sharing similar materials, taut pilasters, aligned cornices, and mansard roofs. Even so, the effects are not the same—the Moran House is much more idiosyncratic than the Fahnestock House, with unusual figural sculptural motifs and surprisingly large windowless panels on what would seem to be the primary floor. The bold tower is an architectural exclamation point terminating one of the city's most opulent blocks. Long serving as the Pakistani Chancery, the house became vacant when a new facility was built in the International Chancery Center.

P7 Embassy of the Republic of Cameroon (Hauge House)

2349 Massachusetts Avenue, NW

1907 George Oakley Totten Jr.
1934 Addition: Smith Bowman Jr.

This romantic limestone château marks the western end of Massachusetts Avenue's great turn-of-the-century Beaux-Arts residences, a procession that begins with Jules Henri de Sibour's Wilkins House at 17th Street. Christian Hauge, a Norwegian diplomat, commissioned the mansion shortly after he was appointed his nation's first minister to the United States in 1905 (the year Norway gained its independence from Sweden). Hauge died in 1907, while snowshoeing back home, but his Kentucky-born and quite rich widow stayed on in the house, holding sway as one of the city's more influential hostesses until her own death in 1927.

P8 Woodrow Wilson House

2340 S Street, NW

1916 Waddy B. Wood
1921 Remodeling: Waddy B. Wood
2005 Exterior restoration: Archetype

TEL: (202) 387-4062
www.woodrowwilsonhouse.org

President and Mrs. Wilson occupied this Georgian revival house, which was inspired by the work of the eighteenth-century Scottish architect Robert Adam, from the end of his latter term as president, in 1921, until his death in 1924. Mrs. Wilson called it "an unpretentious, comfortable, dignified house, fitted to the needs of a gentleman," and she continued to live here until she died in 1961. Although the Wilsons did not commission the house—they purchased it from its builder, businessman Henry Parker Fairbanks—it is the only one the couple ever owned.

Waddy Butler Wood, from a prominent family of Virginia, enjoyed a successful career as one of upper-class Washington's favored architects and designed more than thirty mansions in the Kalorama area alone. He was a particular favorite of the Wilsons, perhaps because they shared his deep Old Dominion roots, and he was chosen to design the inaugural stands for both of Wilson's inaugurations. Wood's professional views were quite conservative—in an unpublished essay, he decried originality for its own sake, which he termed "Architectural Bolshevism."

P9 Codman-Davis House

2145 Decatur Place, NW

1907 Ogden Codman Jr.

The entry courtyard of this mansion would be at home in Paris, but the house itself is more in the English Georgian style. The building's prim aspect is hardly surprising, since Codman was Edith Wharton's collaborator on that classic book of architectural dos and don'ts, *Decoration of Houses* (1897), in which the authors purse their lips and take a firm stand against such modern horrors as the "electric light, with its harsh, white glare." (They encouraged their readers to rely on wax candles instead.) The building now serves as the Thai ambassador's residence.

The stairway just west of the house, connecting 22nd Street to S Street and nicknamed "the Spanish Steps," is one of Washington's hidden treats.

P10 Friends Meeting House

2111 Florida Avenue, NW

1930 Walter F. Price; Rose Greeley, landscape architect
1950 Addition: Leon Chatelain II

Made possible by a gift from a Rhode Island Quaker, and built in part to accommodate President and Mrs. Herbert Hoover, who were also Quakers, this simple stone meeting house recalls similar structures that dot rural Pennsylvania, the religious sect's historic center. The structure is faced with Foxcroft stone, a material once found in abundance throughout the District but now unavailable. One of the ground-floor rooms includes ceiling beams that had been installed in the White House when it was repaired after the War of 1812, but were later removed during another renovation. Greeley designed and planted the informal, tranquil grounds to resemble a small private park; she also produced a sundial for the upper terrace inscribed with the query, "I mind the Light, dost Thou?"

P11 Lothrop Mansion

2001 Connecticut Avenue, NW

1909 Hornblower & Marshall

Alvin M. Lothrop and Samuel W. Woodward founded the business that eventually became the prominent local department store chain, Woodward and Lothrop, which sadly was subsumed by a national retail company in the 1990s. Lothrop commissioned this forty-room house for one of the most spectacular residential sites in the city, commanding the view down Connecticut Avenue. The main façade is actually the rear of the house, designed purely for the public impression; the entrance is on the opposite side, facing a small courtyard.

P12 2029 Connecticut Avenue

1916 Hunter and Bell

What Gilded Age mansions are to Massachusetts Avenue, elegant apartment houses are to Connecticut Avenue. Some of the earliest luxury apartment buildings in the city are found on this stretch of the street, and none can surpass 2029 Connecticut for opulence. With just three huge apartments on each of the main floors, it has long been a favorite of Washington's elite, from former president William

Howard Taft to entertainer Lena Horne. The velvet-voiced Horne occupied one of the units facing the avenue, running the entire width of the building and featuring a forty-three-foot-long foyer, a thirty-three-foot-long living room, and five bedrooms. The base and top of the building are sheathed in glazed terra cotta, as are the two projecting porticoes, whose decorative sculptures include salamanders and fleurs-de-lis, favorite symbols of French King Francis I.

P13 The Dresden

2126 Connecticut Avenue, NW

1910 Albert H. Beers
1974 Renovation: Peter Voghi
1996 Restoration: Oehrlein & Associates Architects

While serving as the chief architect for developer Harry Wardman (a position later held by Mihran Mesrobian), Beers designed a large number of apartment buildings all over Washington. The Dresden is distinct because of its curving neo-Georgian façade, holding the street line of the avenue. One of the side effects of the curve is that the apartments running along that façade contain rooms that are slightly tapered in plan.

P14 Woodward Apartments

2311 Connecticut Avenue, NW

1910 Harding and Upman

Not long after Mr. Lothrop built his mansion at the corner of Connecticut and Columbia, his partner Mr. Woodward developed this apartment house. Generally designed in a tame Spanish Colonial mode, it does have an elaborate neo-Baroque, glazed terra cotta entrance, and is crowned with a little villa in the sky. The building is notable as one of the earliest in Washington to contain duplex apartments, though there are just a few of them facing Connecticut Avenue.

P15 The Lindens

2401 Kalorama Road, NW

1754 Robert "King" Hooper, owner-builder
1934 Moved to Washington
1935 Restoration: Walter Macomber

This wood-frame Georgian house defensibly claims the title of oldest building in Washington, even though it was not built here. Its complex history begins with Robert Hooper, a prosperous Yankee merchant, who erected the house in Danvers, Massachusetts. More than a century and three-quarters later, Mr. and Mrs. George Maurice Morris bought the building, dismantled it, moved it in sections, and reconstructed it on a sloping Kalorama lot, where it immediately seemed at home among its eclectic neighbors.

The house's entrance bay, carried up three stories to the pedimented attic and partially defined by the flanking Corinthian columns, adds a surprising vertical thrust to the otherwise foursquare dwelling. The pale pink rusticated wooden façades were covered in sand-infused paint to resemble more expensive ashlar stone.

P16 Embassy of Oman (Devore Chase House)

2000 24th Street, NW

1931 William Lawrence Bottomley
1965 Addition: Douglas Stenhouse

Bottomley, a specialist in creating "new-old" houses, is perhaps best known for the James River neo-Georgian brick villas he built in and around Richmond in the 1920s and 1930s. Covered in textured limestone, the Devore Chase House suggests more of a French influence, though traces of the Georgian are still evident in its overall demeanor of extreme restraint.

P17 Turkish Embassy

2525 Massachusetts Avenue, NW

1999 Shalom Baranes Associates

The Turks must like the neighborhood, since they built this new embassy just down the street from their ambassador's residence on Sheridan Circle. The building cuts into a steeply sloping site, resulting in massive retaining walls visible at the sides. Eschewing the usual hierarchical grandeur that one associates with such buildings, the chancery seems unusually domestic in scale, comprising two almost independent pavilions linked by a very low-key connector. (One result is that a house located up the hill behind the chancery actually figures very prominently in the view from the avenue.) References to vernacular Turkish architecture are subtle, and largely consist of abstract geometrical patterns that suggest the intricacies of traditional Mediterranean and Islamic decorative motifs.

P18 Japanese Embassy

2516 Massachusetts Avenue, NW

1931 Delano & Aldrich
1960 Tea house: Nahiko Emori

The main building of this complex, which was, unlike most of its contemporaries, designed expressly as an embassy, has a simple, pedimented Georgian revival façade that makes the structure seem modest by comparison with the architectural stage sets that dominate this stretch of Massachusetts Avenue. Note the "swept eaves," which curve up slightly as if lifted by a light breeze, and the unusual radial arch above the main door. The widely praised gardens contain an authentic tea house that was built in Japan, taken apart, shipped to America, and reassembled on this site; the little structure marks the hundredth anniversary of diplomatic relations between the two nations.

P19 Islamic Center

2551 Massachusetts Avenue, NW

1957 Egyptian Ministry of Works with Mario Rossi; Irwin Porter and Sons, associated architects

Officially serving as the religious center for all American Muslims, this steel-framed mosque was built through a joint initiative of the ambassadors of the leading Islamic countries. While the main façade of the building follows the line of Massachusetts Avenue, the mosque proper, in the center, is canted so that the mihrab, or altar-like niche, is oriented toward Mecca. Persian carpets cover the floors, the ebony pulpit is inlaid in ivory, stained glass sparkles in the clerestory, and verses from the Koran are rendered in mosaics around the entrance, throughout the front courtyard, and atop the 160-foot minaret. Still, the Egyptians did make a few concessions to the neighborhood, particularly in deciding to face the mosque in limestone, the favorite material of Massachusetts Avenue's château builders. Visitors of any or no faith are welcome, provided that they observe customs of dress, which guides can explain to those not in the know.

P20 Embassy of Italy Chancery

3000 Whitehaven Street, NW

2000 Sartogo Architetti Associati; Associated architects: Leo A Daly

An abstract rendition of a Tuscan palazzo, the new Italian Chancery is perched rather mysteriously up a fairly steep hill from Massachusetts Avenue. Between the avenue and the chancery is a somewhat forlorn fenced lawn (the fence was added after the terrorist attacks of September 11, 2001), with a gate and a sidewalk implying that one might actually enter that way, but clearly that is not the case. The building itself is marked by warmly colored stone walls, punctuated by vibrantly green copper panels and a wing-like roof. In plan, the structure is essentially a square split diagonally by a glass atrium that serves as the primary gathering and orientation space. This arrangement alludes to the original, ten-mile-square plan of the District of Columbia, with the central atrium suggesting the swath of the Potomac River.

P21 Danish Embassy

3200 Whitehaven Street, NW

1960 Vilhelm Lauritzen; Associated architects: The Architects Collaborative 2006 Renovation design architects: Vilhelm Lauritzen; Architects of record: VOA Associates

An excellent example of coolly rational Scandinavian modernism, the Danish Embassy combines chancery functions and the ambassador's residence in a single building. While visiting the newly finished embassy, Lauritzen, who is perhaps best known for his design of two generations of terminals at Copenhagen's airport, wrote in a letter home that "[Benjamin] Thompson from [The Architects Collaborative] was here yesterday and said that it was the only building in Washington worth looking at." Lauritzen went on to write, "I would like to show the servants' wing to the Americans. They say that we are socialists and perhaps we are; here they can see how it works." Unfortunately, the parking lot at the entrance compromises the initial impression of the elegant and pure building.

P22 Brazilian Embassy (McCormick House)

3000 Massachusetts Avenue, NW

c. 1910 Ambassador's residence: John Russell Pope 1971 Chancery: Olavo Redig de Campos

Built as the Washington lair of retired diplomat Robert S. McCormick, of the Chicago newspaper clan, the Brazilian ambassador's residence presents another variation on

Pope's palazzo formula. Here the architect created a recessed entrance, derived from Peruzzi's Palazzo Massimo alle Colonne in Rome, and canted the plan so that all of the main rooms face the quiet side street (and enjoy southern exposure).

To the north of the residence is the chancery, a classic example of space-age glass modernism seemingly hovering just off the ground. Note the swooping spiral reception desk just inside the lobby.

P23 British Embassy

3100 Massachusetts Avenue, NW

1928 Sir Edwin Lutyens; Associated architect: Frederick H. Brooke
1930–39 Gardens: Lady Lindsay

With its great wings reaching out to the avenue, the British Embassy is simultaneously imposing and welcoming. The plan is actually quite unusual, and reflects the building's original dual purpose as chancery and residence (before the banal new chancery was built next door). The ambassador's study was placed to create a second-story link between the public offices and the private residence. The main axis flows into the original residence, where it is then reoriented ninety degrees to face the elegant gardens.

As earnest revivalists were sweating to create classical references to an idealized (and largely fanciful) American past, Lutyens, who called architecture "the great game," impishly chose colonial American associations for the new embassy. The Massachusetts Avenue façade is a pastiche of Williamsburg—then very much in the news—and Sir Christopher Wren, while the garden façade, dominated by a giant Ionic portico, suggests Hollywood epics about the Old South.

P24 Finnish Embassy

3301 Massachusetts Avenue,
NW

1994 Heikkinen-Komonen
Architects; Associate
architects: Angelos Demetriou
& Associates

When it comes to architecture
and design, the Nordic coun-
tries put most of the world to shame. Finland, in particular, derives a
great deal of its national identity and pride from design excellence. From
cell phones to light fixtures to museums, good taste in the land of Aalto
and Saarinen is as common as double vowels.

Finland's embassy is organized as a series of linear zones running
parallel to the main façade. First comes the porch-like layer defined by
an ivy-laden copper trellis. Just inside is a zone of security and reception spaces, followed by the main circulation spine. A graceful but dramatic curving staircase breaks the rectilinear geometry, connecting the
lobby to the main public event space. A porch runs the length of the rear
façade. The backyard surprise is a pier-like walkway that juts into the
woods, affording visitors a view back to the building, which is particularly spectacular when lit at night.

One press counselor for the embassy remarked, "I had no idea a
building could be such an important diplomatic tool." The Finns take full
advantage of that tool, graciously hosting exhibitions, receptions, lectures, and other events for Washingtonians who enjoy spending time in
such a serene and classy place.

P25 Washington National Cathedral (Cathedral Church of St. Peter and St. Paul)

Massachusetts and Wisconsin avenues, NW

1907 George Frederick Bodley
1907–17 Henry Vaughan; Arthur B. Heaton, superintending architect
1921–44 Frohman, Robb & Little
1944–72 Philip Hubert Frohman
1971–73 Superintending architect: James E. Godwin
1973–81 Superintending architect: Howard B. Trevillian Jr.
1981–90 Superintending architects: Anthony J. Segreti and Robert Calhoun Smith
1989 Landscape architects, West Front: EDAW Inc.

TEL: (202) 537-6200   www.cathedral.org

The notion was preposterous, really: to build from scratch a "true" Gothic cathedral, icon of feudal Europe, in the capital of the world's first modern democracy, at a time when the city was the epicenter of the classically inclined City Beautiful movement. Having overcome this improbable genesis and the infamously protracted construction process that ensued, the Washington National Cathedral stands majestically today atop Mount St. Albans, one of the highest points in the District of Columbia.

The idea for a cathedral in Washington dates back to L'Enfant, who envisioned a "great church for national purpose . . . equally open to all"; but distrust of the commingling of church and state kept the project on hold until 1893, when President Benjamin Harrison yielded to congressional pressure and established the Protestant Episcopal Cathedral Foundation. To get the cathedral going, the Episcopal hierarchy first had to do some politicking and create a new diocese, since Washington was then part of the Diocese of Maryland. Then came a years-long search for the right site, followed by design competitions, or, rather, a series of what the former clerk of the works, Richard Feller, calls "wranglings": church officials came within one vote of adopting Ernest Flagg's plans for a domed, Renaissance-style cathedral. Bishop Henry Yates Satterlee, a devoted Gothicist, traveled to England to persuade the aged George Frederick Bodley to come up with sketches for a Gothic building. Then came the inevitable fundraising, a process helped initially by Charles Carroll Glover, president of Riggs Bank. Finally, in 1907, Theodore Roosevelt tapped the cornerstone into place and cried, "God speed the work!" But the work was anything but speedy—construction continued in spurts for eighty-three years until the building was essentially finished in the fall of 1990.

The building is full of fascinating moments. The strangely erotic sculptures by Frederick Hart in the tympanum areas over the main doors seem strikingly modern in comparison to the structure they adorn. Around the north side, note the colonnade, shielding a garden with an abstract modern fountain—the column capitals are adorned with highly unusual motifs reflecting aspects of American culture and geography, from animals to igloos. Inside, there is the famous stained glass window with an embedded Moon rock. A subtle surprise is the kink in the plan of the nave, best witnessed from the choir area behind the altar—curiously, this minor failure of surveying and construction goes a long way toward making the cathedral seem genuinely Gothic.

The cathedral is, as one might expect, the centerpiece of an enclave of gardens, school buildings, and other attendant structures. Notable among these is the thoroughly modern Tennis Club for the St. Alban's School, designed by Hartman-Cox in 1971.

Foxhall

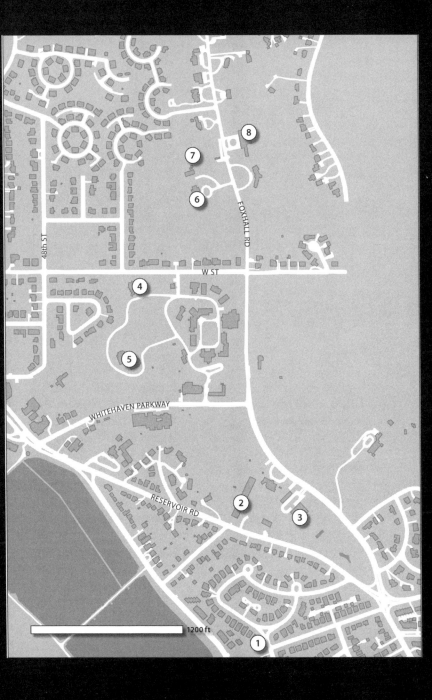

The thoroughly suburban—at some points almost pastoral—character of the Foxhall area belies its proximity to Georgetown and central Washington. Indeed, it was not all that long ago that much of the property along Foxhall Road was open farm country. As recently as the 1920s and 1930s, cows from the nearby Palisades Dairy Farm grazed the land now occupied by the Mount Vernon Campus of the George Washington University.

The neighborhood takes its name from Henry Foxall (without the *h*), whose family farm, Spring Hill, was near where Foxhall Road and P Street now intersect. Foxall was a close friend of Thomas Jefferson's—the two occasionally met for violin duets—and also a major cannon manufacturer. His foundry, located in what is now Glover Archbold Park, was an obvious target during the War of 1812; when a timely thunderstorm prevented British troops from attacking the place, Foxall credited divine providence, and in gratitude, established the Foundry Methodist Church, which initially stood at 14th and G streets and later moved to its current location on 16th Street, NW.

Agricultural enterprises became increasingly impractical within the District of Columbia during the late nineteenth century, and the Foxall farm was sold in 1910. By 1927, construction was under way on the neo-Tudor Foxhall Village (with the *h*—according to legend, a careless sign-maker bears responsibility for the misspelling) just below Reservoir

Much of the Foxhall area was quite rural in character well into the twentieth century, as evidenced by this house on Reservoir Road made partially of logs and dating to the early 1800s.

Road, and station wagons, cocktail parties, and bridge games soon supplanted plows, cattle, and chicken coops.

Q1 Montedonico/Lasky House

4622 Charleston Terrace, NW

1987 Cass & Pinnell
Architects
2002 Renovations: Lisa Van Dusen

This towering house takes full advantage of a difficult, steeply sloping site. The modest street front contrasts with the glassy rear façades through which the residents enjoy expansive vistas. The house's big secret is a basement swimming pool, from which there is a clear view to the Georgetown Reservoir and the Virginia bank of the Potomac.

Q2 Embassy of Germany Chancery

4645 Reservoir Road, NW

1964 Egon Eiermann

The two major buildings in the German Embassy complex, the chancery and the ambassador's residence, both reflect the Teutonic penchant for precision and orderliness, but with strikingly different results. The sleek and finely detailed chancery, one of the most underappreciated buildings in Washington, demonstrates that rationalist, hard-edged modernism can also be visually rich and inviting. Eiermann skillfully obscured the bulk of the building by nestling it into the sloping terrain and stepping down its mass at both ends. The intricate façade, composed of layered grids in wood, metal, and glass, further dematerializes the structure. An influential architect in post–World War II Germany, Eiermann was perhaps best known for his hauntingly beautiful additions to the ruins of the Kaiser Wilhelm Memorial Church in Berlin.

Q3 German Ambassador's Residence

1800 Foxhall Road, NW

1994   O. M. Ungers

In contrast to the delicate chancery, the German ambassador's residence is monumental and forbidding. Despite its almost sepulchral severity, however, the building does have its charms. Many of the forms and patterns visible in the residence, such as the repeated grids of open squares, recall the starkly elegant motifs of Josef Hoffman and the Viennese Secession. Architect O. M. Ungers, who studied under Egon Eiermann, is notoriously obsessive—his contract for this project included language dictating the exact and unalterable placement of all furniture in the building's public spaces.

Q4   Florence Hollis Hand Chapel

George Washington University,
Mount Vernon Campus
2100 Foxhall Road, NW

1970   Hartman-Cox Architects

Conceived as the last element of a master plan for an independent college (now a satellite of the George Washington University), the Hand Chapel was actually the first new structure to be built, following a gift from a generous benefactor. From the main entrance, one descends through a sequence of spaces that offer glimpses of the main sanctuary, which is used for both religious and secular purposes. Inspired by the restrained interiors of American colonial churches and by the work of Alvar Aalto, the unpretentious main hall is, by day, awash in remarkably even light that enters through a series of stepped clerestories, which also carefully frame the views from within.

Q5   Pelham Hall

George Washington University, Mount Vernon Campus
2100 Foxhall Road, NW

1971   Hartman-Cox Architects

Like the Hand Chapel, this slate-roofed dormitory presents a more typically institutional façade toward the main campus, but then steps down
dramatically in the direction of the adjacent residential neighborhood.
Careful planning and a generous supply of balconies afford virtually all
dorm residents sylvan views.

Q6   Belgian Ambassador's Residence (Anna Thomson Dodge House)

2300 Foxhall Road, NW

1931   Horace Trumbauer

Mansions are almost common-
place in Washington, but few
can compete with this one for
sheer Gatsbyesque opulence.
The house's stately façade was inspired by that of the early eighteenth-
century Hôtel de Rothelin-Charolais in Paris. Architect Horace Trumbauer, whose prolific Philadelphia-based firm designed palatial houses
for many of America's wealthiest families, was also involved in the design
of the imposing Philadelphia Museum of Art and the campus plan for
Duke University.

Q7 Spanish Ambassador's Residence

2350 Foxhall Road, NW

2003 José Rafael Moneo;
Moneo Brock Studio

Pritzker Prize–winner José Rafael Moneo tends to rely on the inherent beauty of high-quality materials to lend character to his buildings, and such is the case with the unadorned walls of narrow Roman brick that define this very large but unassuming residence. Several interior spaces stand out, including the barrel-vaulted reception hall whose bold, simple dormers are visible from the street, and the skylit orangerie adjacent to the baronial formal dining room. Without resorting to literal historical quotation, Moneo imbued the residence with a distinctly Spanish feel through such devices as the use of Moorish-inspired tiles, reflecting the influence of seven centuries of Muslim presence on the Iberian peninsula during the Middle Ages.

Q8 Kreeger Museum

2401 Foxhall Road, NW

1967 Philip Johnson and
Richard Foster

TEL: (202) 338-3552
www.kreegermuseum.org

When insurance executive David Lloyd Kreeger and his wife Carmen commissioned Philip Johnson to design a house that could accommodate their burgeoning art collection, they were already planning for its eventual conversion into a museum. Johnson's design strongly evokes ancient Mediterranean villas, with travertine walls, outdoor sculpture terraces, and groin-vaulted interior spaces reminiscent of the great Roman baths. Inside, the unusual choice of cotton carpet as a wall covering serves two practical purposes: it enhances the acoustics for musical performances and facilitates the rearrangement of paintings.

Arlington National Cemetery

Though outside the current boundaries of the District of Columbia, Arlington National Cemetery is so integral to the identity and
character of the capital's monumental core that it warrants inclusion in
this book. The green hills of the cemetery provide a placid backdrop for
views from the Capitol and other spots along the Mall, and its principal
architectural elements are important satellites of the city's network of
landmarks.

· ARLINGTON MEMORIAL BRIDGE ·

Abutment #1   Pier 1   Pier 2   Pier 3   Abutment 2

*Arlington House is barely visible as a light-colored speck on a hilltop in the cen-
ter background of this annotated 1927 photograph, which shows the construction
of the Arlington Memorial Bridge.*

R1   Arlington Memorial Bridge

1932 McKim, Mead & White;
Sculptors: Leo Friedlander,
James Earle Fraser, and C. Paul
Jennewein

Proposals for a bridge at this site
date back at least to President
Andrew Jackson, who suggested
a structure that would symboli-

cally and physically link North and South. In the late nineteenth century, military engineers developed various schemes for a bridge beginning near the foot of New York Avenue, but in 1902, the McMillan Commission, citing the planned placement of the new Lincoln Memorial, issued a statement supporting the current alignment of the bridge. It was not until the 1920s, however, that the firm of McKim, Mead & White was finally chosen from a short list of architectural candidates and construction began.

The elegant result completely transformed the adjacent areas on both sides of the river into the coherent visual experience that had been envisioned by Charles Moore, secretary to the Senate Park Commission, who recalled the group's directive "that the Memorial Bridge be a low structure on a line from the site of the Lincoln Memorial to the Arlington Mansion—a monumental rather than a traffic bridge, but a significant element in an extensive park scheme." Consisting of eight reinforced concrete arches covered in granite, plus a central bascule drawbridge span made of steel decorated to resemble stone, the bridge is an elongated cousin of Paris's many elegant classical spans across the Seine.

R2   Arlington National Cemetery

Arlington, Virginia
Established 1864

TEL: (703) 607-8000
www.arlingtoncemetery.org

In 1864, the Union army's quartermaster general, Montgomery C. Meigs, proposed that the federal government appropriate Robert E. Lee's family estate overlooking Washington and turn a portion of it into a cemetery. The first person buried there was actually a Confederate prisoner who died in a local hospital, but he was soon followed by thousands of Union soldiers. After the war, General Lee's heir, Custis Lee, claimed ownership of the land and successfully sued the federal government, which ultimately paid him $150,000 for title to the property. Today, Arlington Cemetery includes the graves of nearly three hundred thousand war dead, high-ranking government officials, and other dignitaries (including Pierre Charles L'Enfant), on a total of 624 acres.

The cemetery, Arlington House, and the Lincoln Memorial, all linked by the Memorial Bridge, constitute one of the nation's great Beaux-Arts set pieces. Subsequent building in and around the cemetery has generally adhered to the Greco-Roman theme. The classically inspired Memorial Amphitheater is the site of major rituals, such as the annual Memorial Day ceremony. The Tomb of the Unknowns takes the form of a sarcophagus; its effective and restrained decoration is limited to three chaste figures representing valor, victory, and peace.

President Kennedy is buried on a beautiful hillside beneath a slab of fieldstone from his beloved Cape Cod; he admired the site only days before he was murdered in Dallas. Architect John Carl Warnecke, who had worked with the First Family to save Lafayette Square, discussed the treatment of the grave at length with Mrs. Kennedy; they eventually settled on a modest, essentially landscapist approach that emphasizes the eternal flame. As Warnecke said, "The flame is the primary symbol at the grave, stronger than any sculpture or any structure that might be added to it." The president's assassinated brother, Robert, his widow, Jacqueline Kennedy Onassis, and two children who died shortly after birth, are buried nearby.

One noteworthy new structure at Arlington is a maintenance facility at the southern end of the cemetery. Despite its mundane purpose, the building achieves great dignity through its high-quality materials, its segmented plan, and its modest but distinctive profile.

R2A John F. Kennedy's Grave
1966 John Carl Warnecke & Associates

R2B Memorial Amphitheater

1920 Carrère & Hastings
1992 Restoration: Einhorn
Yaffee Prescott

R2C Tomb of the Unknowns

1921 Lorimer Rich; Thomas
Hudson Jones, sculptor

R2D Facility Maintenance Compound

1996 KressCox Associates

R3 Memorial Gate/Women in Military Service for America Memorial

1932 McKim, Mead & White
1997 Weiss/Manfredi Architects; Preservation architects: Oehrlein & Associates Architects

The apse-like Memorial Gate was conceived by McKim, Mead & White as the terminus of the new axis defined by the Memorial Bridge and as the ceremonial entrance to the cemetery. Essentially an elaborate, concave retaining wall, the structure always fulfilled its urbanistic role majestically, but never really worked well as a gate.

In the 1980s, a new organization sought and received permission to create a memorial to women in military service, to be built behind and within the existing Memorial Gate structure. A subsequent design competition produced a spectacular winning entry by Weiss/Manfredi, which called for a series of simple glass spires, dubbed "the Candles," that would have served as skylights for the exhibition spaces by day and beacons of light by night. Though well conceived and beautifully presented, these bold gestures made a lot of people nervous, and unfortunately, they were eliminated from the final design. In the finished building, the exhibition space is lit by shallow, tilted skylights that are covered by an additional layer of thick glass panels, some of which are engraved with quotations. On a sunny day, the engraved words cast shadows on the white marble interior wall, sometimes clearly, at other times quite abstractly. Opposite the marble wall is the original concrete retaining wall—now exposed—that was once hidden behind the ornate Memorial Gate. Penetrating the arcing space is a series of staircases that are not accessible from inside; they connect the original plaza with an upper terrace affording views across the Memorial Bridge to the Lincoln Memorial. Although the exhibits in the memorial are still rather thin, the injection of a new purpose into an underused structure, coupled with an excellent overall design, have turned what was once a mere beautiful wall into a visually rich and moving work of architecture.

R4 Arlington House (Custis-Lee Mansion)

1803 George Washington Parke Custis, owner-builder
1818 George Hadfield
1925 L. M. Leisenring

One of the earliest American examples of Greek Revival architecture, Arlington House remains among the most impressive. George Washington Parke Custis was a grandson of Martha Washington (Martha had two children with her first husband, Daniel Parke Custis, who died in 1757; she and George had no children). He began the hilltop house as the seat of his 1,100-acre plantation, building first the wings, with their slightly recessed arched windows; but then he hesitated before beginning work on the center block, perhaps because he knew how prominent his house would be. Arlington's hillock overlooks the national capital, and conversely, the site is visible from virtually any spot in town. Custis hired George Hadfield, who had worked on the Capitol, to devise an appropriately imposing structure. Hadfield did just that, placing a sixty-foot-long, twenty-five-foot-deep Doric portico across the mansion's main façade. Robert E. Lee, who later owned Arlington, once remarked that the porch made the place "a house any one might see with half an eye."

Lee moved to Arlington when he married Custis's only surviving child, Mary Ann Randolph Custis, in 1831. According to the *Dictionary of American Biography*, Lee once wrote, "My affections and attachments are more strongly placed [at Arlington] than at any other place in the world." The couple and their eventual seven children lived in the house until the Civil War broke out. Since 1933, Arlington House has been maintained by the National Park Service as a memorial to the Confederate general, who has always inspired a degree of admiration even among those who fiercely opposed his cause.

Other Places of Interest

This chapter presents a selection of architecturally significant buildings scattered around the District's less central neighborhoods, and, in the case of the first entry, a network of structures that spans the entire metropolitan area.

In this engraving from about 1910, the campus of Howard University and the McMillan Reservoir (at lower right) are situated amid a pastoral landscape.

S1 Metro System Stations

Throughout the City

1976–Present Harry Weese Associates
2002–Present Exterior station canopies: Lourie & Chenoweth

To the typical American in the 1960s, the word *subway* would have evoked images of a dark, Stygian netherworld that was entered at one's peril. Conscious of such overwhelmingly negative stereotypes, a number of the federal officials planning the new subway system for Washington, later named Metro, strongly advocated spending extra money to ensure that the system's stations were pleasant and inviting places. Even President Lyndon Johnson weighed in, sending a letter to the National Capital Transportation

Agency in February 1966 directing the organization to "search world-wide for concepts and ideas that can be used to make the system attractive as well as useful. It should be designed so as to set an example for the Nation."

The next month, Chicago architect Harry Weese was hired to design the individual subway stations, and he soon developed a prototype featuring a coffered concrete barrel vault that was enthusiastically received by design review authorities and the general public. When the first of the airy stations based on this prototype opened, they became instant icons and contributed to the then-common view that Washington was an exemplary city for modern architecture. The cleverest aspect of Weese's design is the combination of coffers and indirect lighting. Not only do the coffers make sense structurally—note how they grow shallower at the sides of the vault, where the forces acting on the tunnel are smaller—but when lit from below, they create a simple pattern of light and shadow that makes the scale of the space understandable and adds visual interest to what would otherwise be an undifferentiated expanse of concrete.

In 2001, the Washington Metropolitan Transit Authority conducted a competition for the design of a prototypical canopy to cover exterior escalators at many Metro stations, which have long been prone to breakdowns. The winning design was a vault of glass and stainless steel—recalling the form of the stations themselves—supported by slim steel struts. Canopies based on this prototype are gradually being built across the system.

S2   England/Hechinger Houses

2832/2838 Chain Bridge Road, NW

1952 The Architects Collaborative
1993 England House addition and renovation: Winthrop Faulkner & Partners

This pair of houses was designed for John Hechinger, of the Hechinger hardware chain, and his sister, and their respective spouses. Built on a dramatically sloping site, the two houses are articulated as a series of simple, taut geometric forms exemplifying the Bauhaus principles of Walter Gropius, leader of The Architects Collaborative.

The houses were designed and constructed during an extraordinary era in American residential architecture. Ludwig Mies van der Rohe's Farnsworth House, Philip Johnson's Glass House, and even The Architects Collaborative's own noteworthy enclave of houses at Six Moon Hill in Lexington, Massachusetts, were all built around the same time. Perhaps inspired by such revolutionary works, the Hechingers and Englands commissioned what were arguably the first capital-M-Modern houses in Washington. Complementing the structures themselves are various sculptures from Hechinger's large collection of art based on tools, his stock in trade.

S3 Dreier-Barton House

2927 University Terrace, NW

1977 Hugh Newell Jacobsen

Local architect Hugh Newell Jacobsen became famous for his houses designed as series of simple, gabled pavilions, but this is the only example of such a project in the District of Columbia. In this case, each pavilion is slightly offset from the next one, creating a serrated plan and making the house appear larger than it actually is. Jacobsen's trademark gutterless, eaveless roofs yield pure forms suggesting a child's archetypal drawing of a house.

S4 Cyrus & Myrtle Katzen Arts Center

Massachusetts Avenue at Ward Circle, NW

2005 Einhorn Yaffee Prescott

American University's new Katzen Arts Center brings some much-needed architectural definition to Ward Circle, an otherwise undistinguished roundabout along this leafy stretch of Massachusetts Avenue. Occupying a long, skinny site and incorporating a number of widely divergent functions, the building easily could have ended up as either a monotonous fortress or a mishmash of competing forms. Instead, the architects successfully used dynamic, curvilinear elements to break up the building's 660-foot length and to differentiate its myriad spaces. Although large expanses of the façades are windowless, the skin retains visual interest thanks to subtle variations in the color and pattern of the French limestone cladding.

The building's plan is reminiscent of a cubist painting of the human body, with a rounded "head," nearest the circle, housing the primary public exhibition space. In the "torso" are a recital hall, theater, and studio spaces, while the "legs" contain classrooms and other academic facilities for the university's visual and performing arts departments.

S5 Cityline at Tenley

Wisconsin Avenue and
Albemarle Street, NW

1941 John S. Redden and
John G. Raben
2005 Renovation and addition:
Shalom Baranes Associates

A classic, Art Moderne former
Sears store, with a swoopy canopy
and soaring display window at the
corner, now serves as the podium for a condominium apartment building with more than two hundred units. While the materials, fenestration patterns, and details of the new and old elements of the complex are quite dissimilar, they are nonetheless aesthetically complementary. The striations of the aluminum panels on the apartment structure reinforce the characteristic, horizontal emphasis of the original building, while the new structure's broad, gentle arc plays off against the more acute curves of the Art Moderne elements.

S6 Brown House

3005 Audubon Terrace, NW

1968 Richard Neutra
1993 Renovation and addition: Cass and Associates

Richard Neutra helped to define the "California style" of residential architecture in the early twentieth century, which, in turn, influenced do-

mestic design across the country. Open floor plans, asymmetrical compositions of simple forms, and large expanses of glass blurring the distinction between indoors and outdoors yielded houses that epitomized the informality that became a hallmark of American domestic life.

Donald and Ann Brown commissioned Neutra to design what turned out to be his last single-family house. To understand his clients' needs and desires, the architect instructed them to keep a diary of their activities and take an inventory of all their possessions, and even insisted on living with them for two weeks. Though often frustrated by Neutra's notoriously difficult personality, the Browns were thoroughly pleased with the house he designed for them, which came in exactly on budget.

The house retains a remarkably pure silhouette thanks in part to the lack of railings at the edges of the balconies—the Browns simply did not let their children out onto the balconies until they were old enough to avoid tumbling over the edge. A large new music room, added under the direction of architect Heather Cass, seamlessly extends the structural and spatial character of this classic house.

S7 Hallet House

4542 28th Street, NW

1996 Stanley I. Hallet

This residence appears rather like a very large tree house, with a straightforward structural system and exposed joinery. The warmth and texture of wood elements, including beams made of cypress, contrasts with the slightly industrial, machined character of steel columns, bolts, and connector plates. The house incorporates a pair of studios—one for the architect who designed it and one for his wife, a filmmaker.

S8 Washington Theological Union

6896 Laurel Street, NW

Original buildings: Dates and architects unknown
1996 Renovation and additions: KressCox Associates

This seminary, known as a relatively liberal outpost of the Roman Catholic Church, occupies an agglomeration of buildings that formerly served as the headquarters of the Seventh Day Adventist Church. Early work on the renovation revealed a number of surprises related to the previous occupants' apocalyptic worldview, including nuclear fallout shelters filled with large supplies of aspirin and vitamin C. Moreover, what had been thought to be four primary buildings turned out to be an incredibly complicated warren of countless conjoined structures—presumably, the Adventists were not interested in long-range planning, and therefore built out their headquarters on an incremental and haphazard basis.

The renovation architects enclosed the disused courtyard and turned it into the library, making it both the symbolic and physical core of the institution. A pergola was added along the eastern elevation to define the entrance. Finally, the entirely new Connelly Chapel of Holy Wisdom, connected to the main building by a glazed breezeway, was built at the southern end of the complex. With tall walls of buff brick and large clerestory windows separated by white aluminum-composite fins, the chapel has an almost industrial feel, which is augmented by the coincidental presence of a nearby brick smokestack. The interior is bright and neat, rendered in light-colored materials such as unstained maple. The ceiling of the sanctuary features a giant cross articulated by two pairs of steel beams and a smooth plane of acoustical plaster.

S9 St. Paul's Church

Rock Creek Cemetery
Webster and 3rd streets, NW

c. 1775 Architect unknown
1864 Renovation: Architect
unknown
1922 Restoration: Delos H. Smith

The original chapel on this site, built
around 1719, was the first church
in what later became the District of
Columbia. It was replaced in 1775;
the replacement was then remodeled in 1868, but that version burned to
the ground in 1921. The present one-story brick church, with its central
entrance tower and projecting chancel, is a reconstruction incorporating
surviving walls of the 1775 building.

S10 Rock Creek Cemetery/ Adams Memorial ("Grief")

Rock Creek Cemetery
Rock Creek Church Road, NW

1890 Statue: Augustus Saint-
Gaudens; Base: Stanford
White

Henry Adams commissioned
this heavily shrouded bronze as
a memorial to his wife, Marian, after her suicide, and it almost immediately became one of the most revered works of art in Washington.
Lorado Taft, who sculpted the Columbus Fountain near Union Station,
said that to look on the figure's face was like "confronting eternity";
Saint-Gaudens himself felt the sculpture "beyond pain and beyond joy.
It is the human soul face to face with the greatest of all mysteries." The
figure sits on a rough stone base with a simple bench in front. Henry
Adams died in 1918 and was buried here beside his wife.

S11 Armed Forces Retirement Home– Washington (U.S. Soldiers' and Airmen's Home)

Rock Creek Church Road at Upshur Street, NW

1843 Lincoln Cottage: Architect unknown
1857 Main buildings: Barton S. Alexander
1869 Addition and alterations to Sherman Hall: Edward Clark
1897, 1923 Alterations to Lincoln Cottage: Architects unknown
2005 Restoration of Lincoln Cottage: Hillier Architecture

Lincoln slept here. Actually, several mid-nineteenth-century presidents used Anderson Cottage—now called Lincoln Cottage—on the grounds of what was then known as the Soldiers' Home, as a retreat from the White House. It was here that Lincoln wrote the final draft of the Emancipation Proclamation. The cottage was built by banker George W. Riggs, and later named in honor of Major Robert Anderson, the Union commander at Fort Sumter when the first shots of the Civil War were fired.

The Soldiers' Home was established on the site in 1851 by General Winfield Scott, hero of the Mexican War, who used a portion of the tribute paid to him by the Mexican government to create what is now the oldest veterans' home in the country. The most notable of the other structures on the vast property is Sherman Hall, a neo-Romanesque castle with a tall, central clock tower.

S12 The Catholic University of America

620 Michigan Avenue, NE

1989 Edward M. Crough Center for Architectural Studies: John V. Yanik et al.
1994 Columbus School of Law: Florance Eichbaum Esocoff King Architects
2003 Edward J. Pryzbyla University Center: Bohlin Cywinski Jackson

Washington, D.C., is home to the largest collection of Roman Catholic institutions and facilities outside of Rome, many of them concentrated in an area of the city's Northeast quadrant that is sometimes called the "Little Vatican." At the heart of the precinct is the Catholic University of America, which was founded by Pope Leo XIII in 1887 and is officially the national university of the American Catholic Church.

The campus includes several buildings of note, including the School of Architecture and Planning, which occupies a renovated former gymnasium. The initial plan for the renovation was developed by students in the school under the direction of Professor John Yanik. Other prominent structures include the Columbus School of Law, a quietly contextual affair, and the new Pryzbyla Center, marked by a roughly 250-foot-long, undulating, glass-and-steel façade.

S13   Basilica of the National Shrine of the Immaculate Conception

400 Michigan Avenue, NE

1920–59 Maginnis and Walsh (later Maginnis, Walsh and Kennedy); Associate architect (1920–32): Frederick V. Murphy

TEL: (202) 526-8300
www.nationalshrine.com

Despite being the largest Roman Catholic church in the country, and one of the largest churches in the world, seating more than six thousand people, this is technically not a cathedral. It is rather a shrine dedicated to the Virgin Mary as patron saint of the United States. Designed and built over a period of forty years, it is ostensibly a combination of the neo-Byzantine and neo-Romanesque styles, but the finished structure—particularly the interior—somehow conveys more than a whiff of 1950s Beverly Hills Moderne.

The colorful dome and tall, slender carillon make the shrine one of the major landmarks on the Washington skyline. The main sanctuary, which was very loosely modeled after St. Mark's in Venice, features brightly colored mosaics and a succession of small chapels depicting the various incarnations of Mary. The basement houses an astonishing shop full of religious paraphernalia.

S14 Pope John Paul II Cultural Center

3900 Harewood Road, NE

2001 Leo A Daly

TEL: (202) 635-5400
www.jp2cc.org

The Pope John Paul II Cultural Center, which houses exhibition galleries and an interfaith think tank, is a startlingly modern building that eschews trite symbolism and knee-jerk monumentality. It is impressive without being overbearing, dignified without being stuffy.

The building is a balanced but dynamically asymmetrical composition in both plan and elevation. The primary façade is enlivened by the visual interplay between two projecting forms—a stout cylinder containing the main entrance at ground level and a boardroom above, and a rather enigmatic three-dimensional puzzle of planes and volumes enclosing a small chapel. Behind these foreground elements is the main body of the building, a long and solid bar offset by a wing-like, patinated copper roof, held aloft from the main structure by slender struts. The crowning touch is an attenuated, gold-leaf cross that engages a rectangular bay window before piercing the roof plane. Inside, the center affords visitors a number of rich spatial experiences, including a generously scaled bank of sloping walkways that connect the exhibition spaces on the three lowest levels.

S15 Franciscan Monastery

1400 Quincy Street, NE

1899 Aristides Leonori
Various alterations: Architects
unknown

TEL: (202) 526-6800
www.myfranciscan.com

This highly romanticist complex—official home of the
"Commissariat of the Holy Land for the United States"—contains copies of shrines to evoke Jerusalem and Bethlehem, copies of catacombs to evoke Rome, and the Portincula Chapel to evoke Assisi. In all, the monastery comprises forty-four acres of buildings, woodlands, and gardens.

S16 McMillan Reservoir Sand Filtration Plant

Michigan Avenue and North Capitol
Street, NW

1905 Lieutenant Colonel Alexander
M. Miller; Landscape architect for
park: Frederick Law Olmsted Jr.

This former water filtration facility is
now Washington's most intriguing ruin,
and surely one of the most popular sites
for local architecture school projects,
thanks to the irresistible challenge of figuring out how to incorporate the
facility's strange remnants into some sort of new development. The District of Columbia bought the site from the federal government in 1987,
and has been trying to figure out what to do with it ever since.

S17 Howard Hall

Howard University
607 Howard Place, NW

1867 Architect unknown
1996 Restoration: Oehrlein &
Associates Architects

This structure, built of hollow white
bricks later painted a succession of colors, was the home of General Oliver
Howard, founder of Howard University
and a commissioner of the Freedmen's
Bureau. The university purchased the house in 1909 and, after years of
neglect, it has now been fully restored. It is the oldest extant building on
the Howard campus.

Other noteworthy buildings at the university include the Founders
Library, whose tower dominates the campus, and the neo-Gothic Rankin
Memorial Chapel.

S18 LeDroit Park

Florida and Rhode Island avenues
between 2nd and 7th streets, NW

1873–77 James McGill
2001 Multiple renovations and new
houses: Sorg and Associates

Though originally built as an exclusively white neighborhood, LeDroit
Park has long played a key role in the
cultural and social life of historically
black Howard University. The neigh-
borhood was developed by Amzi L. Barber, one of the university's founders, who was white. In 1888, a group of African Americans, frustrated by
having to walk around what was, in effect, a gated community, tore down
part of the fence that surrounded it, and within a few years, the remaining fences and walls were dismantled and the area was integrated. It
became a center of African American cultural life in the early twentieth
century, with residents including the poet Paul Lawrence Dunbar.

James McGill designed many of LeDroit Park's houses in the highly
popular romantic styles of the period: Gothic Revival, Italianate, and Sec-

ond Empire. The area remains largely intact, with fifty of McGill's original sixty-four dwellings still standing. The neighborhood was once marked by pastoral street names—Elm, Maple, and so on—that were later officially changed to fit the District's rational system of letters and numbers.

S19 Eckington Place

1500 Eckington Place, NE

1915–72 Architects unknown
2002 Renovation: CORE; Interiors:
STUDIOS Architecture

One of Washington's few true industrial buildings to be converted to office use, Eckington Place is a former printing plant that now houses the headquarters of XM Satellite Radio, among other tenants. Actually a complex of at least ten separate structures, the project has served as a catalyst for redevelopment in the area. The radio network's hip offices and studios were designed, appropriately enough, by STU-DIOS Architecture.

S20 Gallaudet University

7th Street and Florida Avenue, NE

1866 Master plan: Olmsted, Vaux
and Company
1868–81 Various buildings: Frederick
C. Withers/Vaux, Withers and
Company
1993 College Hall restoration:
Einhorn Yaffee Prescott
1995 Kellogg Conference Center:
Einhorn Yaffee Prescott
1999 Chapel Hall restoration:
Einhorn Yaffee Prescott

Gallaudet University was founded in 1864 as the Deaf Mute College, the first institution of higher learning for the deaf in America. Later named for Thomas Hopkins Gallaudet, a pioneering educator of the hearing-impaired, the university occupies a park-like setting removed from the bustle of the city. The campus plan by Frederick Law Olmsted and Calvert Vaux is a masterpiece of informality. While the buildings generally harmonize with each other and with the landscape, many also possess great individual character—both Chapel Hall (Frederick C. Withers with Calvert Vaux), built of contrasting-colored stone and possibly the earliest Ruskinian Gothic college structure in America, and College Hall (Frederick C. Withers), built of brownstone and brick, merit special attention.

S21 Hecht Company Warehouse

1401 New York Avenue, NE

1937 Abbott, Merkt & Co.
1948, 1961 Additions: Abbott, Merkt & Co.

The finest work of streamlined, Art Moderne architecture in Washington, and one of the greatest such buildings anywhere in the United States, the Hecht Company Warehouse is a glistening layer cake of glazed bricks and glass block. The surfeit of the latter material, which would now be considered almost indulgently decorative, actually derived from the practical desire to bring natural light to expansive interior spaces in a structure where views to the outside were unimportant. Still, it is difficult to explain the beacon-like, multifaceted corner tower as anything other than a magnificent gesture just for the fun of it.

S22 United States National Arboretum

24th and R streets, NE

1963 Administration building: Deigert & Yerkes & Associates
1976, 1978, 1980 Revisions: Sasaki Associates Inc.
1990 Corinthian column garden: Russell Page, with EDAW Inc.
1993 Bird garden and grove of state trees: HOH Associates

www.usna.usda.gov

The National Arboretum comprises 446 hilly, green acres, incongruously adjacent to a gritty stretch of New York Avenue. Lobbying for an arboretum began at least as far back as 1901, and in 1927 Congress approved legislation to "establish and maintain a national arboretum for purposes of research and education concerning tree and plant life." Since then the institution has grown into one of the largest, most advanced of its kind in America. The arboretum maintains diverse educational programs, and, thanks to the staff's interest in plant propagation, many local gardens now boast new, hardy species of camellia, crape myrtle, and azalea hybridized by arboretum scientists.

One of the arboretum's more recent landscapes incorporates the nearly two dozen thirty-four-foot-tall sandstone Corinthian columns that were removed from the U.S. Capitol during expansions in the 1950s. The columns, designed by Benjamin Henry Latrobe and erected under the supervision of Charles Bulfinch, seemed, despite that pedigree, to be destined for some local landfill, until Mrs. George Garrett intervened and rescued them. After years of negotiations, the columns finally were taken out of storage and placed in the arboretum, and landscape architect Russell Page designed a setting for them on a knoll near the main entrance. Page died in 1985, but EDAW faithfully carried out his low-key plans: a small fountain adds gentle noise and movement to the composition and spills over to form a reflecting pool below.

S23 Langston Terrace Dwellings

Benning Road and 21st Street, NE

1938 Hilyard R. Robinson; Associated architect: Paul Williams; Sculptor: Daniel Olney
1962 Addition: Leroy Brown

The first public housing project in the District of Columbia, Langston Terrace was built under the auspices of the Public Works Administration expressly for low-income African American families. The design by Hilyard Robinson, one of Washington's most prominent early African American architects, was heavily influenced by the famed Karl-Marx-Hof housing estate in Vienna, Austria, and other avant-garde projects that Robinson had visited on a European tour. Though built on a very modest budget, the complex includes relatively elaborate sculptural elements, including bas-reliefs by Daniel Olney depicting "The Progress of the Negro Race." The development was named after John Mercer Langston, a former congressman who also served as acting president of Howard University.

S24 Frederick Douglass National Historic Site (Cedar Hill)

1411 W Street, SE

1859 Architect unknown
1878–93 Various additions: Architects unknown
1972 Restoration: Architect unknown

TEL: (202) 426-5961   www.nps.gov/frdo/freddoug.html

Frederick Douglass, author, abolitionist, and editor, moved to this house in 1877 when he became U.S. marshal of the District of Columbia. He named the picturesque cottage to honor the cedar trees that shaded the house (most are now gone) and lived here the rest of his life. In buying property in what had been a segregated neighborhood, Douglass launched the first serious attack on the city's racist housing laws.

Born into slavery in Talbot County, Maryland, in 1817, Douglass was taken by his owner to Baltimore, but in 1839 he managed to escape. He fled to New England, where he purchased his freedom and started the antislavery newspaper *North Star,* whose masthead bore his credo, "Right is of no sex—Truth is of no color—God is the Father of us all and we are all Brethren." Douglass died here in 1895 from a heart attack suffered during a women's rights meeting. His widow, Helen, opened Cedar Hill for tours in 1903; and in 1962 the property was acquired by the National Park Service, which maintains it as a memorial to its most prominent occupant.

S25 St. Elizabeths Hospital

2700 Martin Luther King, Jr., Avenue, SE

1853–74 Main building: Thomas U. Walter
1902 "Letter Buildings": Shepley, Rutan and Coolidge

Outraged by the shameful condition of the nation's homeless and mentally ill during the mid-nineteenth century, Dorothea Dix lobbied the federal government to improve the condition of the "many persons from various parts of the Union, whose minds are more or less erratic," and who "find their way to the metropolis of the country [and] ramble about . . . poorly clad and suffering for want of food and shelter." Congress heeded her pleas and approved funds for what was initially known as the Government Hospital for the Insane. Working closely with the hospital's first chief of staff, Dr. C. H. Nichol, architect Thomas U. Walter created the first building, a dignified structure whose brick façades are enlivened by a stone belt course and splayed stone window arches, and whose rooms are shaded by rambling arcades and two-tier porches.

Over the years, thousands of men and women have been treated here. One of the most noted residents was the American-born poet Ezra Pound, who had lived in Italy for much of his life and was an ardent fascist. In the wake of Mussolini's execution in 1945, Pound was arrested by Italian partisans, turned over to American authorities, and later admitted to St. Elizabeths after he pled insanity in order to avoid a trial for treason. Released in 1958, Pound returned to Italy, declaring, "All America is an insane asylum." The most infamous modern patient is John Hinckley Jr., who shot Ronald Reagan in an attempt to impress actress Jodie Foster.

In 1854, partly to provide housing for hospital workers, land developers laid out Anacostia. Known as Uniontown until 1886, and predating Baltimore's Roland Park and Philadelphia's Chestnut Hill, Anacostia is arguably America's first planned suburb, long before that term was widely used.

Index

Getty, Robert, 226–227; house, 227
GGA.Ehrenkrantz Eckstut & Kuhn Architects, 164
Ghequier, T. Buckler, 49
Gifford, James J., 142
Gilbert, Cass, 13, 39, 161, 165
Gilbert, Cass, Jr., 39
Gilded Age, 167, 170, 243, 251, 310
Gilman Building (F4), 117, 126
Gilpin, Richard A., 175
Giuliani Associates Architects, 215
Glover, Charles C., 291, 323
Glover Archbold Park, 326
GMR, 160
Godwin, James E., 323
Golding, Stuart, 133
Goodhue, Bertram Grosvenor, 183
Goodman, Charles M., 65
Gordon & Greenberg Architects, 143
Gordon, Tracy, and Swartout, 139
Gothic Revival style, 5, 12, 52, 145, 212, 231, 239, 261, 270, 323–324, 353
Government Printing Office (GPO), (A12), 25, 43
Grace Church (K20), 206, 223
Grad, Frank, 59
Graham, Jay, 303
Graham, Robert, 81
Graham, Anderson, Probst and White, 42
Graham Building, Jackson (E15), 97, 112
Graham, Burnham & Company, 42
Graham Gund Architects, 44, 109
Grant, Ulysses S., 100, 156, 236; house (K41), 206, 236; statue, 35
Grant Memorial (A2), 25, 34–35
Graves, Michael, 119–120
Greeley, Rose, 314–315
Greenberg, Allan, 168
Green Building Council, U.S., 44
Greenleaf, John, 58, 65
Greenleaf Point, 66
Gregory, Waylande, 114

Greyhound Bus Station, Old, 149
Grigg, Wood, and Browne, 285
Guerin, Jules, 83
Gugler, Eric, 158
GUND Partnership, 44, 109
Gurney, Robert M., 287

Hadfield, George, 6, 27–28, 54, 113, 176, 239, 337
Haiti, Embassy of (P5), 307, 312
Halcyon House (K13), 206, 218–219
Hallet, Stanley I., 344; house (S7), 344–345
Hallett, Marcus, 285
Halprin, Lawrence, 81–82
Hammel, Green and Abrahamson (HGA), 93
Hand Chapel, Florence Hollis (Q4), 325, 328
Hanks Center, Nancy (F11), 116, 129–130
Hansen, Ramm, 286
Harbeson, Hough, Livingston & Larson, 27
Harbour Square (C11), 56, 58, 65–66
Hardenbergh, Henry, 133
Harding, Clarence L., 285
Harding and Upman, 316
Hardison, Fred L., 27
Hardy Holzman Pfeiffer Associates, 133–134
Harkness, John C., 145, 270
Harris, Albert, 187
Harrison, Wallace K., 183
Harrison & Abramowitz, 183
Harry Weese and Associates, 17, 41, 63, 340
Hart, Frederick, 324
Hart, Philip, 6
Hartman, George, 88
Hartman-Cox Architects, 38, 43–44, 81, 83, 105, 107, 109, 122, 126–128, 151, 185, 196–198, 223, 236, 246, 266, 295, 299, 328–329
Hartman Design Group, 295

Trentman House (K33), 207, 230
Trevillian, Howard B., Jr., 323
Trowbridge, Alexander Breck, 38, 179
Truman, Harry, 160, 168, 216
Trumbauer, Horace, 264–265, 329
Tudor Place (K40), 206–207, 214, 234–235
Turkey, Embassy of (P17), 307, 318
Turkish Ambassador's Residence (P2), 307, 309–310
Turpin, Wachter and Associates, 42
1250 24th Street, NW (J20), 190, 203
21 Dupont Circle, NW (L5), 240, 246
2164 Florida Avenue, 251
2300/2400 N Street, NW (J21), 190, 204

Ukraine, Embassy of (K14), 206, 219
Underwood, Bayard, 105
Ungers, O. M., 328
Unification Church (N9), 279, 286
Union Station, Capitol Traction Company (K11), 206, 217
Union Station and Plaza (A10), 14, 25–26, 41–42, 71
Union Trust Building, 147
University of the District of Columbia (O12), 104, 289, 298–299
Upjohn, Richard, 9
Urban, James, 73, 218
U.S. Botanic Garden (A3), 25–26, 35–36
U.S. Capitol. *See* Capitol, U.S.
U.S. Court of Claims, 169
U.S. Soldiers' and Airmen's Home, 347
U.S. Tax Court Building (E19), 97, 114
Uzbekistan, Embassy of Republic of (L18), 241, 256–257

Valmarana, Mario di, 186
Valtchev, Ivan, 134
Van Dusen, Lisa, 327
Van Ness Mausoleum, 239
Van Ness Station building, 299
Vaughan, Henry, 323
Vaux, Calvert, 9–10, 86, 233, 353

Vaux and Company, 352
Vaux, Withers and Company, 352
Venturi, Rauch & Scott Brown, 132
Venturi Scott Brown Associates, 236
Vercelli, Peter, 220–221
Verizon Center (E14), 97, 111
Vietnam Veterans Memorial (D16), 68, 83, 85–86
Vietta Group, 149
VOA Associates, 125, 143, 320
Voghi, Peter, 316
Volta Bureau (K3), 206, 212–213
von Ezdorf, Richard, 170
Voorhees Walker & Smith, 164
VVKR, 268

Wadsworth, Herbert and Martha, house, 254
Waldron Faulkner House (O18), 289, 304
Walsh-McLean House, 248
Walter, Thomas U., 8, 10, 27, 30–32, 105–107, 109, 160–161, 163, 356
Warder-Totten Mansion (N6), 279, 284
Wardman, Harry, 154, 292, 316
Wardman Park Marriott Hotel, 292
Wardman Tower (O4), 289, 292–293
Warnecke, John Carl, 19, 244, 334
Warner Theatre/Office Building (F12), 116, 130
Warren, Herbert Langford, 261
Warren & Smith, 261
Warren & Wetmore, 194
Washington, D.C.: building height limitation in, 14, 16, 259; center of, 134, 138; establishment of, 1–5
Washington, George, 3–4, 28–29, 52, 98, 106, 176, 181, 227, 249, 305; statue, 70, 90
Washington, Martha, 64, 235, 337
Washington Canoe Club (K12), 206, 217–218
Washington Chapter/AIA, 241, 266
Washington Club (L13), 240, 242, 253
Washington Convention Center (E5), 16, 97, 103–104

Photo Credits

Photographs in this volume are by Alan Karchmer, except for those on the pages listed below. All illustrations are reproduced by permission.

Aaron, Peter / Esto 109 (bottom), 151, 196, 342 (bottom); Andersson, Eve Astrid (www.eveandersson.com) 23; Arthur Cotton Moore/Associates 225; Becker, Brian 295; Blessing, Hedrich 244 (bottom), 300 (top); Bonstra, Bill 273 (bottom); The British Embassy and Ambassador Sir Robin Renwick 308; The Catholic University of America 348 (top); CORE 342 (top); Cott, George 72; Cox Graae & Spack 335 (bottom), 345; Cunningham, Dan 35, 149 (top), 260, 272; Dersin, Michael 149 (bottom), 256; Devrouax & Purnell 66 (bottom), 104; Dumbarton Oaks Research Library 237; Feldblyum, Boris 33 (middle, bottom), 34, 40, 43, 44, 51 (top), 55 (top), 61, 63 (top), 74, 81 (bottom), 82, 83 (top), 85, 87, 88, 94 (top), 99, 100, 107 (bottom), 114 (top), 124 (bottom), 128 (bottom), 129 (bottom), 143, 144, 152, 153, 176, 193, 197, 198 (top), 199 (bottom), 200, 201, 202 (bottom), 217 (top), 220 (top), 221, 223 (top), 224 (top), 250, 257 (top), 259, 274, 275 (bottom), 282 (top), 284 (bottom), 285 (top), 302 (top), 303 (top), 310, 312 (bottom), 315 (bottom), 316 (top), 319 (bottom), 321, 322, 328 (top), 330, 349, 353 (top), 354; Fleming, Gary 147 (bottom); Foster & Partners, courtesy of the National Portrait Gallery and Smithsonian American Art Museum 22; Fred Sons Photography 252 (top); General Services Administration 60; Hartman Cox 223 (bottom); Heine, Julia 216 (bottom); Hellmuth, Obata + Kassabaum 222 (top); Highsmith, Carol 126 (top), 140 (bottom), 145 (bottom); Hochlander, Anice 124 (top); Hochlander Davis Photography 53; Honarkar, Ali 276; Houlahan, Michael 50 (bottom); Hoyt, Wolfgang / Esto 300 (bottom); Hursley, Timothy 188; Jamison, Alex 258 (bottom), 286 (bottom); Lautman Photography 77, 169, 198 (bottom), 329 (top), 344 (top), 350 (bottom); Library of Congress Prints and Photographs Department 4, 6–11, 13, 14, 26, 28–32, 48, 58, 70, 90 (bottom), 91, 98, 101, 118, 138, 157, 159, 174, 208, 242, 269 (top), 280, 290, 326, 332 (top), 340 (top), 346 (bottom); Mackenzie, Maxwell 45 (bottom), 49 (top), 71, 110, 150, 166 (top), 179 (top), 202 (top), 263 (bottom), 271 (bottom), 301 (bottom), 318 (top), 327 (top), 343; Michael Graves & Associates 119; Moran, Michael 275 (top), 352 (top); Odom, Sonny 45 (top); Oesch, James 62 (top); O'Rourke, Ronald 244 (top), 261 (bottom), 266, 296 (top), 298, 311, 341; Patel, Prakash 111, 112 (bottom), 141, 187 (bottom), 263 (top), 301 (top); Patterson, David 148 (top); Portlock, Phil / WMATA 340 (bottom); Randlett, Mary 309 (top); Redmond, Dan 273 (top); Shalom Baranes Associates 130; Skidmore, Owings & Merrill 129 (top), 148 (bottom), 203 (top), 204; Smalling, Walter, Jr. 166 (bottom); Solomon, Ron 164; Sorg and Associates 228 (top); Stoller, Erica 195 (bottom); Stoller, Ezra 95; Suzanne Reatig Architecture103 (top); Warchol, Paul 287; Wyner, Ken 103 (bottom), 105 (top).